My Paris Dream

ILE DE BRÉHAT

DALIBOT
LOCATION DE VÉLOS
22870 ILE DE BREHAT
TÉL. (96) 20.03.51

GILLES & MURIEL...

MIRAVIL...

RESTAURANT...

46.34.07.7...

MURIEL ET GILLES ÉPIÉ, 25 QUAI DE LA TOURNE...
FERMÉ SAMEDI MIDI, DIMANCHE...

"KARL, CAN I GET YOU A WEINER?"

"WHY YES."

PARIS   1-91

Madame Kate Belts

My Paris Dream

AN EDUCATION IN STYLE, SLANG, AND SEDUCTION IN
THE GREAT CITY ON THE SEINE

Kate Betts

SPIEGEL & GRAU

NEW YORK

Copyright © 2015 by Katherine Betts

Published in the United States by Spiegel & Grau, an imprint of Random House, a division of Penguin Random House LLC, New York.

SPIEGEL & GRAU and the HOUSE colophon are registered trademarks of Penguin Random House LLC.

Grateful acknowledgment is made to Hal Leonard MGB s.r.l. for permission to reprint a lyric excerpt from "Douce France" by Charles Trenet, copyright © 1943 Editions Salabert-Paris. All rights reserved. Reprinted by kind permission of Hal Leonard MGB s.r.l.

Library of Congress Cataloging-in-Publication Data
Betts, Kate.
My Paris dream: an education in style, slang, and seduction in the great city on the Seine / Kate Betts.
pages cm
ISBN 978-0-679-64442-2
eBook ISBN 978-0-679-64443-9
1. Betts, Kate.   2. Betts, Kate—Homes and haunts—France—Paris.   3. Young women—France—Paris—Biography.   4. Americans—France—Paris—Biography.
5. Women journalists—France—Paris—Biography.   6. Fashion—France—Paris—History—20th century.   7. Fashion designers—France—Paris—History—20th century.
8. Paris (France)—Social life and customs—20th century.   9. Paris (France)—Biography.   10. Coming of age—France—Paris.   I. Title.
DC705.B48A3 2015
944'.361092—dc23 2014040620
[B]

Printed in the United States of America on acid-free paper

www.spiegelandgrau.com

9 8 7 6 5 4 3 2 1

First Edition

Book design by Caroline Cunningham

For Oliver and India

One's destination is never a place, but a new way of seeing things.

—HENRY MILLER

CONTENTS

My Paris Dream

CHAPTER ONE

Seeds of the Dream

In the summer of 1982 I discovered Paris for the first time. I was on a high school graduation adventure with my boarding school roommate, Maria, and her sister Johanna. We bought Eurail passes and spent two months traveling around France, Italy, Germany, and Czechoslovakia. We arrived in Paris on a hot June morning, bunked in a youth hostel on the rue des Barres behind the Hôtel de Ville, and made a beeline for Berthillon, the ice cream parlor on the Île Saint-Louis that Johanna's worldly older boyfriend had told her had the best ice cream in the world. It was true. I still remember the intense flavor of the side-by-side scoops of raspberry and lemon-lime sorbet. Everything about Paris was more intense, from the sorbet flavors to the cornflower-blue sky stretched over the sharp spire of Sainte-Chapelle to the scarlet poppies poking out of green grass squares in the Luxembourg Gardens to the acrid smell of urine in the long, white-tiled Métro corridors.

For two weeks we walked and walked, restlessly roaming from Right Bank to Left, through lush displays of dahlias and roses in the Île de la Cité flower market, past the stout Gothic turrets of the Conciergerie, and over the Pont Neuf to the boulevard Saint-Michel. We walked from

the Jardin des Plantes to the Eiffel Tower and then crossed the Seine again on the Pont de l'Alma, taking in the golden shadows of Paris at dusk. Every streetscape and boulevard seemed to shimmer in the heat and summer light like an Impressionist tableau. We visited the Louvre, Notre Dame, and Sacré-Cœur. We rolled down the grassy hillside of the Parc des Buttes-Chaumont and ate buttered baguettes with thick slabs of boiled ham. In the evening we counted out chunky ten-franc coins and splurged on steak au poivre and cheap Beaujolais at Aux Charpentiers.

Something about the majestic landscape moved me in ways I didn't quite understand: the shock of history. Everywhere I looked, the past was present. On the sides of the limestone buildings, brass plaques memorialized fallen soldiers and members of the French Resistance. The parks, the broad, slick paving stones on the boulevards, even the light had been immortalized by the Impressionist painters. So much texture and flavor! Twenty kinds of bread were splayed out in bakery windows; boisterous cafés spilled over with students, professors, prostitutes, and *ouvriers,* workers in their cobalt-blue jumpsuits.

When the summer ended, I headed off for my freshman year at Princeton and was immersed in an all-American preppy campus that was a world apart from the bohemian Paris that had moved me to my soul. Within a few weeks, I fell in love with a sophomore named Will who, like me, had grown up in the prep school tradition of the East Coast. Will was confident about his place at Princeton, not intimidated by ambitious classmates or the grind for grades. He laughed at me for trying to read every book on every syllabus, for rushing over to Firestone Library after dinner. On weekends we'd go to drunken parties in the basements of eating clubs like Cap and Gown or the Tiger Inn, where masses of people would dance to one-hit wonders. *"Everybody wants to rule the world,"* we sang along, punching the air with our hands and skidding around the beer-soaked tile floor in our acid-washed jeans and Laura Ashley blouses. Yeah, we were gonna rule the world, at least until 2:00 A.M., when many of the party animals were vomiting in the gutter.

I was interested in fashion, and that made me a bit of an anomaly on campus. Style was part of my upbringing. New York in the seventies was defined by larger-than-life style icons like Bianca Jagger, Halston, Diane von Furstenberg, and Andy Warhol.

My mother and father had divorced when I was six. I was never sure why exactly—we didn't talk about it—but I remember a kid pointing at me in second grade and whispering to her friend, "Her parents are *divorced.*" In those days, at that school, divorce was rare. A few years later my mother moved my sister, my brother, and me into an apartment on East 63rd Street just off Park Avenue, across the street from Halston. Warhol lived two blocks up; my brother and I would see him with Liza Minnelli in the butcher on Lexington Avenue. We stayed with my dad every other weekend and on Wednesday nights. He was an architect and had a strict aesthetic inspired by Le Corbusier, Louis Kahn, and the

Color Field painters of the 1950s. His apartment, across the street from the Museum of Modern Art, was all white, with recessed lighting and the latest Eames chairs. He was passionate about art and architecture and would take us on excursions to the Museum of Modern Art or to SoHo and would talk endlessly about painters like Frank Stella and Franz Kline and the art scene in the sixties. He loved to tell the story of a trip to Paris as a newlywed, when my mother dragged him to a concert. It was Édith Piaf's

last. "You never know," he would say, "what you might learn or see." He was strict and aloof in a way that my mother was not, but he cared about education—cultural education. "You are barbarians!" he would say when my brother and I complained about yet another museum.

As a teenager I devoured copies of *Vogue* and French *Elle* and Carrie Donovan's pages in *The New York Times Magazine*. From my mother I learned the power of fashion to lift a mood or transform a moment. She always said that shopping was better than therapy. If things got tense in our family, if she was fighting with my father over alimony or if my brother was expelled from yet another school, she would dash off to Bergdorf's to console herself with a new Jean Muir dress or a Pucci scarf. Like many young women, I used fashion to try on different personas—one day preppy, the next day punk. In college it was a way of defining myself among the valedictorians and All-Ivy athletes. I wasn't wearing anything radical—no Mohawks, no combat boots—but the fact that I cared about how I looked, that I paid attention to my appearance, mystified my roommates. They were varsity athletes—rowers, lacrosse players, and soccer forwards. Blow-drying my hair and putting on makeup made me something of a freak among freshmen.

Four years later, on a hot June day, I was standing under the ancient ash tree on Cannon Green, a new college graduate posing for pictures with my parents, my sister, and my grandmother. My brother had cooked up some excuse to avoid this family event. Anyone could see the unhappiness in that picture. My mother and father had been divorced for over a decade, and the years of conflict and disappointment are written in my beautiful mother's sad blue eyes. My father's posture is awkward, almost mechanical, but he's smiling his goofy smile, and his fierce brown eyes are filled with pride. I'm smiling, too, a weary smile brought on by too many champagne parties and the futile feeling that I would always be caught in my parents' tug-of-war. Only my eighty-two-year-old grandmother, once statuesque but now hunched over with age, seems oblivious to the tension.

"I have something for you," my grandmother said after my mother and father had retreated to their separate corners of the green. She thrust a small box into my hand. "Make sure you read the card."

In the box was a pair of small perfect round diamond studs. My grandmother believed every young woman should mark important occasions with talismans, preferably beautiful jewelry.

"Oh, thank you, Libby!" I kissed her on her soft, powdery cheek.

The note card had four dates scrawled in her loopy handwriting: "1986, 1956, 1926, 1893." The years my father, and his father, and his father before him had graduated from Princeton. Looking down at those numbers, all I could think was, *Get me out of this equation.* I wanted to get as far away as possible, not just from my unhappy parents but from the expectations the legacy conferred on me.

At Princeton I was the emissary of a family tradition. When I had tried to find my own way as a teenager—for a while I had my heart set on becoming a dancer—my father steered me back onto the college path and eventually toward Princeton. Some people are immensely proud of their family legacies; mine haunted me with the implication that I was qualified not on my own merits but because of the line I had been born into.

Everything in my life had been so predictable, so bound up in traditions I was supposed to uphold without even knowing quite what the implications were. I wanted to swerve off the path marked out by that succession of dates, to do something adventuresome and unexpected. I wasn't a rebel in the usual sense of breaking rules, but I had a hunger to learn something about myself—what that was, I didn't exactly know.

The thing that intrigued me was journalism. As a kid, I'd watched Barbara Walters on the *Today* show every morning, reporting on the war in Vietnam. She was authoritative and glamorous—an intoxicating combination. As a freshman I had joined the staff of *The Daily Princetonian*. I admired the paper's star reporter, Crystal Nix, a brilliant six-foot-tall African American woman who made reporting look effortless, filing story after story while the rest of us in the newsroom scrambled around frantically, chasing campus news. My only front-page byline was attached to a story about zoning restrictions on a local Wawa convenience store. It was hardly what they call a Cheerio choker.

As a senior, I took a course called Politics and the Press, taught by the Vietnam correspondent Gloria Emerson. Emerson had started on the women's pages of *The New York Times* in the 1960s, reporting on events like Marc Bohan's Oriental-inspired collection at Dior or the arrival of longer suit jackets and ostrich trim at the Fontana sisters in Rome. By 1968, she was so fed up with the fashion beat, she asked to be transferred to Vietnam.

In my delusions of grandeur—or out of desperation—I thought I could make that jump, too. I could parlay my Wawa exclusive into a *Time* magazine gig in Paris and then transfer to Rome and end up in some remote, exotic place like Hanoi. Aspiring to become a war correspondent was romantic and sounded good on paper, but secretly, when I played out that fantasy in my head, I never made it past Paris. I was in love with fashion and culture, specifically *French* culture.

And yet, like most bewildered souls graduating from college, I didn't have a clue as to how to make it happen. I had no plans, no strategy. My friends had signed up for interviews with advertising firms like J. Walter Thompson or had applied and been accepted to law school or were taking the Foreign Service exam. They knew their starting salaries and what the next five years of their lives would look like. I knew I was supposed to make a choice and plant a flag somewhere, to locate myself physically in a way that announced I was "starting my life." But all I had was an instinct that harkened back to that feeling of elation I'd experienced in Paris four years before. I knew virtually nothing of the practical aspects of living in Paris, but I could see myself there. I could see myself in a walk-up in some exquisite limestone building on the Île Saint-Louis. I couldn't say what I thought I'd find there, but I knew Paris would give me something I couldn't find anywhere else.

Princeton Playlist

"I Would Die for You," Prince

"What I Like About You," the Romantics

"Tainted Love," Soft Cell

"Everybody Wants to Rule the World," Tears for Fears

"Don't You Want Me," the Human League

"Our Lips Are Sealed," the Go-Go's

"I Ran," A Flock of Seagulls

"I Melt with You," Modern English

"Save It for Later," the English Beat

"Borderline," Madonna

"Avalon," Roxy Music

"Road to Nowhere," Talking Heads

"Everyday I Write the Book," Elvis Costello

"Do You Really Want to Hurt Me," Culture Club

CHAPTER TWO

Just Go

In the months following graduation, I talked endlessly and with great bravado about my plan to live in Paris. I would find a job and learn to speak French fluently. I told my boyfriend, Will, that I'd be gone for just a year. A year seemed like enough time to figure out what to do with the rest of my life. It certainly sounded more appealing than a year in some entry-level cubicle at J. Walter Thompson.

Secretly I was not so sure. The security of family and friends in New York made a European adventure seem daunting. I vacillated back and forth: I didn't know many people in Paris. Then there was the job, or, rather, the lack of a job. What would I do? I was not going to Paris to be a *flâneur*, or the female version—one of Manet's immaculately coiffed ladies whose sunlit garden and nineteenth-century finery were financed by her industrialist husband. I was not Hemingway or Janet Flanner, banging out newsy dispatches from a café over a bottle of cheap wine. All I had was an impulse to go.

My godmother, Sandy, lived in a rambling corner apartment with sweeping views of the gilded dome and esplanade of Les Invalides. She was a footloose bohemian who loved a good party and, on a whim many years earlier, had followed her boyfriend, Bob, an editor at the *International Herald Tribune,* to Paris. Bob kindly gave me the phone number of a woman named Maggie Shapiro, who ran the internship program at the *Trib,* and she offered me a *stagiaire.* I signed up for French classes at the Sorbonne, solicited reference letters from professors and former employers, and filled out a stack of forms for a student visa. My friend Tanya connected me with a French family who rented rooms to American students. I sold my car, had my wisdom teeth pulled, and typed up a French résumé. I booked a ticket on a cheap charter flight to Paris: one-way.

And then a bomb went off.

I was sitting on a rattan stool in my mother's kitchen when I saw the news flash on TV: an explosion in Paris. This was the fifth one in just ten days. Terrorists had been planting bombs in cafés and Métro stations. A grisly attack had occurred at a police station and another one at a post office in the Hôtel de Ville.

"Europeans are very used to this," my mother said. She came from the Keep Calm and Carry On school. As a parent she had done what she could, all she could, and probably sensed that her work was nearly done. She had taught me table manners, the imperative of good posture, and how to speak clearly from my chest, not my nose. She stressed the importance of being kind to elderly people. She had exposed me to New York City's cultural treasures, including the Alvin Ailey American Dance Theater—where I had studied—Martha Graham, and the New York City Ballet. She had enrolled me in dance classes at a young age because she felt it would give me confidence and focus. She had been a great teacher and, like all great teachers, she knew when to push the fledgling out of the nest.

Looking back, I see now that my mother feared I might shortchange myself by choosing an easy, conventional path. She didn't want me to depend too much on a boyfriend, on things that weren't mine. She didn't want me to make the same mistakes she had made, defining herself by her husband, becoming emotionally or financially dependent on someone else. She knew I needed to let go of everything I might cling to in fear of the unknown, including her.

"The Irish bombed London all the time in the nineteen-seventies. It was no big deal," she said two weeks later when we heard that another round of random terrorist acts had destroyed a police station near the Louvre.

But it was a big deal. I hung on the news, growing more agitated with each new attack. News stories referred to Paris as "Beirut on the Seine." Parisians, celebrated for their *sangfroid,* were shaken. Many readjusted daily routines, avoiding the Métro or staying out of cafés and cinemas. President Mitterrand had instructed everyone not to give in to the terrorists. "If you are afraid, if you change your routines, then they will have won," he said.

I called Bibiane, the mother of the French family I planned to live with, and asked how she was managing. "*Ça va,*" she said, "it will be fine."

I packed my bags: a few oversized sweaters, the acid-washed jeans, a handful of gold hoop earrings, my hair dryer, some flannel pajamas from L.L.Bean.

But I was hardly resolved. The bombings had inflamed my fears about the whole endeavor. I delayed my departure for a week. Every night I checked the news. Several days following my original travel date in early September, two terrorists driving a black BMW up the rue de Rennes, a few blocks away from where I would be living, tossed a bomb out the window onto the crowded sidewalk in front of a discount department store. Carnage and panic ensued. Dead bodies were sprawled on cobblestones. Police helicopters hovered overhead. Seven people were dead and seventy-five injured. What seemed even scarier was the timing of the attack: a Wednesday afternoon, when kids were out of school and accompanying their mothers on errands. Parisians were afraid. The Champs-Élysées was deserted. Newspapers were reporting that people were holed up in their homes. So much for the life of the *boulevardiers.* So much for the glamour of the great city on the Seine.

"You can always come back," my mother said. "Just go."

CHAPTER THREE

17, Rue de Grenelle

The early-morning mist had settled on the golden patchwork of farms below as my plane circled over Charles de Gaulle Airport. I could make out the Eiffel Tower in the distance, a tiny metal toy punctuating a vast urban landscape of limestone and slate.

I took a taxi into town, past the dull gray suburbs and toward the Paris of my dreams, the Paris of bustling open-air markets and curvy nineteenth-century balustrades, of Haussmann's grand boulevards, and of clipped linden trees marching alongside the Seine. As the taxi crossed the Périphérique, entering the city, I fantasized about what it would be like to live in an apartment with views over a sun-dappled square, floating above a leafy canopy of chestnut trees. Along the boulevard Malesherbes, men in sleek suits were emerging from their stately apartment buildings, shooting their cuffs, checking their watches, with just enough time for a morning crème at the corner café.

The taxi's worn velvet seats reeked of cigarette smoke. The driver accelerated, swerving into the chaotic Place de la Concorde, and I glimpsed the postcard-perfect vista down the Champs-Élysées, the imperial Arc de Triomphe vibrating in the sunny haze. Continuing over the bridge, we crossed the Seine, and there it was! The Eiffel Tower, popping up next to the gilded dome of Les Invalides like a cartoon. I had arrived.

We pulled up in front of a carved mahogany door at number 17, rue de Grenelle, in the elegant 7th arrondissement, with its pristine neoclassical façades and carefully tended window boxes. I paid the driver, peeling off a crisp pink bill from a wad of French francs I had changed dollars for at the airport. My unwieldy suitcase landed with a thud on the freshly scrubbed sidewalk. I pushed the door. It didn't budge. I nudged it again with my shoulder. My palms began to sweat. *Don't tell me,* I thought.

To the left of the door was a small brass plate with a grid of numbers on it. Nervously, I pushed every button on the grid until one of them elicited a click. I heaved the door open and dragged my suitcase across the threshold, into the cool, dark marble lobby. The elevator, a cage at the end of the hall, was barely big enough for my purse—forget about my suitcase. I headed up the worn wooden snail-shaped staircase.

My college friend Tanya had spent her junior year in Paris and urged me to rent a room from the same young couple she had lived with, at least for the first couple of months. The Deschamps and their two children inhabited a sprawling second-floor apartment overlooking the rue de Grenelle. My Paris fantasy revolved around my very own apartment somewhere near the Odéon, convenient to shopping trips on the rue de Buci for fresh lychees and Camembert; it would have a tiny kitchen with a gas stove, where I could whip up dinner like French women did—with just a few eggs, some salad, and a crunchy loaf of fresh bread. I envisioned this dreamy apartment as the ultimate expression of my independence and self-reliance, free at last from my family's dysfunctional malaise. The last thing I wanted to deal with in Paris was somebody else's family.

"The kids will teach you slang; you'll speak fluently," Tanya had said. I pictured a bunch of sullen teenagers in skinny jeans listening to Serge Gainsbourg and smoking Gauloises. Kids had no place in my Parisian fantasy.

So I was surprised when a frazzled-looking young woman with a long braid and a warm smile leaned over the banister on the landing as I lugged my bag up the shallow steps to the second floor. I guessed she was the Deschamps' au pair. She wore a striped velour sweatshirt and leggings; a black velvet bow was perched on top of her head in the preppy fashion of what the French call BCBG, *bon chic, bon genre*. Good style, good family.

She smiled, rattled off a long string of words—what to me, with my senior year French, was an indecipherable greeting—and beckoned me inside. I could hear the piercing screams of an angry child behind her. Nodding as if I understood every word, I hoisted my bag onto the landing just as a red-faced toddler burst through the open door. I leaned down to greet him.

"Caca prout!" he shouted, a pair of Chiclet-sized teeth protruding from his mouth and a shower of spit spraying over me.

"Maxime," said the au pair, cringing. *"Non! On ne dit pas caca!"* She leaned in to offer me the French *bises,* a peck on each cheek.

"You are very tire-*red*?" She must have realized that my French comprehension was dim and switched to English. She gestured with her hands as if laying her head on a pillow.

"No, *je* ..." I said, shaking my head and then nodding my head. I didn't know what to say. French words had skedaddled from my jet-lagged brain.

She pushed the front door wider, reached for my suitcase, and moved inside the vestibule, with its creaking parquet floor and lofty twelve-foot-high ceiling. Another round of unintelligible questions and she swooped down to pick up Maxime, now bawling and kicking and throwing his head back.

Was she saying something about a roommate? My flight? Maxime? I hadn't heard her name properly but couldn't summon the necessary reflexive verb in French. *"Comment vous appelez-vous?"* Tanya had said Bibiane was young, but not this young. I followed her through a pair of leaded-glass doors into an enormous room that looked like it was at one time a formal dining room. But instead of the customary table and chairs, a lumpy single bed was pushed up against one wall next to a big desk. My room. A tiny door led to the closet-sized room where Susan, another American renter, lived. The tall windows looked out on the dirty gray wall of a courtyard. Paris, city of a thousand grays.

We continued on to the kitchen, past the WC—the only toilet in the apartment—and out into the back hall, through another heavy door. I tried to summon the words to ask the smiling young woman her name, but she kept talking, explaining where everything was and pointing to a washing machine next to the refrigerator. The kitchen was big and bright, painted daffodil yellow. Dishes were piled in the sink. Open jars of jam, glasses, and dirty plates crowded the counters. A huge pile of laundry spilled out of a basket next to the sink. Mademoiselle What's-Her-Name put Maxime down and yanked a bag of Tater Tots out of the freezer and dumped them into a skillet. Maxime, suddenly enraptured with a tiny toy truck, pulled up a plastic stool. She kept talking, fast, as she lit the burner and shook the skillet over the flame, simultaneously opening the fridge and pouring some juice. Her words ran together, without pause, without any identifiable syllables or sounds to which I could respond. *"Tuneveuxpasquelquechose?"* Four years of college French, completely useless. I nodded enthusiastically.

"Capish?"

Um.

"Petit déjeuner," she continued. *Oui.* Help myself to breakfast, she was saying, pointing to a shelf with a few boxes of cereal. In the fridge there was an area where I could put my own food. She picked up a clunky gray phone receiver and wagged her finger. No phone calls out. No *linge,* either, she said. *Linge?* She pointed to the washing machine: *les vêtements!* Clothing, she said, grabbing a shirt that was hanging over the washing-machine door. No doing laundry here. I understood no shampooing *tous les jours*—every day—and something about the keys. She would give me a copy of the keys later. And the code, *en bas*—at the bottom. I tried to memorize it as she rattled off a bunch of letters and numbers in quick succession: A-B-6-2-4-0. Maxime interrupted with bursts of nonsensical dialogue. She had her hands full.

I found my way back to my room and sat on the lumpy bed. My bulging suitcase, sprawled on the threadbare carpet, seemed excessive. There was only one small closet and a few drawers in a bureau. I started to unpack, feeling a pang of homesickness at the sight of my familiar things—the L.L.Bean pajamas, my Canon portable typewriter, my hair dryer with the wrong plug. The artifacts of another life. They looked jarringly out of place here. The usual cues of language and dress and behavior and achievement did not translate. Choate, Princeton, New York City—all of the carefully checked boxes on my résumé meant nothing. I thought I knew Paris, but suddenly everything was new. The language, the young family, the ramshackle apartment—I had spent months imagining this place, convincing myself I needed to be here, visualizing a life in this magical city. And now Paris, that faraway dream, was crushingly real.

The babysitter, as I was calling her in my mind—I would get her name soon enough—reappeared in the doorway, holding Maxime in her arms. He yanked on her earring while she swatted his hand away. *"Ça va?"*

"When will Madame Deschamps return?" I asked, speaking slowly. She frowned and cocked her head to one side.

"C'est moi, Bibiane!"

The rest of the family trickled in throughout the afternoon. Bibiane brought her daughter, Guillemette, home from school and settled in to *le goûter*—snack time—in the kitchen. Bibiane's husband, Antoine, returned from work that evening. He looked like a really short brother of David Bowie and spoke English pretty well. Turning up the volume on his stereo in the salon, he asked me if I knew a band called Les Rita Mitsouko. *"Andy, dis-moi oui,"* the nasal-sounding female vocalist's voice pleaded, alongside a thumping bass. Antoine liked to turn the volume way up, to earsplitting decibels, until Bibiane would come rushing into the salon, her hands covering her ears.

"Antoine! Mer-duh!"

Antoine managed a rock band called Baraka on weekends and rode a scooter to his day job as the director of a vocational school. His uniform, a faded denim jacket and black boots, disguised his deeply bourgeois roots. He and Bibiane had married when she got pregnant at eighteen. They both admitted it was too young, but Bibiane knew Antoine was the love of her life. She just *knew*. She had Guillemette at nineteen, and Maxime followed three years later.

They couldn't afford to live in such an expensive apartment, so they rented out two rooms to Americans to help pay the rent. Bibiane had lucked into the apartment through a childhood friend whose grandmother—a grumpy woman named Madame de Froment—owned the building. Twenty people had vied for the place, but Bibiane jumped to the front of the list; she was *pistonnée,* connected. Everything in Paris's posh 7th arrondissement was about connections.

I asked Antoine if he was nervous about all the terrorist attacks around Paris. Bibiane had said she usually didn't get nervous but this time was different. The afternoon of the explosion on the rue de Rennes, she had taken the kids to her aunt's house nearby and was planning to go to Tati, the discount store where the bomb had been tossed, but she was tired so they just went home. She marveled at her luck.

"Ah!" she said, as she made crêpes for the kids, whisking a bowl of eggs, flour, and sugar. "It could have been something else. *Tu imagines?*"

I couldn't imagine, still shaky about the idea that another bomb could go off at any minute.

Antoine was more philosophical. "We are *fataliste,*" he said, pausing to puff on a cigarette as he lounged on the sofa. "Life has to go on."

That first night in Paris, I didn't know what to do. I was dog-tired from jet lag and from the effort to comprehend a language I thought I knew. Susan, the other American *locataire,* had returned late from classes. She was taking her junior year abroad, and her French wasn't so great, either. She turned in early to study.

I grabbed the keys, scribbled the code on a scrap of paper, and ventured downstairs. The rue de Grenelle was a narrow street tucked behind the boulevard Saint-Germain and lined with antiques shops, cafés, and grand private houses with enormous courtyards hidden behind heavy, lacquered doors. A few intrepid fashion boutiques had infiltrated the village-like atmosphere of the street, staking out the corners nearest to the bustling Bar de la Croix Rouge. Sonia Rykiel's headquarters were housed in an ancient building with low-slung timbers; her popular striped velour sweatshirts hung in the window. Down the block, electric-blue neon lights flashed on and off in the windows of a new Claude Montana shop. Along the quiet street I noticed the white metal shutters on all the windows were closed, and all I could hear was the loopy sound of a television game show coming from inside a concierge's ground-floor apartment.

I remember thinking it was better to avoid busy boulevards and brasseries, because of the bombs. So I chose a small touristy restaurant down the block. The place was nearly empty. Parisians were staying home. Onion soup and steak were the only familiar items on the menu. Waiting for my food to arrive, I felt painfully self-conscious and alone. I imagined writing a letter to my friends back in New York: *Paris is great! Having so much fun eating alone in restaurants. And bombs are going off. It's great!*

I paid the bill quickly and went back to the apartment. I punched in the code, pushed the door, and found the button for the light. When I was halfway upstairs, the light went out. I fumbled around in the pitch-black stairwell, looking for another switch, but couldn't find it, so I felt my way up each step, hugging the wall. I had yet to learn that the timer—

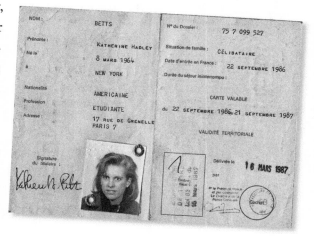

the *minuterie*—on the light switch was set for only a minute. I was not a tourist anymore. I was a student with a *carte de séjour,* a freshman, starting over, with a different kind of hazing, or *bizutage.*

I slipped into the apartment, changed into my pajamas, and fell asleep as the lights of the city quietly went dark. My room with a view—of a gray wall.

The next morning Maxime burst in through the glass doors and promptly hurled a toy truck at my head. *Bonjour!* When I tried to say something to him, stammering a string of nonsensical French words, he raced back into the living room to assume his place on the floor in front of the TV. It was Saturday and the kids woke at six and scurried across the parquet to their parents' room. I could hear a rumbling and a door opening and Bibiane turning on the television. For the next few hours, while the parents slept, the kids sat parked like two baked potatoes, mesmerized by a television show called *Madame Pepperpote.*

Tanya was right: Maxime and Guillemette became my primary French teachers, especially in the lessons of slang. On my second night, Bibiane put me to work babysitting.

"Voilà," she said, grabbing her keys off the mantel and applying a quick slash of red lipstick. "All you have to do is give the bath and *au lit!"*

Put the kids to bed. Easy.

"Merci, ma Kate-uh!" she said, adding the Parisian extra syllable to my name before slamming the door behind her with a thud.

We eased our way into the kitchen, flicking on the lights. The kids sat on their plastic stools obediently.

"Moi, je veux des frites!" Maxime half screamed, as was his way. Fries! Just fries! He kept saying it. I tried to mimic what I'd seen Bibiane do—dumping the frozen fries into a pan of hot oil and then shaking the pan. I lacked her confidence, and the kids picked up on this. My fries were not nearly as crunchy. Maxime doused his in ketchup, but to no avail. The half-eaten steak I'd cooked disappeared into the garbage can, too. *"Berk! Dégueulasse,"* he said, grinning. Disgusting.

When the magical hour of seven-thirty arrived, Maxime scurried into the bathroom and began shouting impatiently. *"La flotte, la flotte,"* he screamed, pointing to the bathtub. I tried to make sense of it, but he just kept shouting. Finally, Guillemette turned on the faucet. *La flotte* was slang for water. Maxime simply wanted me to draw his bath.

My name was not easy to pronounce in French, so Antoine started calling me *Quéquette*, which sort of sounded like Kate but actually was slang for penis. Maxime and Guillemette threw their heads back and shrieked with laughter. Antoine added a word that sounded like my last name: *Bite,* also slang for penis. From then on I was *Quéquette Bite*— penis penis.

I picked up French by hanging around the house with Bibiane and her friends. She worked part time as a temp at the American Hospital, but she always collected her kids at school and invited other moms back for tea in her salon. They would gossip about in-laws, vacation plans, and recent shopping sprees. They never, ever spoke about work. Bibiane's best friend, Brigitte, was obsessed with fashion. She spent hours searching for the best deal on the latest Robert Clergerie boots or Il Bisonte handbag. She spoke carefully with a Southern accent, from Aix, pursing her lips and sucking in her breath while saying *"oui."* There were a million different ways to say *"oui"*—the Parisian *ouais,* or other iterations such as *d'ac,* which was short for *d'accord,* or agreed.

Sometimes Bibiane's mother, Bénédicte, would join these impromptu tea parties. Bénédicte always wore a neat navy pencil skirt, low heels, and a snug tweed jacket. She lived in the posh 16th arrondissement with her husband, Gérard, and had the same warmth and sincerity as her daughter. She spoke slowly in elegant, proper French and scolded the others for teaching me slang. I liked listening to her, because I could understand most of what she said. Bénédicte liked to tell stories about her family and about growing up in the rural southwestern region of Limousin. As for many French people of Bénédicte's generation, World War II was the central point of reference in her life: Everything was either *before the war, during the war,* or *after the war.*

"The thing about Americans is that they are easy to meet but they do not remain your friends forever," she said, shaking her head and clucking. "French people are hard to get to know, but once you know them you will be their friend for life."

Her pronouncement reminded me of a story I had once heard about a family that had hidden an American soldier in their backyard for several months. On V Day, they ran to the tree where he had lived, but the soldier was gone. The family could not understand why they had never heard from him again. When I repeated the story in broken French, Bénédicte nodded silently.

"They risked their lives to save him," she said, shrugging.

I didn't have the vocabulary yet to explain that the American soldier had risked his life to save them, too.

Bénédicte's memories of the war were vivid. She could still hear the sound of machine guns in the village and remember her mother saying the Lord's Prayer as she closed the shutters in the salon of their house. She could still recall the *thunk, thunk* of the German soldiers' boots on the parquet as they burst through the front door. To this day, Bénédicte cannot abide loud sounds, because they remind her of those machine guns—*les mitraillettes*.

"Are you a student?" Bénédicte asked me in her high-pitched, sing-song voice.

"*Non, je cherche un travail,*" I said tentatively.

"*Un boulot!*" exclaimed Bibiane. "*Un* job!" She laughed, her eyes widening as if to say, "How absurd to be looking for a job!"

"*Du travail,*" Bénédicte corrected, using proper French.

Yes, I was looking for a job. Two days after arriving, I had called Maggie Shapiro, the head of internships at the *Trib*, to ask her when I should report to work. It turned out they no longer needed another intern. She was very sorry. She took my phone number just in case something opened up.

I hung up the receiver and slumped down on the floor of the phone booth on the corner of the boulevard Saint-Germain, where I went to make calls. *Merde.* I had been counting on the internship at the *Trib*, not just for the money but also for the sense of belonging and purpose it would bring. What would I do now? How would I find a job? A place to go? A sense of identity? I wanted desperately to belong in Paris. And I wanted to be able to tell my friends back in New York that I had a good job and a paycheck, a career and a *raison d'être*. But this was Paris, not Princeton. I had yet to learn that in Paris nobody cares what you do for a living.

For days I scanned classified ads in the *Trib,* looking for bilingual-secretarial jobs. I typed up cover letters in the formal French I copied from examples borrowed from Antoine. I applied to banks, law firms, and insurance agencies. Bibiane and Antoine marveled at my focus. "You work so hard!" Bibiane said. "I am sure you will be a success."

One rainy morning I took the RER train out to La Défense, the vast modern complex of skyscrapers in the suburbs west of Paris. I had secured an interview for a secretarial position at a Middle Eastern bank called Bank BAII. I found my way through the wasteland of broad, empty concrete plazas and granite lobbies to the fifteenth floor of a 1970s-style glass tower. A dead-eyed receptionist gestured for me to wait in the reception area, where a plastic ashtray filled with cigarette butts spilled over onto a chrome-and-glass coffee table. This was not Hemingway's Paris.

Madame Pelouard, the HR person, was a birdlike woman with stringy hair and wire-rimmed glasses that she reflexively pushed up her nose every fifteen seconds.

"Why you did not put the information *plus* important *ici?*" she asked in broken English, stabbing my résumé with her finger. "*Taper à la machine?* What *vitesse?*"

Typing speed? I had never typed on a French keyboard, which had the A and Q reversed. I took the test anyway. My work was incomprehensible. *Non,* Madame Pelouard said, shaking her head vehemently. I did not have the correct skills. I unfurled my umbrella and headed back to Paris—my Paris, Hemingway's Paris, city of a million café crèmes, not the Paris of dead-end jobs in the sad and sordid suburbs.

The parents of a friend in New York had been helpful, supplying me with a list of their Parisian contacts. A few days after I arrived, an art dealer they knew invited me to a *vernissage* at an elegant townhouse off the Champs-Élysées. I bought a black miniskirt at a discount store in Les Halles and wore it with a pair of opaque tights and heels. I could have been mistaken for one of the catering waitresses. The other women, all much older and more elegant, were dressed in bright-red silk blouses with billowing sleeves or pink tweed Chanel suits with giant gold buttons. They were drenched in expensive perfume, their necks wrapped neatly in Hermès scarves. Someone introduced me to the director of a historical preservation foundation called Friends of Vieilles Maisons Françaises. She offered an internship but then never took my calls. A week later, at a dinner at Le Bœuf sur le Toit with the parents of another New York friend, I met a vice president of the beauty company Orlane. He talked about job opportunities in their marketing department. Alas, I didn't have working papers. Every connection seemed to lead to a dead end.

Letters from friends back home recounted office parties, weekend flings, and gossip. Paris was *great,* I responded; everything I'd hoped, I lied. Paris was hardly glamorous. I was schlepping to the corner phone booth to make calls and carrying my laundry on the Métro to a cheap laundromat in Saint-Michel. When Susan and I felt homesick, we would sneak off to McDonald's and feast on Big Macs. We went to American movies like *Top Gun* and *Down by Law,* in *version originale,* English.

After two weeks of pounding the pavement, interviewing for secretarial jobs, it dawned on me that a sales job in an American shop was probably more realistic. I applied to the Polo store on place de la Madeleine. As I sat on a giant tufted leather couch, waiting for my interview, a blond saleswoman thrust her hand out at me and introduced herself. Nikki was about my age. She had come to Paris from Perth, Australia. She had working papers because her mother was Scottish, and anyone with a European passport was allowed a special working visa in France. We laughed about the French and how far from home we often felt. I was relieved to make an English-speaking friend. We exchanged phone numbers.

I didn't get the job, but I called Nikki a few days later and we met for brunch. We talked about our love of Paris, our loneliness, and our ambition. She had confidence and spoke French with a thick Australian accent. Her sentences were peppered with expressions like "I reckon" and "hey?" She was amused by my desire to ingratiate myself with Parisians.

"Forget it, they'll never accept you!" she said. "You'll always be a foreigner, hey, never a native."

Nikki didn't care much for Parisians, but she loved Paris. At that age when most people are trying on different selves, Nikki already knew who she wanted to become. By day she was the top-grossing salesperson at the Ralph Lauren shop, in plaid prairie skirts and button-down silk shirts. At night or on the weekends, she transformed into the sporty Parisian in riding boots and hacking jackets. She told me stories about how lonely it was to travel home to Australia, because she would inevitably have a layover in a city like Kuala Lumpur. I'd never even heard of the Malaysian capital. She was fearless and game for anything.

I was still hovering between two worlds. I missed my friends and my family, but I had no desire to go home. My college boyfriend would call occasionally, usually early in the morning Paris time, after he had been out drinking with friends. Our conversations were awkward, broken up by a long-distance delay. How could I explain my new life? I missed him, but in a selfish way, in the way that one misses seeing a familiar face.

Bibiane and Antoine were generous with their invitations. If they were having a dinner party, they invited Susan and me to join the group. We sat on the floor around their coffee table, drinking cheap red wine and smoking.

Bibiane's bohemian approach to life was not at all in sync with her background. She had grown up a few blocks away, on the rue de Rennes, the oldest daughter of an aristocratic family. She hardly fit the stereotype: She was not a dutiful churchgoer; she had never adopted the appropriate preppy uniform of snug tweed suits, crisp button-down shirts, and silk scarves. Even when she was flambéing crêpes for dinner for her kids, she wore big dangling earrings, black leggings, and tacky pumps with cone-shaped heels.

Bibiane was unorthodox in that she rebelled against the idea that you could be defined by your name alone. She explained that in France, if you had *de* in front of your name, you were either judged as a kind of *aristo-con,* or asshole, for being from a good, old family or, worse, people were nice to you only because of your name. Bibiane hated that.

Antoine was grittier and insolent. He came from a bourgeois provincial family, the second of eight kids. His father had been in the military, and the children had grown up in the Loire Valley city of Saumur, home to the Cadre Noir, the famous equestrian school that once supplied officers to the French cavalry. Antoine considered himself the black sheep of his family. He blasted hard-rock music and chain-smoked Philip Morris Ultra Lights, filling huge square ashtrays on the coffee table with cigarette butts night after night. He would play his favorite songs from Les Rita Mitsouko over and over, ignoring the loud taps on the ceiling from Madame de Froment upstairs.

For her informal dinner parties, Bibiane would serve theme meals—taco night, couscous—or typical French dishes like blanquette de veau. She could cook as easily for twenty people as she could for two. The guest list was usually a spontaneous mix of friends and family. And if more people showed up unexpectedly, Bibiane would reach into the freezer and pull out fillets or chocolate cake from a nearby frozen-food market called Picard Surgelés. Her friend Stéphane was a frequent guest and a former student of Antoine's. Balding and insecure about the fact that he was a hairdresser's son from the provinces, Stéphane had a wicked sense of humor and played the clown to Antoine's cool cat. It took me a while to understand their comic routine. Stéphane would patiently repeat slang words and explain them to me. Money was *espèces,* or *liquide, blé, la thune, fric, sou, pognon,* or *le pèze.* Car was *bagnole, caisse, tire.* In France it was impolite to talk about money, but you could talk about cars all day long.

On special occasions like birthdays and anniversaries, Bibiane and Antoine would host costume parties. The French love to dress up, to radically transform themselves, just for one night. I was always amused by the themes they chose for these parties, like Sex or Kitsch or Legends. The more BCBG and uptight, the more radical the metamorphosis.

It was in these moments of disguise, when the guard was down and the identities of these people were less fixed to their social rank, that I understood the depth and complexity of French, and not just the spoken language. To express oneself fluently involves more than simply speaking the language properly. It includes inflection, voice, posture, gestures, and clothing. All of these elements add up to an individual's personal expression. They are the elements of style.

"Ce n'est pas à mon goût." This is not my taste, Bibiane would say, trying to define her own look or compare her style to mine.

"*Très Américaine,*" she and her friends would say, sizing up my style. "*T'es tellement Américaine!*" So American. They couldn't identify exactly what gave me away—was it the way I cut my hair, in a short bob, but not quite short enough or slanted enough to have that Gallic chic? Or was it my shoes, scuffed lace-up oxfords, classic pumps with worn-down heels? Or the slouchy bag, a splurge I bought on sale at Il Bisonte on the rue du Cherche-Midi? I tried so hard to shed my baggy American collegiate look for a sleeker, more refined Parisian silhouette.

What I lacked in style, I made up for in my effort to speak French. I wanted to crack the codes, master the gestures and manners that could not be learned in a textbook or a classroom. The codes defined you, just as the *de* particle in front of Bibiane's maiden name defined her. Even the smallest gestures mattered. Hands always on the table, never in the lap, in case some funny business was going on under there. (All those years of my mother instructing me about hands in the lap . . .) As a guest in someone else's home, you never opened the refrigerator. Never made references to bodily functions, such as, "I'm eating breakfast," or "*Je suis en train de manger.*" You took breakfast—*prendre le petit déjeuner*—or you lunched or you dined or you supped. Never took off your shoes and walked barefoot on grass, even in the countryside. Never, ever walked on grass in the city. It was not for use; it was for appreciation. And never addressed an elder as anything but *vous*.

I studied these codes, making the inevitable mistakes and learning. At a party one night, I helped myself to a beer. "*Sale Américaine,*" someone whispered. Dirty American. How was I supposed to know women of a certain class in France don't drink beer?

I listened patiently to dinner conversations; I listened to the kids; I listened to French pop music on Antoine's stereo, replaying Vanessa Paradis's hit song "*Joe le Taxi*" over and over again. "*Vas-y Joe,*" she sang in her tinny Lolita voice.

I had been in Paris for about three weeks when Maggie Shapiro from the *Trib* called to say that in fact they did need an extra intern— could I start immediately? My title would be *aide-documentaliste,* or glorified paper pusher. My godmother's boyfriend had pulled strings. I was *pistonnée,* too.

Paris Playlist

"Tchiki Boum," Niagara

"Les Cactus," Jacques Dutronc

"Marcia Baïla," Les Rita Mitsouko

"Les Brunes Comptent Pas pour des Prunes," Lio

"Asimbonanga," Johnny Clegg

"Joe le Taxi," Vanessa Paradis

"Evidemment," France Gall

"Là-Bas," Jean-Jacques Goldman

"Andy," Les Rita Mitsouko

"Il Est Cinq Heures," Jacques Dutronc

"Quand Paris s'Éteint," Jean-Louis Aubert

"C'est la Ouate," Caroline Loeb

"Toi Mon Toit," Elli Medeiros

"Bascule avec Moi," Marc Lavoine

CHAPTER FOUR

Dual Citizenship

The job description of an *aide-documentaliste* was anything but glamorous: sort mail, type manuscripts, take dictation. Three interns worked a six-month *stagiaire,* which consisted of a thirty-nine-hour week that paid about six dollars an hour. After those first few weeks of living in Paris, feeling my way around blindly— like a fool stuck in a stairwell when the *minuterie* times out—the *Trib* was a place to go and a reason to show up every morning at nine-thirty sharp. I ranked lowest on the totem pole because I didn't have working papers. The two other interns, Phil and Catherine, were half French, so they had dual citizenship and working papers. Working papers conferred status; they *belonged* in France. I was

a foreigner; I had a *carte de travail temporaire,* a blue index card bearing my name and address. Not everyone belongs, but everyone is accounted for.

An American in Paris! I was following in the footsteps of generations of diplomats, painters, writers, and *flâneurs* who beat a quick path to Paris when life stateside became predictable and dull. Oliver Wendell Holmes wrote that he went to Paris seeking relief from the "sameness" of his life. I could relate. I had come seeking some kind of foreign adventure. Paris represented an opportunity for reinvention, and in that new persona, I hoped, I would also shed the traces of my family's unhappy history. Of course, I was still relying on my parents and any connections or guidance or cash they could supply. I was still an adolescent, running from fears I couldn't face. But Paris in that moment seemed like a beautiful, if impenetrable, sanctuary.

"Good Americans, when they die, go to Paris." I jotted down all those Paris quotes from Appleton, Emerson, Hemingway, and Henry Miller in the spiral-bound journal I bought at a kiosk on the boulevard Raspail. Next to each inspirational quote I taped a postcard depicting the city's mystical pearly light as seen through the eyes of the great American painters who had honed their craft in Paris: Mary Cassatt, John Singer Sargent, James Whistler.

Like Thomas Jefferson, James Fenimore Cooper, Samuel Morse, I was discovering those funky French dualities that everyone encounters in Paris, what Cooper called the appalling dichotomy of "dirt and gilding . . . bedbugs and laces." The grandeur of the gilded dome of Les Invalides and the gigantesque Louvre seamlessly juxtaposed with the small, labyrinthine medieval streets of Le Marais or the cubbyhole shops along the rue de Grenelle.

Every morning I pulled open the heavy door at number 17 and walked out to the rue du Bac Métro stop. Every day the same route: past the locksmith window filled with chunky brass keys and ancient locks; past the teenage girls peeking out behind long curtains of hair, loitering outside the Lycée Louis-le-Grand before class; past the antiques shop selling carved wooden canes and billiard balls, and past the café where red-nosed *ouvriers* in cobalt-blue jumpsuits gathered around the *zinc* for a *ballon de rouge.* In the morning, the gutters overflowed with water running like a river alongside the sidewalk. Occasionally a street sweeper in a bright-green jumpsuit would push the water along with his plastic broom, collecting cigarette butts and discarded yellow Métro tickets in its wake. On the boulevard, buses with open-air platforms at the back roared by, while Vespas slalomed gracefully around slow-moving taxis and cars.

Everything was new and foreign and exciting. Even the mundane morning rituals of Paris thrilled me: the cleanliness of the street sweepers, the formal greeting from the café bartender—
"*Bonjour, mademoiselle*"—and the

discipline of the Métro riders moving swiftly through the long, tiled corridors at the Place de la Concorde, seemingly oblivious to the awful, acrid urine and tobacco odor. Even in the chaotic Métro, the French clung to their rules, hugging the right side of the corridor as they hustled from one platform to the next. I fell in line behind *la foule,* the Parisian herd. Only a fool would disturb the orderly rhythm and risk being trampled.

The office of the *Trib* was on the edge of Paris in the suburb of Neuilly; the building perched over the avenue Charles de Gaulle, a busy thoroughfare that extended west from the Champs-Élysées. The Bauhaus-style glass, chrome, and marble offices hadn't been renovated since they were built in the 1960s. A threadbare entryway hung with framed copies of famous front pages of the paper led to the newsroom on the second floor. Twenty desks piled high with stray newspapers, books, and mail clogged the middle of the room, while glassed-in private offices lined the perimeter. Interns reported to the mail room, a cubby overlooking the bullpen. You could hide in the mail room and peek out through the mail slots at the editors slouched down in their swivel chairs, staring blankly at the screens of their clunky word processors.

The *Trib* was its own universe, a world apart from Paris. The editors existed in an expatriate bubble. They enjoyed the daily pleasures of Paris but seemingly had no desire to become Parisian. They lived the American expat dream: They dined at La Coupole, Hemingway's favorite Montparnasse brasserie, where they slurped platters of oysters with a chilly Sancerre. They jogged listlessly through the Luxembourg Gardens on sunny Saturday mornings. They rushed to WHSmith, the English-language bookstore on the rue de Rivoli, to buy American magazines. Most of the editors spoke very little French—just enough to order coffee, have a phone line hooked up, or navigate the *préfecture de police.*

In my own cloud of delusion, I found the isolation of this expatriate life pathetic. Even after years of living in Paris, my godmother, Sandy, was no different. She would wave away my suggestions that she socialize with Parisians. "I don't speak French!" she would say with a shrug. "They aren't interested in anyone who doesn't speak their language."

Dinners at her apartment were inevitably limited to American expats and visiting friends from New York or California. She was big-hearted and loved to entertain, preparing elaborate buffets of fabulous food and serving excellent wines.

"Don't you love it?" she would gush, with a nervous, boozy laugh, thrusting open the doors to her balcony and gesturing to the expansive view of Paris aglow in the evening light. Sandy had inherited money. Her grandfather had founded the Underwood typewriter company, or something, and she didn't need to work. And yet her isolation seemed to breed a loneliness that terrified me. How could you live in such a vibrant city and not speak the language, or engage with its inhabitants, or make friends? Sandy's boyfriend, Bob, a jolly Midwesterner who had climbed the masthead at *Time* before being transferred to Hong Kong and then Paris, spoke French well but had few French friends. It seemed odd and insular, a bald-faced rejection.

The den mother of the expat bubble at the *Trib* was Maggie Shapiro, whose official title was *archiviste.* She sat in the cramped library behind a stack of newspapers and dispatched each intern to a different department every couple of days. It's impossible to imagine now, in the digital age, but in the fall of 1986, archives meant pages and pages in oversized bound volumes filled with precise columns of newsprint clippings. Maggie organized all the copy that had been printed in the newspaper in these oversized books. When editors needed to reference past articles,

Maggie would search through the books to find the stories. It was meticulous and tedious work and required an infinite institutional knowledge of the editorial content of the newspaper.

There was not much breaking news to report at the *Trib*—mostly the paper reprinted stories from *The New York Times* and *The Washington Post*. Occasionally something big would happen in Paris, like the string of terrorist bombings, and the editor would dispatch a reporter to cover the events. But by early October the terrorist threat had been lowered. The French police had arrested nine people from a radical group called the Committee for Solidarity with Arab and Middle Eastern Political Prisoners. They had claimed responsibility for the bombings. Paris started to feel safe again.

Apart from the business desk, which was responsible for converting currencies on the stock listings, the only people I ever encountered who filed stories on a regular basis were the fashion critic and the art critic, but they rarely set foot in the office. Most of the editors—former bigwigs on the mastheads of the *Times* and *Post*—rolled into work at around 11:00 A.M., spent a few hours hunched over their word processors, and then ambled out the door for long Parisian lunches. What they lacked in editorial cachet, they made up for with airy nineteenth-century apartments wrapped in wrought-iron balconies and splendid views. It was a graveyard, a cushy but nebulous reward for career journeymen.

At the *Trib* I was first sent upstairs to the supplements department, where features editors cobbled together arts coverage and special advertising sections. My boss was a patient Australian woman named Marian who trained interns, teaching us how to run the shift known as day copy; this consisted mostly of sorting mail and entering copy or manuscripts into the system. For the first week I typed for eight hours every day, stopping only for a half-hour lunch break. Sometimes Marian would ask me to take dictation from the snooty art critic, who called in his copy from London. He spoke excruciatingly slowly, enunciating each word as if I had never before heard English spoken. He didn't trust anyone with his precious copy, so he spelled out every word.

"The," he would say. "T. H. E."

When an editor yelled at me for making too many typos in my transcripts, I'd be reassigned to the mail room to help Catherine or Phil file the afternoon mail and clip newspaper articles for the library. At lunchtime I ate by myself in a grim sandwich shop nearby, paying with the free lunch checks—the *chèque déjeuner*—every workplace was obligated to distribute to employees. The pay wasn't great at the *Trib,* but plenty of perks made life in Paris more affordable. The paper also offered discounts at health clubs like the nearby chain Le Gymnase Club. I signed up at a branch just off the Champs-Élysées. The place was painted bright green to evoke grass and sport. It was a joke, because French people didn't work out; the machines—treadmills, a few weight-lifting rigs—were primitive. Most of the members were American expats who worked at law firms and investment banks nearby.

The first night I went to the gym, I met a young French woman named Hélène. She was on the treadmill next to mine, groping frantically at the speed buttons, trying to slow down. She wore a perfectly pressed Lacoste shirt and khaki shorts; her hair was held back in a velvet headband. The French have a uniform for everything except exercise.

"Vous êtes Américaine?" Hélène asked, speaking slowly in French, her blue eyes wide with wonder. She cocked her head to the side, pursed her lips, and examined me, up and down.

I nodded, out of breath from the treadmill.

"Vous venez de quelle ville?" she asked, knitting her brows together with a look of great concern. When I told her I was from New York, she nearly fell off the machine. She stared at me, speechless, climbing down off her treadmill to get a better look.

"New York!" she said with a big smile, her eyes lighting up again. "I do not know it! But I've seen it in the movies. Do they really have the smoke coming out of the street like you see in the *cinéma?*" she asked, incredulous.

We ran into each other several more times, once on the Métro on the way home. She was with her friend Bénédicte. They were secretaries at a bank near Le Gymnase Club. They wore long cashmere cardigans and pearls and blue mascara, a look most often described as *coincé,* or uptight. They laughed at me for washing my hair every day. Why didn't I just go to the salon and have a *brushing*—or blow out—once a week, like most French women? Hélène lived with her parents and her brother in a ground-floor apartment on the boulevard Montparnasse. She had the habit of repeating everything you said and then attaching a question to it, like a language teacher. "*Alors*, Kate, you are living with a French family in the seventh arrondissement but you are not an au pair or an *étudiante, oui?*"

One Saturday afternoon Hélène invited me to her house for tea. She introduced me to her parents, who stared at me, unable to speak any English and seemingly afraid to speak French.

"*Beh, alors!* She speaks French *couramment*," Hélène said, imploring her mother to speak.

She addressed her parents formally, with *vous,* and introduced me to her older brother, whom she dismissed with a wave. He was a nerd, *"pas cool, débile,"* she said. *"Allez, on va bavarder."*

She motioned me down the hall to her room, where we sat on her bed, gossiping beneath a wooden crucifix hanging on the wall. Hélène confided that her parents were very religious, and strict. She wanted to get out from under their grip. But it was clear that she was the pride of her family, the socially adjusted and aware child who might marry well. Even though it was common in France to live at home at her age, Hélène's ambition in life was to find a husband and be free of the watchful gaze of her parents. Although we had little else in common, we shared a desire to escape the confines of family expectations. I liked Hélène for her curiosity and her forthright attitude, and in a foreign city one is less discriminating when it comes to making friends.

One evening in early December on my way home from work, I heard people on the Métro talking about a *manif,* or demonstration. Strikes were common occurrences in Paris, especially with a socialist like Mitterrand as president. Students at the Sorbonne had been demonstrating for a week. They were protesting a government plan to make state universities more expensive and more selective. The protestors called the plan elitist. Nothing irritates the French more than a whiff of unauthorized elitism.

The previous evening, the protest had erupted in violence over by the boulevard Saint-Michel, and the CRS—French armed police—were called in with their tear gas and their riot gear. The rumor was that one student had died, supposedly beaten by the police (later it was revealed that the kid had suffered a heart attack). In response, thousands of students were expected to protest at the Sorbonne that evening. I was intrigued and excited about the events. I had written my senior thesis at Princeton on the student riots of 1968 and the impact of student-worker action on French political consciousness. My adviser, a specialist in European intellectual history, had dismissed the incident as a minor upheaval with little historical significance. But to me, the idea of rioting in the streets, of questioning authority, was a French political rite of passage, and the Sorbonne protest planned for that evening was a must-see demonstration of French political fervor.

I called Hélène to see if she wanted to walk up the boulevard Saint-Michel to check out the burning barricades and the hurled pavement stones up close.

"*Tu es dingue?* Are you crazy?" She laughed. "*Non,* there are cops everywhere. It's dangerous! These students are just *voyou,* hoodlums. They are Communists!" She thought it was strange and hilarious that I wanted to go into the crowd of rioting students just to see it.

"This is not the *Mona Lisa!*" She laughed again, then, in a serious tone, she warned me about thugs from the suburbs who came into the city at the slightest sign of upheaval and vandalized stores or beat up innocent bystanders. "They are usually Algerians," she whispered. "*Tu piges?* You know what I mean?"

I decided to go anyway. Walking up the boulevard Saint-Germain, now empty of cars, toward the intersection of boulevard Saint-Michel, I could see the overturned cars and smoking piles of rubble in the distance. Two telephone booths on the corner had been smashed. Cafés were closed, the door handles chained shut, the rattan chairs tucked safely inside, stacked up in neat columns.

Police swarmed the street, brandishing shields and spraying tear gas into the crowds. Along the sidewalks, right-wing *casseurs,* or provocateurs, wearing motorcycle helmets pitched paving stones through store windows. Rumor had it they were brought in by the police to discredit the students.

The streets looked like a war zone. Whether they were serious or just out for a good vandalism spree, the students had wreaked havoc on the neighborhood. There was something so exhilarating about the nervous, violent energy of the street. Maybe it was because I was seeing history for the first time come to life.

The next day *Le Matin,* a socialist newspaper, reported that an older group of *soixante-huitards*—people who had participated in the riots of 1968—was seen showing the new generation of younger students how to set cars on fire and build barricades. Like any French ritual that was passed from one generation to the next, the rituals of rebellion and protest were also taught. Perhaps my thesis adviser had a point. These riots were insignificant in the grander scheme of French history. This was not the Bastille circa 1789. No guillotines, no decapitated monarchs, and no altering the course of history. This was just another French strike that had spiraled out of control. The government had responded swiftly, and eventually the prime minister rescinded his proposed reform. By Saturday morning the students had retreated to their smoky cafés, savoring a crème and a pack of Philip Morris Ultra Lights.

Although I was hardly manning the barricades, I recognized something in those rangy students in their denim jackets, hurling paving stones. I shared their impulse—to a less violent degree—to rebel against the people and institutions that had shaped them. Hadn't I fled Princeton, rejecting the notion that such an institution would empower me? I wanted to go my own way, without relying on the ballast of tradition. But deep down I lacked confidence in my choice. I had rejected one path without choosing another. I didn't have a clearly articulated passion. I certainly didn't have the visceral confidence of those rioting students. I was still trying on new personas and experimenting with a new voice—a French voice.

At work a few days later, while sorting faxes of photos coming over the wires, I found one showing two demonstrators being carried off by police. I slipped it into my journal and took it home. That night I wrote a letter to my thesis adviser and enclosed the fax of the photo. At the bottom I printed, "1986 = 1968," like the graffiti I'd seen on a wall in the Latin Quarter.

I was determined not to go home for the first year I lived in Paris. I was looking forward to the Christmas season. Big department stores, like Printemps and Galeries Lafayette, decorated their windows with elaborate installations and festooned their façades with ribbons of lights. Along the boulevards, each branch of each tree and the curlicues of every lamppost were articulated by tiny lights. In every square, a Christmas tree glowed. Rows of stalls at Christmas markets sold chestnuts and wreaths and delicate glass ornaments.

"We'll come to you!" my mother exclaimed on the phone. I was calling late one night from the phone booth on the boulevard Saint-Germain.

"It will be great to see you, and we can celebrate New Year's Eve with Sandy and Bob!"

She had it all planned out. I could hear it in her voice: This was not a last-minute, spur-of-the-moment decision. My mother had given me space and time to find my way in my new home, but now she had her chance to breach the divide. Plus, she had her own romantic notions about Paris. She needed an escape from issues that had plagued her for some time. She and her then-boyfriend had invested in a weekly newspaper in northwestern Connecticut. She had naïvely thought running a small-town paper would allow her to flex her photojournalist muscles, taking pictures of the prosaic countryside, writing columns about neighborhood issues. But she quickly fell into managing a dysfunctional staff of disgruntled reporters, editors, and printers. Every day brought a new crisis: firings, budget cuts, angry board members. She was eager to get away. She enlisted my older sister to join her. Liz had just moved to New York from Washington and was studying graphic design. She was curious about Paris but perhaps less enthusiastic about traveling, particularly with Mom.

I booked a room at the Hôtel des Saints Pères, a small establishment around the corner from the Deschamps' apart-ment. I met Mom and Liz at Orly Airport, and we shared a taxi into town. Jet-lagged, Liz begged off for a nap, while my mother and I caught up over café crèmes on the carrefour de la Croix Rouge. She was tired but didn't want to waste a minute of her time here. She listened closely to stories of Bibiane and Antoine, the *Trib,* and the excitement of meet-ing new friends. It was such a relief to see her smile, to feel her warmth. I didn't realize until then, staring at the December rain pelting the win-dow of the café, how much I had missed her.

For the next few days we walked and walked under gray skies and drizzle, stopping for a crème and pillowy croissants at the Café de Flore or for tiny balls of raspberry and lime sorbet at Berthillon on the Île Saint-Louis. My sister brought her camera and took photos of the Art Nouveau Métro signs and the perfectly geometric alleys of chestnut trees in the Luxembourg Gardens. My mother complained about the Parisians' habit of bumping into tourists on the narrow sidewalks.

"Am I bumping into them?" she asked, perplexed. "I feel like such a clumsy American."

"No, no," I corrected. "That's their way of saying hello."

President Mitterrand had recently inaugurated the Musée d'Orsay, and we spent an afternoon reveling in the majesty of Gustave Courbet's great masterpiece *A Burial at Ornans,* Manet's *Le Déjeuner sur l'Herbe,* and Van Gogh's tiny, jewel-like portrait of his brother Theo. We ordered chèvre salad at the restaurant, under the iconic clock, and I took a picture of my mother sitting on the edge of a bench inside the sleek, modernist interior of the vast museum, a former train station that had been completely gutted and redesigned by the Italian architect Gae Aulenti. I drew out itineraries of different neighborhoods where we could walk and explore and then end up at a museum or restaurant or, better yet, a department store. We shopped, of course, returning several times to Galeries Lafayette, with its huge Christmas tree reaching up to the Belle Époque glass-domed roof. The dressing rooms were hot and small, but I tried on pair after pair of Dorothée Bis pants, oversized Joseph Tricot sweaters, and tiny snap-front Agnès B. cardigans in every color. A midnight-blue shearling coat caught my eye and I slipped it on, pulling the fuzzy collar up around my neck. A luxurious cocoon, the best insulation from Paris's damp winter chill.

"Get it!" my mother urged, wanting to indulge me. "Buy yourself something nice! I'll pay for it. This is Paris, after all." She believed in the idea that beautiful clothes could boost your confidence. Back in New York she went on legendary shopping sprees, buying up two or three pairs of shoes at a time. But when all the packages were undone and the latest outfit hung in the closet, an aura of emptiness lingered over these extravagances.

In Paris my mother embraced the fashion consciousness that mysteriously wraps itself around you like a silk scarf. "I have nothing to wear!" she exclaimed, astonished that her clothes from New York felt completely wrong on the boulevards of Saint-Germain. She bought a Jean Muir sweater and a straight black skirt from Rodier. At Kenzo she scooped up armfuls of colorful paisley scarves, African beaded necklaces, and ropes of amber beads, piling them on, one over the other.

"French women know how to accessorize," she would marvel as we traipsed from one bead store to another on the Île Saint-Louis. "They never buy anything new, they just change the jewelry and the scarves."

I thought of Bibiane, who every once in a while would splurge on a new sweater or pair of high heels at the discount stores along the rue de

Sèvres. Rushing in the front door after a shopping excursion, intoxicated by some great deal, she would announce her latest find—"fifty francs!"—and triumphantly brandish the spoils. *"C'est insensé!"*

Sabbia Rosa was a tiny jewel box of a shop tucked into a corner of the rue des Saints-Pères, next to the hotel. They sold beautiful hand-finished silk negligees to Frenchmen who shopped discreetly for their mistresses. The walls were covered in green jacquard fabric. Racks hung with delicate bras and panties flanked either side of two glass cases filled with more silk-satin treasures. A tall redhead with wild curls and a glamorous slash of red lipstick stood behind the counter, deftly unfolding satin negligees in luscious shades of pale peach, lime green, turquoise, lavender, chocolate brown, magenta, one more beautiful than the last. Each piece was edged in black or ivory lace as fine as netting. My mother took us back twice, insisting we each buy something—a negligee, a *porte-jarretelle,* a lace bra—in beautiful shades of emerald or fuchsia. I chose a short raspberry silk slip with spaghetti-thin straps. What on earth would I do with a silk negligee? Such a skimpy swath of silk would require a sexier assignation than my lumpy bed at Bibiane and Antoine's. But I played along with the French film-noir fantasy running through my mother's mind.

Every night we went to a different restaurant—La Coupole, with its Art Deco columns and worn red leather banquettes; Brasserie Lipp, where the tourists are quickly shuttled upstairs; and Brasserie Balzar, next to the Sorbonne, the only place open on Sunday nights. We feasted on thick *pavés* of steak with salty frites and fresh avocados filled with shrimp. We were Americans in Paris, retracing Hemingway's steps, lingering over café crèmes and ambling around the fountains and the alleys of chestnut trees in the Tuileries, Michelin Guide in hand.

We celebrated New Year's Eve at my godmother's apartment. Sandy greeted us with champagne *coupes* filled with delicate bubbles. Bob was shucking Belon oysters from Brittany on the wraparound terrace, imploring us to join him.

"Bienvenue à Paris! Voilà, the emperor's tomb!" he bellowed, sweeping his hand around to take in the magnificent view from the Grand Palais to the gilded winged horses cantering above the Pont Alexandre III

and the glittering dome of Les Invalides. The glow of candles and a roaring fire warmed us as we huddled around the fireplace, happy to be together. Later, at the dinner table, Bob raised a glass to the New Year, 1987. "Here's to perestroika and glasnost and the new chunnel," he said. All the talk in Paris that fall and winter had been about a new tunnel that would connect France to Britain with a high-speed train, whisking passengers from Paris to London under the English Channel in three hours.

"The world is getting smaller!" Bob declared. *"Cin cin!"*

My mother raised her glass and smiled warmly. "To old friends!" she said. "Well, not *old*—we are not old. To *good* friends!"

They'd been through so many milestones together: marriage, babies, divorce, their children's adolescent dramas, college applications, and the death of Sandy's parents at a very young age. Both glamorous beauties in their youth, they had shared adventures, traveling abroad, throwing parties in Sandy's vast Central Park West apartment in the early 1970s, wearing djellabas from India and floral print dresses from Biba in London. I thought of my college roommates. What were they doing now? Studying law, teaching underprivileged kids on Indian reservations in Albuquerque. Would our friendships endure the hardships and triumphs the way Mom and Sandy's had? Or had we already drifted apart, unhinged by time zones and the vast distance between us? I hoped Bibiane's mother was right when she insisted that the French, once you got to know them, remained your friends forever. I couldn't imagine not knowing Bibiane and Antoine. In that moment I felt my emotional allegiances shifting closer to my newfound French friends.

Just after 1:00 A.M. we tottered out onto the boulevard de la Tour-Maubourg, tipsy from too many tiny goblets of Armagnac. At the far end of the rue de Grenelle, the lights of the Eiffel Tower blinked off. I thought of the lyrics to a cheesy French pop song I loved. *Quand Paris s'éteint.* When Paris goes dark.

On their last night, my mother and sister came to Bibiane and Antoine's for dinner. Bibiane cooked my favorite French dishes: roast chicken, pommes dauphinoise, and île flottante—an airy island of whipped meringue floating in rich crème anglaise. Instead of sitting around the coffee table on the floor, we sat at a more formal glass table in the corner of the living room. Impressed by my mother's elegance, the Deschamps made an effort to speak English.

"So, anyway, you know what I mean?" Antoine said, mimicking my expressions. "Your daughter is *très* French," he said. "Isn't it?" These were private jokes Bibiane, Antoine, and I shared.

My mother smiled blankly and sipped a glass of white wine. She looked uncomfortable.

"Well, I speak Engleesh a little bit," said Bibiane.

"Your English is great!" my sister said, chiming in. We poured more wine.

"Kate is like a second daughter for me! You are like *famille*! Please, come and stay here if you want-uh. Anytime, *vraiment!*" Bibiane must have thought it was up to her to communicate, to move the stilted conversation along.

"I think it's wonderful the way you welcome so many American students into your home." My mother was trying to express her gratitude that her daughter had found such a friendly household. And yet I could hear a hesitation in her voice, a resistance to the idea that I could be happy in Paris.

When I think of my mother now, poised on Bibiane's couch in her turquoise-blue Jean Muir sweater, a smile frozen on her face as she nodded, pretending to follow the chaotic conversation, I think about what she must have seen in me at that moment—my fluency in French slang, the BCBG black velvet bow in my hair, the big dangly earrings. I was breaking away, finding my footing in a foreign culture, but also finding a new home in another family. I had a habit of looking for refuge in the homes of friends. Throughout my childhood, I spent afternoons and weekends and vacations with friends. In college, Will's family in Greenwich became my safe haven. At the time, my mother knew better than I did that I was looking for a happy, whole family to replace mine, the family that had fallen apart.

But the Deschamps family was different, or so I thought. They represented more than a refuge; they were part of my education, accomplices in the creation of my new identity.

With my sister and mother marooned in my new life, sitting tentatively beside me at the Deschamps' dinner table, I struggled to unite two disparate sides of myself. I was not French, and yet I was becoming less American. I could feel a strange duality growing within me—the uncomfortable divide between the reality of who I was and the dream of who I wanted to become.

The next morning I picked my mother and sister up in a taxi and accompanied them to Orly Airport. We dawdled over a final crème, and I bought my mother a bottle of Annick Goutal Gárdenia Passion perfume at the duty-free shop. She dabbed a splash of it on her wrist, and the sweet, intense smell of night-blooming flowers filled the space between us. At the customs gate, I hugged them goodbye and, holding back tears, walked away, turning around every few steps to see if they were still there. When my mother rounded the corner and disappeared behind the security checkpoint, I felt a pang of longing and the urge to run and join her.

Bibiane's Recipe for Pommes Dauphinoise

Ingredients:

    2 pounds of Idaho potatoes
    4 large onions, thinly sliced
    4 generous tablespoons of crème fraîche
    1/2 cup of shredded Gruyère cheese
    Salt

Preparation:

Preheat the oven to 350 degrees.

Peel the potatoes and the onions and slice very finely with a mandoline. Place the potato slices in a pot of salted boiling water and cook for 20 minutes. When cooked, drain the potatoes and layer them with the onions and crème fraîche in a shallow baking dish. Cover the top with Gruyère cheese and add a pinch of salt. Cook at 350 degrees for 30 minutes. Serve warm with red meat—a roast or a steak—and a bottle of Bordeaux.

CHAPTER FIVE

87, Rue Saint-Dominique

Two words in my journal on February 24: *"Journée affreuse."* Awful day.

My contract at the *Trib* was coming to an end. Although Maggie Shapiro kindly kept me on for a few weeks beyond the expiration date on my *carte temporaire,* the thought of finding another job filled me with dread. February was the cruelest month in Paris, the time when the gray clouds, or *grisaille,* touched down on the boulevards too early in the afternoon, suddenly turning the sky an inky, velvety black.

In the city of a thousand grays, *grisaille* has its own special place. It can elicit a melancholy sadness, but it can also evoke a more sinister mood. That winter I experienced what I called "Paris poignancy attacks" all the time: at the sight of an old man swaying unsteadily at a zinc bar at ten o'clock in the morning, or the look on the face of a teenage prostitute standing in the doorway of a cheap hotel on the rue de Budapest. How could such a magnificent city harbor such desperation?

On nights when I felt so lonely I couldn't hold back tears, I would gather up a handful of ten-franc coins and steal out of the apartment, walking quickly up the narrow rue des Saints-Pères to the corner telephone booth. Ten or twelve coins would get an international line and I could call my mother or Will. Standing in that glass phone booth at midnight, calling home, I felt isolated and exposed. I couldn't explain my loneliness to my French family or friends. There is no word in French for loneliness.

"Well, sweetie," my mother would say, trying to comfort me from three thousand miles away, "go to bed, and tomorrow will be a better day."

Usually she was right. Usually the next day would bring a newfound sense of vigor and appreciation for the small things, the Parisian rituals that reminded me why I loved the city so much. But the more comfortable I became with my life in Paris, the more exposed I was to some of the sinister aspects of the city.

I began working part-time for the managing editor of *Paris Passion,* an English-language magazine for expats and tourists. Su was a quirky Brit who spoke fluent French and fluent cockney and drove a Moby-lette around Paris. She sent me on errands and asked me to proofread copy. The offices, on the second floor of a decrepit building in Les Halles, were cramped, stacked with back issues of magazines and boxes of office supplies. There wasn't much to do; *Passion* was the landing pad of almost every English-speaking English major looking for something to do in Paris. Recognizing that I needed to make some money, Su offered to bring me along on the night shift of a job that paid cash, working as an *animatrice* for a Minitel service.

Minitel was the early French version of the Internet, a way to communicate by text through the telephone line. Subscribers received a terminal—like a miniature laptop—to hook up to their phone; with a special code, they could access the phone directory, shop for groceries, make train reservations, and look up stock quotes. With a subscription to magazines like *Le Nouvel Observateur,* the left-leaning newsweekly, they could also engage in conversation in chat rooms, which were billed by the minute, like long-distance phone calls. This was the most lucrative side of the business. Magazines would host their own chat rooms and charge a rate.

Su's job was to spark up conversations in those chat rooms, using pseudonyms and fake names to create realistic-sounding callers who would chat to lonely guys, engaging them in slightly provocative conversation in order to keep them on the line for as long as possible without giving away her false identity.

"Easy money," she said.

I met Su one night at the *Nouvel Obs* offices, around 8:00. We sat in a room crowded with desks and stacks of magazines and worked until midnight, chatting to lonely men around France. We made up names—Marie-Laure, Françoise, Anne; the more generic, the better. The idea was to sound like young women looking for dates, but mostly we would say things like, "What's going on?" or "What do you think of the new Jim Jarmusch movie, *Down by Law*?" or *"T'es sympa, toi."* We would blast Los Lobos and Run-D.M.C. on a boom box in the corner and keep four or five conversations going at once, typing in bad French and giggling about the callers who tried to wheedle information out of us. The first step was always *le rendez-vous*. They wanted to meet, get our address. *Voulez-vous rencontrer?* If we refused, they would get personal: "How tall are you?" Or "What color hair do you have?" Or "Do you like it doggy style?" When conversations turned raunchy, we clicked out of the chat room and came back in with a different name, a whole new identity.

Inevitably, the men on the chat line would recognize our spelling mistakes and ask us if we were French. The whole premise was creepy. What if these guys figured us out? What if they got our codes or traced our calls? Su didn't care; she was thick-skinned and industrious. But I felt weird and exposed. I wasn't that desperate for the money.

After a month I quit.

On Saturday nights, Nikki liked to go clubbing at places like Le Palace and Les Bains Douches, a fashionable club near Les Halles. We would meet at her studio apartment on the rue du Gros Caillou near the Eiffel Tower and change into outfits we hoped would pass muster with club bouncers—skinny black leggings, Equipment silk shirts, and cheap high-heeled stilettos we bought at a knockoff place called Jet Set. Nikki would strip off her preppy Ralph Lauren cable-knit sweater and plaid skirt and squeeze into tight Chipie blue jeans and a big blazer. I wore miniskirts I bought at Claudie Pierlot, on the rue de Sèvres. Any extra cash I had in those days financed Saturday-afternoon shopping sprees at Agnès B. in Les Halles or Naf Naf on the boulevard Saint-Michel.

We rode the Métro up to Pigalle or Les Halles and sat around in sleazy cafés, drinking red wine until the clubs opened. Without connections, we often had to wait in line or deal with snarky French doormen. Usually we got in by paying the hundred-franc entrance fee. In other words, *pas cool*, not *branchée* or hip. Every Saturday night there was a theme and a roomful of trendy French kids dancing to local punk-rock bands. Nikki and I would buy drinks and dance, scanning the room for cute French guys. Sometimes we would bump into Nikki's friends from work or other interns from *Passion*.

One night, Nikki and I went to Les Bains Douches for La Nuit Informatique—computer night. French kids were dressed up as robots, in sleek silver unitards and funny makeup. The DJ played techno music. I decided to leave early, at around 1:00 A.M. Nikki had found some friends and wanted to stay out later. Outside, on the boulevard de Sébastopol, other club kids heading home were looking for taxis, too. The Métro had been closed for an hour. There wasn't a taxi in sight. Although the neighborhood was sketchy, I wasn't that far from home. I was wearing my Jet Set heels and a very short skirt, but I was twenty-two and this was Paris, not New York. I decided to walk.

The boulevard was busy with people walking home from clubs; cars were speeding by. I ambled over the Pont des Arts and watched the Eiffel Tower lights blink off. As I crossed the quai, the buildings suddenly grew dark. Shutters were closed tight. Café doors were locked with double-knotted chains. The streets were barren. My familiar neighborhood felt eerie and frightening. I picked up my pace as I reached the rue des Saints-Pères. Halfway down the street, I heard a car pull up from behind. When I turned to look, a black BMW rolled to a stop alongside me. A preppy-looking middle-aged guy sat in the driver's seat, smiling at me. Perhaps he was a friend of Bibiane and Antoine's, offering me a ride? I stopped and looked inside. He had his pants pulled down to his knees and he was playing with himself!

My heart thumped like the DJ's techno beat. I took off running up the rue des Saints-Pères, toward the boulevard Saint-Germain, past the kiosk locked up tight, past the ominous 1940s façade of the medical school. There was no place to go but home, but I couldn't outrun a car. Quickly, I thought to turn right on Saint-Germain, a one-way street. He couldn't follow me there.

The boulevard was empty. No cars or taxis to flag down. Not even a bus. I could scream, but who would hear me? At two in the morning, the neatly coiffed *dames* of the 7th arrondissement were sleeping behind their shutters. I stopped and yanked off my cheap heels, one in each hand, and started to sprint: past the dark vitrines of the Roche Bobois furniture store, past the Crédit Agricole bank with its metal grille pulled down, past the abandoned pump of the gas station.

This was it, then. This was how my Paris dream ended: trapped in the trunk of a stranger's car, in a sordid Parisian suburb. I kept running. My stockings ripped and my feet were raw from the rough pavement. *Merde.* The rue Saint-Guillaume was only a block away. I could turn left there and be sure to lose him. I dropped my shoes and tore all the way to the rue de Grenelle, only a block or so from home.

Rounding the corner, I slowed to catch my breath. And there was the black BMW again, parked alongside the narrow sidewalk. He had seen me turn down the rue Saint-Guillaume and had taken another route to the rue de Grenelle. He had followed me. The car door was open and he was waiting at the end of the street, leaning against the car, blocking my path. I wanted to crumple down on the sidewalk in a ball and cry. My breath was so loud in my chest, I couldn't hear what he was saying. He smiled a creepy smile as he tried to grab my arm, but I pushed past that sleazeball, shoving him hard with my shoulder and elbow and then stumbling another block to the heavy mahogany door at number 17. I punched the code in over and over again. *Merde.* What was the code? I didn't have time to fumble around for the key. Bibiane and Antoine were away. I could hear the car motor approaching, backing up. *Just get in the door.*

Finally the lock clicked and I pushed the door open and, just as forcefully, slammed it shut. Sliding down onto the cold marble floor, I curled into the fetal position; my hands were shaking and my chest was heaving. I felt as if I was going to vomit. The car was idling right outside. I closed my eyes, counted my blessings, and crawled up the stairs in the dark.

For the next few weeks I stayed in at night. Nikki kept calling, hoping to make plans. "Look, it's no big deal," she would say. "Now you know and it won't happen again, hey?"

But the incident had shattered my sense of security. The city took on a new, menacing dimension. Returning home from work late, I would make a point of racing up the stairs before the *minuterie* timed out. Who knew what creeps could be lurking in the shadows?

Paris was also not the glamorous bastion of liberal thought and artistic spirit I had imagined. The city's bohemian history—from Sartre to Gertrude Stein to the *soixante-huitards* of May 1968—gave me the impression that most Parisians leaned to the left. They had helped elect a socialist president, after all. And their history was littered with the triumphs of the left.

In the spring of 1987, all the talk over dinner tables in Parisian parlors was of the Klaus Barbie trial. The Butcher of Lyon, as he was called, was finally standing trial for his war crimes—forty years later. The list of his hateful acts was so long that the prosecution took an entire day to read it. The trial brought Barbie's terrible crimes into the courtroom and, for the first time, televised them for all to see. But it also brought the French collaboration to light. Barbie had succeeded with the help of French informers, and his defense used that fact to shine a light on the dark corners of French history. Headlines in newspapers announced the trial with damning phrases like BARBIE ... AND FRANCE GO ON TRIAL. The French wanted Barbie to pay for his crimes and to receive the ultimate punishment, but any reminder of their collaborationist past made them apoplectic. Some disagreed with the idea of reopening past wounds, on the grounds that it was too painful.

Everywhere you went—at corner cafés, fancy dinner parties, even on the Métro—heated political discussions followed. Bibiane and her friends argued passionately about history and forgiveness. Should France be on trial, too? The subject was particularly difficult for the generation that had lived through the war. They were still haunted by vivid memories of that time and the choices and sacrifices they had made. They wanted nothing to do with any reminders of war criminals like Barbie.

The discussions surrounding the trial made me aware of the mounting strain of nationalism in France. I noticed graffiti on walls of Métro stations: VOTE FOR LE PEN or FRANCE FOR THE FRENCH. Even in early-morning boulangerie lines, conversation turned to racist anti-Arab sentiments and criticisms of the socialist government.

The Parisians I knew were disgusted by the behavior of the extreme right. They didn't believe in the violence and racism propagated by politicians like Le Pen. But privately the same Parisians guarded their French identity from foreigners. Like a collective national tic, they wanted to preserve their Frenchness, preserve their daily routines, their weird incongruent dualities, their language, their traditions, and their own history—what they liked to call their patrimony. The *patrimoine* of France, as they saw it, was what every foreigner admires—the sense of civilization, rigor, discipline, and self-preservation. But that powerful sense of identity thrived precisely because it was exclusionary.

I got a closer look at French patrimony as it is expressed in the most sacred of French institutions—the family—when I started dating Antoine's younger brother, François. A gregarious blue-eyed charmer in his second year of business school, François lived with his grandmother—Bonne Maman—near the Eiffel Tower. He rode around town on a Vespa. He invited me to parties and to classical music concerts at the Salle Pleyel. He had a big group of friends—a *bande*—including Jerome and Patrick, two classmates from business school. They were all in the same *rallye,* an exclusive organization that hosted dances on weekends.

François didn't give a hoot what I did professionally. When I told him I had been pitching American magazines as a freelancer, he just shrugged and said, *"C'est ça, oui,"* as if I was bullshitting him, a kind of cynicism only Parisians can muster. What mattered to François was his family. Every Sunday he went to the *déjeuner à domicile*—lunch at home—at his parents', with his seven brothers and sisters and all of their kids. Every few weekends he would head off to Saumur, where Bonne Maman had a windmill and a big house on a hill overlooking the vineyards.

His social circle consisted mostly of BCBG kids from the 7th and 16th arrondissements. They would throw parties—or *un pot*—in their parents' apartments and everyone would drink *pinard*—cheap wine— and dance Le Rock, the French version of the Lindy, a partnered dance where you swing your arms back and forth like windshield wipers and twirl your partner around in circles. François was a great dancer and he taught me how to swing around the dance floor with him, effortlessly sweeping my arms back and forth and twirling in, swinging out, holding my back and head straight and moving only my limbs. Mastering Le Rock was another *bizutage*. If I could talk and dance with the French, then perhaps I was acceptable. But François was much more traditional than his brother Antoine. He would say things to me like *"Ça ne se fait pas"*—no, that is not done—or *"On ne dit pas"*—we don't say that. Beneath every gesture lies an inculcated discipline.

For all of his French superciliousness, François was a lot of fun. He would bring an extra helmet and drive me to a trendy nightclub called La Locomotive on weekends. He was funny, but he was also very French. His interest in me was only as an exotic kind of conversation piece, and once the conversation was over, he disappeared. I found myself alone at fancy cocktail parties, surrounded by people who all knew one another, people who had no interest in speaking to an American. Often, separated from the group, I would go home by myself. Or François would ignore me completely and then drive me home on his Vespa and maul me in the stairwell outside Bibiane and Antoine's front door.

Even though our relationship was mostly platonic—apart from the make-out sessions in the stairwell—I began to fantasize about what it would be like to marry a Frenchman and have French-speaking kids. I would buy them tiny Shetland sweaters at Bonpoint and take them to the carousel in the Luxembourg Gardens on Saturdays. They would speak *l'argot,* of course, saying things like, *"J'ai la trouille!"* when they got scared riding the ponies around the garden. In winter I would pull navy-blue wool *cagoules* over their heads, the way the mothers in the park did. I would sit on the bench talking to other moms, never playing in the sandbox with the kids. No, French women didn't do that. *Ça ne se fait pas.*

"Why don't you come to my sister's wedding?" François and I were having Sunday brunch at his friend Jerome's house when the subject of his older sister's wedding came up. Marie-Stephanie was to be married in early June at Bonne Maman's windmill house (Le Moulin) in Saumur. All eight siblings, plus aunts, uncles, and cousins, would converge on the property for the weekend.

"It would be *chouette* if you came!"

I wondered if the invitation was real. His family was rigid in the classic way of the French bourgeoisie, completely impervious to outside influences. A foreigner invading the inner sanctum of the family posed the worst possible threat. *Sacrebleu,* not an American! But Bibiane and Antoine insisted, and so I packed a pale-pink linen shift and a pair of white sandals with kitten heels, and late on a Friday night I drove out to Le Moulin with Antoine.

"*Ah!* You are here *enfin!*" Bibiane greeted us at the kitchen door. She took my bag and looked around frantically. "But where is your hat?" It was late and we'd been driving for what seemed like hours, in bumper-to-bumper traffic out of Paris.

"*Beh, alors?* You will be the only one not wearing a hat!" This sartorial oversight did not bode well for the weekend ahead.

No sooner had we crossed the threshold than a crowd of sisters, brothers, sisters-in-law, children, cousins, and François's father swarmed into the cavernous kitchen. A tornado had ripped through the property earlier that afternoon, and they were all eager to share the stories about how the tent had blown over, two trees in the yard had been damaged, the mother of the bride had cut her hand open and was at the hospital getting stitches. One sister-in-law had lost her engagement ring. The tent makers had to go all the way back to Nantes to get new materials. There would be a lot of work to do in the morning to get the place ready. François was nowhere in sight. He had decided to stay in Paris for a party. He would be arriving in the morning.

I was nervous, afraid I would misstep and *tutoyer* someone instead of the formal *vousvoyer*. Every time I opened my mouth to speak, the group fell silent. "Can she really speak French?" Incriminating jokes about François and me punctuated the conversation. Jobs were assigned for the following day.

"Do you know how to make mayonnaise, Kate?" One of the sisters was charged with preparing the hors d'oeuvres for the reception. "*Tu sais,* you cannot make it if you are at that certain time of the month."

"*Oui, oui.*" Bibiane had taught me this mysterious cooking secret as she was preparing one of her dinner parties. The days of reaching for a jar of Hellmann's were officially over.

The following morning I was summoned to the kitchen with two cousins and ordered to make big batches of mayonnaise for deviled eggs. As we whipped furiously at the egg yolks, dripping olive oil into the messy concoction, the sound of a loud crash came from the courtyard outside. François had arrived. Speeding down the driveway a little too fast, he had mowed down four chairs. He burst through the kitchen door.

"*Alors, La Grosse Américaine!* I'm glad you're here." I was so happy to see him. He smiled broadly, kissed me, and then disappeared.

By four o'clock, the wedding party was dressed and assembled in the kitchen. The bride was gleaming in shiny white taffeta, her sister trailing behind with the veil, a big cloud of tulle. The groom wore a top hat and tails, as did most of the men—all but Antoine, who had caused a scene, exploding in fury at his mother when she asked him to shave his side-burns. In defiance, he had removed his hat.

"*Va te faire foutre!* Go fuck yourselves!" He yelled obscenities at the crowd that had formed when they heard the ruckus. "Nobody is going to tell me what to wear or how to look!"

It seemed the women had all told one another what to wear to an early-June wedding. They looked like peacocks, strutting down the grassy hill to the chapel in their spring finery: trim silk suits in bold shades of fuchsia and lime green, frilly chiffon dresses festooned with cabbage-rose prints and trailing scarves. Everyone except me, it seemed, had a big straw hat covered in bright silk flowers, grosgrain ribbon, and feathers. They wore dangly earrings and ropes of pearls. Some even carried white gloves, their hair carefully whipped into fancy chignons that swooped up the backs of their necks, their lips stained red or magenta. I felt like hired help in my simple shift. Not even a tube of lipstick for *La Grosse Américaine.*

Inside the chapel, the air was heavy and humid and the pews were crowded with aunts and cousins and friends. The Mass seemed to go on forever, with guests arriving throughout the ceremony, stretching their necks and offering their cheeks to plant the customary *bises* on familiar faces. Children screamed and had to be carried outside and hushed. At one point, an elderly woman arrived and looked around for a place to put her umbrella. At a loss, she plopped it down in the baptismal font. Peals of laughter echoed in the rafters. Later, as the priest gave his blessing, the bride giggled furiously. It appeared she had lost the top of her bodice and could not recover it soon enough—a wardrobe malfunction *à la française.* Finally, vows were exchanged, the organist pounded out a waltz, sachets of rice and confetti flew through the air, and the wedding party swirled out of the church and up the hill to the windmill.

We stayed up all night dancing, tossing one another across the tent floor, snaking through the tables in conga lines, and gyrating to the tinny pop beat of Vanessa Paradis and Madonna. The champagne flowed; the top of the wedding cake tipped over and crashed to the floor. During dinner, François's mother leaned in to ask me if I was having fun.

"Are you thinking now that you might want to marry *un Français?*" Her clear blue eyes had the same mischievous sparkle as François's, but her smile was cold.

"Non! Mais jamais! Jamais!" Bibiane interrupted. "She must marry an American!"

I nodded vigorously, obeying the code: Hands off François. Beneath their smiles and encouraging conversation lurked a subtle reminder that I didn't belong. They called me *La Grosse Américaine*—ironically, because I was skinny and so much taller than most of François's friends. I was a foreign trinket, charmingly gauche sometimes, and sometimes just gauche. I talked too much about work, or spoke with a funny accent, or didn't know how to make mayonnaise, or didn't wear a hat. Whatever the crime, I was constantly reminded that my acceptance was temporary. Even if I spoke slang and danced Le Rock, I would always be *une étrangère*. They would be my friends, forever, they promised, but they would never be my family.

When summer vacation came, François and I parted ways. Ours was not a story of intense love or heartbreak, merely a fun flirtation that petered out. Not *le grand amour,* as Bibiane would say. François got a job leading an advertising campaign for French wine in La Baule, on the southern coast of Brittany. I got a job as the Paris stringer for *Metropolitan Home,* a trendy interiors magazine that chronicled the lifestyle of New York yuppies in the 1980s. Bob's daughter was the photo editor, and she was looking for someone in Paris to scout stories for the magazine, someone who spoke French fluently. Bob told her that I spoke French like a truck driver.

In late June, the magazine's senior editor came to Paris to interview me. Steven was a tall, dashingly handsome American who had grown up in Rome and spoke Italian. We met at Café Costes, a hip spot in Les Halles that had been designed by Philippe Starck. The place was packed with Parisians in Perfecto jackets and jeans, smoking cigarettes and leaning into their espresso cups. We sat on the banquette, and Steven explained in a world-weary tone that I would have to find interesting cultural stories and worm my way into glamorous apartments in Paris. Did I know anything about food? The magazine's food editor would be coming to town. Could I show him around? I wore a short skirt and barked at the waiter in my best truck-driver French.

"Monsieur, monsieur!" I yelled, waving my arm, trying to catch his attention as he darted through the crowded cluster of tables, ignoring my frantic signals. *"J'en ai marre!* I'm sick of waiting!"

"Je vous écoute." The waiter shrugged as he swiped our table with a wet rag and plopped down a clean ashtray.

"Ouais, moi, je prends un crème," I said, with an exasperated Parisian air, "and also maybe *le petit déj,* breakfast." I looked at Steven—a croissant, perhaps?

Steven was fumbling with the menu, struggling to string together a sentence. His words spilled out in Italian.

"Cappuccino e biscotti?" he said haltingly, affecting a lilting accent that fell on deaf ears.

The waiter scowled, disappeared, and returned a few minutes later with two croissants, carelessly tossing the plate on the table.

"Your *pote,* he is *à côté de ses pompes*! Totally out of it!" the waiter snarled. He was right. My friend didn't understand a thing we had said.

Steven returned to New York and reported that I did in fact speak French beautifully. A week later he sent me a contract and a five-hundred-dollar advance for expenses. On the contract he penciled in my title: "Paris City Editor." He wrote: "Call Andrée Putman, introduce yourself; Look into the I. M. Pei addition to the Louvre. Send us as much information as you can."

Luckily, the world of French design was exploding with young talent. Architects like Jean Nouvel and designers like Philippe Starck were making headlines with their work. Somehow I managed to wrangle an interview with a young architect named Jean-Michel Wilmotte. He was a personal favorite of François Mitterrand and had just landed the commission to design the interiors of I. M. Pei's pyramid at the Louvre. With that interview I was able to parlay myself into the studio of two trendy furniture designers, Mattia Bonetti and Elizabeth Garouste. They had recently completed a quirky couture house on the rue du Faubourg Saint-Honoré for a rising fashion star from Arles. His name was Christian Lacroix. My days of typing manuscripts and pining for a bilingual-secretarial job were finally over.

My days of living at Bibiane and Antoine's were over, too. Bibiane had new students coming in the fall. She suggested I find an apartment; she would help me. We studied the listings in *Le Figaro* and found two places that looked promising farther down the rue de Grenelle, toward the Eiffel Tower. The second apartment, a newly renovated one-bedroom with a view over a courtyard and peach-colored wall-to-wall carpeting, was only 1,200 francs a month. It had a sunny, clean feeling to it. No matter that the entrance to the building was on a narrow side street—a passage—where big gray rats scurried in and out of the gutter late at night.

With a nudge from Bibiane, I signed the lease at 87, rue Saint-Dominique and moved in two days later. I bought a black foam IKEA couch and borrowed a twin four-poster bed from my godmother. Two packing boxes became a makeshift coffee table. I found a cheap boom box and a Bruce Springsteen CD at the local FNAC record store. The kitchen was just big enough to boil a pot of water and make spaghetti. Across the street, a young baker from Bordeaux named Jean-Luc Poujauran had opened up a shop. The interiors and exterior were painted bright pink. He made a Bordelais dessert called canelés, custardy sweet cakes filled with rum and vanilla. His ficelles—long, skinny loaves of organic bread—were lauded in newspapers and magazines as the best new bread in Paris. He was only twenty-four. He was also the best-looking baker in town.

I had an electric bill, a telephone number, and a boulangerie. At last I was a Parisian.

Dictionnaire de l'Argot

(Slang Dictionary)

baraque—house

beauf—thug

bled—village

bordel—mess

bouffe—food

clope—cigarette

dingue—crazy

mec—guy

nase—exhausted

pinard—wine

pote—friend

ringard—tacky

trouille—fear

truc—thing

CHAPTER SIX

Douce France

August is a dreadful month in Paris. The streets are deserted, as residents flee to the turquoise waters of le Midi or the rocky shores of Brittany. Even tourists tire of signs on shop doors that read *de rétour en septembre* and head for the trains leaving the Gare de Lyon destined for Nice, Saint-Tropez, Saint-Malo, fleeing the prix-fixe menus of Montparnasse bistros, the ghastly urine-soaked odor of the Métro, and the chaotic rush-hour traffic along the rue de Rivoli. Anywhere but here.

Something about the August exodus always reminds me of the classic 1970s Michel Fugain hit song, *"Une Belle Histoire,"* about two young lovers who meet on the road to summer vacation in the south of France. The lyrics tell the story of an ill-fated love affair: He's from the north; she's from the south. They have nothing in common, but, what the hell, they're on holiday, liberated for a moment from those crazy social codes.

A new job and plenty of work kept me busy, but I was oppressed by the heat and the vacant boulevards. My grumpy concierge had stopped delivering the mail. Bibiane took the children to her parents' house in Normandy; Antoine was preparing to meet her there. Nikki had decamped to Deauville to manage the opening of a new Ralph Lauren shop behind the resort's jazzy casino. She called occasionally to regale me with stories about intoxicating evenings on the terrace of a local brasserie called Chez Miocque. "You must come visit," she insisted.

I took the train up to Deauville on a stifling Friday afternoon and walked through the seaside resort town that had once been home to high-society Parisians like Coco Chanel and Wallis Simpson. The Ralph Lauren boutique was on the main square in an old timber building, its window boxes overflowing with bright-red geraniums. The town was crowded with tourists and people who looked like they worked at the nearby horse stables. The sun felt warm on my arms, and I was giddy to be out of Paris and in a place where summer was in full swing. Inside the store, Nikki was darting around display mannequins, her high heels crunching on the sisal and her long blond ponytail swishing back and forth as she ferried cashmere sweaters and Polo shirts from shelf to fitting room. She wore a short skirt that showed off her tan legs. She nodded to me to wait, and when her clients finally left she rushed over.

"You made it!" She laughed and gave me a hug. "I reckon we should go back to my place, change, and then go to Chez Miocque for dinner, hey?" She still had her Aussie accent. "I know the owner, Jacques; you have to meet him. He and his wife are so great."

Her studio apartment was on the ground floor of a modern building a few blocks away. We changed quickly into miniskirts and tight T-shirts, brushing Terracotta powder on our faces to fake a deep summer tan.

Chez Miocque was packed with dashing polo players and leathery-looking playboys. The walls were lined with photos of the owner, Jacques, cuddling up to Johnny Hallyday and Alain Delon. Now he cuddled up to Nikki and ushered us to a prime table on the terrace. Flutes of sparkling pink champagne appeared, and we toasted with two well-dressed guys, in Gucci loafers and ascots, at the next table. They were old enough to be our fathers. Nikki introduced me as her friend from New York.

"She lives in Paris!" she said with her big, hearty laugh. *"Elle est jour-naliste!"*

"Mé-tro-pol-i-taine Om," I said slowly, trying on a French accent to

make the magazine sound more familiar. But they were not the least bit interested in my professional résumé.

Nikki winked and they liked that, laughing along with her.

"You mean you are not *mannequin*?" one of the guys asked as he poured more champagne.

"Non!" Nikki tossed her head back flirtatiously and rolled her eyes. "We are not models. *Non, désolée."*

It all looked so glamorous—the warm glow of the brasserie lights, the laughter of young French *minettes* flirting with their elderly escorts, champagne and Calvados glasses scattered across our table, and ashtrays filled with cigarettes. Nikki moved effortlessly between her working life as a shopgirl and this glamorous, louche world of polo players and gigolos in Gucci loafers. She had no inhibitions about mingling with a much-older crowd, taking an unabashed pleasure in flirting with the slick polo players. She was not waiting for someone to tell her what to do, and she was not rebelling against expectations. She was having fun, reaching for a life of glamour and and extravagance. It was certainly one passport into Parisian life. Sitting next to her on the banquette that night, I was drawn to the incandescent glamour and sophistication of Chez Miocque, but I didn't have the chops.

Nikki was a pro. After hours of teasing these groveling playboys, drinking their champagne and laughing at their idiotic jokes, she stood up at 2:00 A.M. and announced that we were leaving.

"On y va, on y va," she said. "We have to work tomorrow." But the leathery old guys kept offering more drinks, more louche invitations.

"Non, we have to go now," Nikki said. She was firm, even after a few too many flutes of champagne. A taxi driver appeared in the front door of the café and we made a clean getaway.

The next day Nikki got up early to go to work.

"Call me when you get to Paris. You have to come back. We have to find you a polo player!" She cackled under her breath and tiptoed out the door. I walked to the train station, my head pounding from the Calvados.

Antoine's friend Stéphane was still in Paris. His job at the TF1 television station afforded him only two weeks of vacation. We went to dinner a few times and saw the movie *The Witches of Eastwick*. Stéphane was always game for dinner and a movie. He would pick me up in his car, dressed immaculately in a blazer and a neat polo shirt, his jeans pressed. Bibiane always whispered about how Stéphane was insecure about his provincial roots and the fact that his father was a hairdresser. But what did I care? I was American, and in America nobody cared if your father was a hairdresser. At least that's what Stéphane imagined.

Unlike many French people I met that first year in Paris, Stéphane was curious about other cultures. He would joke about my hometown, calling it the concrete jungle, and he constantly referenced the Blues Brothers and John Belushi. The French have always nurtured the skewed idea that comedians like Belushi and Jerry Lewis are somehow representative of the average American, as if we all walk around in outrageous personas, performing absurd slapstick stunts.

Stéphane had a bit of Jerry Lewis in him in the way he would imitate people or make fun of French mannerisms—I liked that about him. We both liked Steve Winwood and Madonna, and we argued about French and American politics. He loved to talk about American politics and called President Reagan my Cowboy President. I was too naïve at the time, or just unaware, or, worse, self-involved to see that Stéphane hoped our friendship would grow into something much deeper. I ignored his overtures, because I had no romantic notions about Stéphane. He was a friend, a confidant whom I could call at the last minute to distract me with a joke or a spontaneous adventure.

Met Home didn't have an office, so I worked from my apartment, typing out memos and stories on my portable Canon at my kitchen counter or crouched over the keyboard on the floor. I spent my days scrambling for story ideas, cold-calling architects and decorators and sending formal letters written in the obsequious business lingo I had learned at the *Trib*: "*Veuillez accepter, madame, mes sincères sentiments.*"

The *Met Home* position had come through just in time. All spring I had floundered around, trying to find a proper job. Queries to the Paris offices of American magazines like *Newsweek* and *Elle* produced polite form letters that spelled out rejection in one sentence or less. I tried getting a job at the French newsweekly *Le Nouvel Obs,* but the editor kept postponing the interview. I dropped my résumé at countless magazines—*Harper's Bazaar, City, Time.* Antoine and Bibiane introduced me to a television host on Canal Plus. I went out to dinner with him a few times and to a U2 concert, hoping he might have a job prospect. But his intentions were different.

It was demoralizing not to land a full-time gig. Freelance and *Met Home* were not enough to fill my days. It wasn't the money so much as the security and purpose of a job that I was longing for. Maybe one year in Paris was enough. I thought of Will back home, ordering Chinese food on Thursday nights and watching episodes of *Cheers.* As my resolve was wavering, I got an encouraging letter from my father:

> I think that you can pick almost any place on any part of the globe
> and say "This is where I belong"—without feeling estranged from
> what has traditionally been your home. Five thousand miles is noth-
> ing; doing what you enjoy is everything.

Just when I thought I couldn't take another minute of August in Paris, Antoine invited me to spend a Sunday at his friend Virginie's house in the ritzy suburb of Versailles. Stéphane came, too, and brought a friend of his from Brittany named Hervé. He and Hervé had spent summers together in Carnac, a resort town on Brittany's southern coast, part of a band of kids who had gone to the same sailing and tennis club. They were both from Brittany, but they hung out with a group of Parisians, including Virginie and her fiancé, Alex.

We arrived just in time for lunch at Virginie's parents' country house, one of those ramshackle nineteenth-century manors straight out of a Manet painting, covered in sun-dappled ivy and punctuated with pale-blue shutters. It was hot. Stéphane and Hervé were playing Ping-Pong on the lawn. Virginie, a tall, elegant blonde with impeccable manners, was setting a table under a canvas umbrella with champagne glasses. She loped across the grass to greet us.

"*Beh, voilà,* this is *La Grosse Américaine,*" Antoine said, shrugged, and gestured toward me, by way of introduction to Virginie and the group.

He was wearing Ray-Bans, the ubiquitous *clope*—cigarette—dangling from his mouth. We exchanged the customary greeting, the *bises,* or double kiss. I felt self-conscious in front of this circle of French sophisticates studying me in my Kookaï T-shirt and white chino shorts. They spoke quickly, joking back and forth in slang I couldn't completely understand. It was Hervé who, sensing my unease, came to my defense, with a joke about Antoine.

"Et toi? Le Petit Français?" Hervé countered, pointing at Antoine and covering his mouth mischievously as he laughed.

"Pauvre mec de province! You are just a poor boy from the provinces!" Antoine poked fun at Hervé, who lived in La Rochelle, a port on the western coast of France. "Go back to your small village." Was this the French interpretation of slapstick? I wasn't so sure. I knew it was all in fun, but the subtext of Antoine's ridicule was cutting. Surely there was a knife buried somewhere in the velvet badinage.

Hervé was quick enough to play the clownish version of a rough-edged hick to Antoine's Parisian cynic, or so it seemed to me. I remember thinking Hervé was funny and self-deprecating. He seemed free of Parisian snobbery—he didn't mind that his friends called him DuDu, a diminutive derived from his surname, Dunand. He had a slight lisp and a widow's peak. His hair was short and spiky and his forehead wrinkled like a shar-pei when he laughed. Not a GQ model, but so utterly charming. He pulled up his shirt and slipped it over his head unself-consciously, revealing a six-pack and a surfer's tan. He was solicitous of me; he seemed to like *La Grosse Américaine*. He made fun of the Parisians with childlike rhymes: *Parisien tête de chien.* I liked him. I liked the way he made me laugh, especially at myself.

After lunch we lingered in the shade of the canvas umbrella. I told him how excited I was about going home to New York for a two-week vacation. He asked about life in the concrete jungle and laughed when I told him I was born in the Bronx. He planned to spend the rest of August in Brittany, at his parents' place on the beach in Penthièvre. There was a surfing spot in front of the house, and he and his friends would paddle out to catch the perfect wave.

"*Alors,* what does *La Grosse Américaine* do on weekends in the concrete jungle?"

I thought about it for a minute and lit another cigarette—a habit I had not been able to resist in my eagerness to assimilate. I told him I'd once been a ballet dancer and had hoped to become professional but my father had insisted I get an education. Sometimes on weekends I still took ballet classes at a studio in le Marais.

Now what I mostly did on weekends was worry about finding a job.

"Ah! *Boulot, boulot!* Work! That's all you talk about in the concrete jungle."

I told him how I had felt such pressure after college to do something meaningful, to find a career, to get a respectable job. How I'd been turned down twice for internships at *Time* magazine, how I had this idea that I wanted to become a foreign correspondent.

I told him about my family, my parents' divorce, how I had lived with my mother, how my brother had started drinking too much. His dramas had driven me to be the straight-arrow type, under pressure to make my parents proud. It was strange to be speaking about such personal matters with my French friends, but Hervé's curiosity put me at ease.

"In France we are just, uh, you know, *branleurs,*" Hervé said, using the slightly crude slang word for lazy. His job, selling life insurance for a national company out of La Rochelle, meant little to him. He hated it, in fact. He came up to Paris almost every weekend. He asked me for my phone number and said he would give me a call the next time he was in town.

Two hours flew by, and suddenly Antoine was standing over me, jangling keys in his pocket.

"*Allez,* let's go, *La Grosse. On se casse.*" He was anxious to get back to Paris for his band's practice session that evening.

I bid farewell to Virginie, Alex, Stéphane, and Hervé.

"Have fun in the concrete jungle," Hervé said in English, covering his mouth as he laughed at his bad American accent. *"Reviens vite."* Come back soon.

A few days later I returned to New York. The first night home, I met two of my college roommates at the West 14th Street nightclub Nell's, and we danced until two in the morning. Most of my friends were working entry-level jobs in advertising or in Wall Street training programs. They were putting in long hours but still possessed that youthful impulse to go out every night. I would meet them after work at a cheap Mexican place on Second Avenue and drink margaritas and order plates of nachos. They were still dressed in their corporate uniforms: dull beige Tahari suits, dowdy blouses from Ann Taylor. I felt quite smug about my Parisian wardrobe of miniskirts, shrunken Petit Bateau T-shirts, and high heels. Paris had given me a sophistication, and I was eager to advertise it.

We talked about what college friends talk about: who got into medical school, who was sleeping with whom, and how certain relationships had fared post-college. What was Paris like? they asked. What happened to the French guy, François? It had just been a dalliance, I told them, nothing serious. And Will? Had I missed him?

The sweetest reunion was with Will. He drove down from Boston, where he was working for Time Warner, selling cable subscriptions, and we fell right back into our old habits, going to the movies and taking long walks through Central Park. It felt like old times, and yet my mind kept wandering back to Paris. It was easy for me to fit back into his world, but I couldn't picture him in my Paris life.

One Sunday afternoon I met Will at his parents' place in Greenwich. He was playing golf with his father and brother and had asked me to join. I wasn't exactly dressed appropriately, in ballet slippers and a miniskirt, and I wasn't a golfer, but I was excited to spend time with Will.

"Let's just see you tee off here on the first hole." Will was encouraging, boasting to his father about what he called my "near-perfect" swing. I tried to deliver on that promise, whacking at the tee somewhat wildly and cursing under my breath in French. It didn't help that all of my efforts played out in front of a patio full of patrician country-club members tucking into their shrimp salad. Finally I hit the ball, and it veered off into a shrub. *Merde*. Maybe it was the clubs? I was using Will's, and they were way too big. He offered up a nine iron. Try again. I swung again, now desperate to earn the approval of the patio crowd. I didn't want to embarrass Will, but the country club—with its clipped hedges, striped awnings, and rolling green fairways—felt more foreign to me than the French. Will hit it right down the middle. Nothing had changed. I loved him, but I had no interest in a life of putting greens, golf bags, and shrimp salad.

Still, when the time came to say goodbye a week later, it was hard to leave. Part of me was terrified of being alone again in Paris, and part of me was thrilled at the prospect of going back to my own apartment and to Bibiane and Antoine and my French life. I told Will that I loved him but I needed six more months.

He flew back to Boston. I said goodbye to my mother and my friends and boarded another cheap charter flight to Charles de Gaulle Airport.

It felt like I was heading home.

Hervé turned up again a few weeks later at a dinner at Bibiane and Antoine's. He came with Stéphane and sat on the floor around the coffee table in the living room. I laughed when he and Stéphane ridiculed Antoine's taste in music. He complimented my shoes and my earrings; *"Très Parisienne,"* he said. He dressed in preppy BCBG style, buttoning his Lacoste shirt all the way to the collar and wearing pressed jeans and a tweed blazer. I noticed a fleck of mischief in his forest-green eyes. But from the jokes he made about being a "hick"—the French word he used was *plouc*—he was obviously self-conscious about not being Parisian. He was an outsider like me. In the context of the Parisian dinner party, there was something naïve and vulnerable about him.

By October, Hervé was writing to me from La Rochelle. Every day, the concierge would shove the mail under my door, and I found myself looking eagerly for a letter inscribed with his ragged handwriting. The letters were filled with the same jokes and asides I had found so charm-

ing that weekend in Versailles. I was flattered and excited by his attention, but there was nothing more to our friendship than that. We talked
on the phone a few times. I told him about a trip I'd taken down to
Provence to produce a story on the food writer Patricia Wells, who had
an old farmhouse in Vaison-la-Romaine. We had shopped at the weekly
market, buying fresh Cavaillon melons, and she had cooked ravioli with
sage from her garden. The food and the smells of the region enchanted
me. I told Hervé on the phone one night that I wanted to explore those
kinds of markets, to discover more of the French countryside, to get out
of Paris.

One morning about a week later, I was surprised—astonished,
actually—to find in my mailbox an envelope that contained a round-
trip ticket to Bordeaux.

In Hervé's peculiar handwriting: *"On se retrouve là-bas."* I'll meet you
there.

My heart was fluttering.

What the hell? I thought. *Just go.*

He was standing at the airport gate waiting for me. He had driven down
from La Rochelle and made a reservation at a hotel in town. I was nervous to be alone with him in a strange city and excited to discover
something new, but I played it cool. I had planned my outfit carefully: a
black miniskirt, black tights, an oversized menswear jacket, and an Agnès
B. shirt—not too studied, a little sexy. And, just for the hell of it, I packed
the Sabbia Rosa negligee.

We took a taxi from the station to a small hotel in the center of
town. We stood at the reception desk as Hervé checked us in to separate
rooms, a gesture that seemed to diffuse any lingering trepidation I had
about traveling to a foreign city to meet a virtual stranger.

"Ça va comme ça?" He turned his soft smile to me.

"Yes, yes, of course." My cheeks flushed with embarrassment in front
of the concierge.

We walked through the old part of town, along winding medieval
streets, to a big open square lined with neat rows of chestnut trees—the

Place des Quinconces, with its soaring columns and white marble statues of Montaigne and Montesquieu. The November night was crisp and cool. Hervé offered me his sweater and I wrapped it around my neck like a scarf. It smelled of orange flower and musk, his Hermès cologne.

As we walked, he told me about his childhood in Brittany, growing up as the only child of a domineering and tempestuous father and a devoted mother. They lived in Redon, a small, forgotten town in the south of Brittany. His father had a factory that made cheap tchotchkes for big corporations—rubber key chains, ugly mugs, bottle openers in the shape of the Eiffel Tower. They had money, relatively speaking. To small-town shopkeepers, they were "industrialists."

We got a table at the back of a restaurant where they served Bordelais specialties like magret de canard, garlicky lamb, fresh oysters, and those sweet little custard cakes called canelés de Bordeaux—the ones the boulangerie across from my apartment had introduced to Paris. Hervé knew about wine and explained the difference between Cabernet Sauvignon, Merlot, and Malbec. We must have been inspired by the landscape, because we consumed two bottles of red. We stumbled back to the hotel well past midnight. It didn't take long to tear off those black tights. I never did see the second hotel room.

The next day we drove to Margaux and visited the ancient former priory Château Prieuré-Lichine, with its vine-covered façade. Hervé bought me a 1986 grand cru as a souvenir. We walked bashfully hand in hand through the cobblestone streets of Saint-Émilion, stopping every once in a while to stare at each other and embrace. We found a room at a bed-and-breakfast in a beautiful château surrounded by vineyards. There were peacocks wandering through the yard. I took pictures of the heavy gray November sky and the skeletal vines crisscrossing the fields in front of the Romanesque ruins of the town. The streets were empty; the grape harvest was over. The vineyards glowed golden orange in the waning afternoon light.

Those romantic landscapes stayed with me. I returned to Paris's dreary gray boulevards with newfound buoyancy. I couldn't stop thinking about Hervé and his kind eyes, his gallant gestures, shy smile, his self-conscious shrug. I tumbled down that dizzy roller coaster of love, the one where you feel as light as a cloud. Even the dark, menacing Parisian sky couldn't stop me from smiling.

Back home, my friends were consumed with talk about the epic stock-market crash—508 points. They were obsessing over the prospect of a recession or, worse, a depression just like the one in 1929. The Dow could have gone to zero for all I cared. I was floating on air. Paris *grisaille* was suddenly golden light, the damp gray November days strangely tender and soft. Instead of dreading the long winter ahead, I could only think about spring.

My professional life blossomed, too. *Met Home* finally published one of my stories, the Wilmotte interview. It was pretty bad, bloated with adjectives and lacking any real structure, but what did it matter? I had a byline in a national magazine! My first paycheck came a few weeks later, along with embossed *Met Home* business cards and a sense of professional legitimacy.

Soon Hervé was commuting to Paris by train from La Rochelle on Friday nights. We would kiss on the platform of the Gare d'Austerlitz as commuters rushed past. He always had his bag slung over his shoulder and a surprised look on his face. Then we'd repair to a local bistro called Au Petit Tonneau. The chef was a woman—*cuisine de femme*, as the French call it—who made delicious, simple plates of beef bourguignon or coq au vin. After dinner we would retire to my apartment, where we would make love in the single four-poster bed I had borrowed from my godmother.

On Saturdays we roamed through Porte de Vanves flea market, browsing in the stalls lined with boxes of postcards and tables piled with vintage linens and thick bistro glasses. I started collecting Art Nouveau posters and Thonet chairs. Hervé would search for hunting paraphernalia and old knives and horns. He loved the *chasse à courre,* or running hunt, a uniquely French sport dating back to medieval times and involving hunters on horseback or on foot, chasing down a wild boar or stag with hounds and then killing it with a knife. It sounded like a barbaric ritual, but Hervé assured me it was a noble tradition, an art.

"You must come with me one weekend and follow the hunt," Hervé would say, as he told me stories about the forest of Paimpont, in Brittany, where he hunted with a team called the Rallye Bretagne. It had once been known as the forest of Brocéliande, the original stamping ground of King Arthur and also the empire of the mythical Druids, who supposedly lived there in ancient times, when the Celts ruled Brittany. Hervé loved all of these legends and the romantic history of the area.

During the week Hervé would send me letters, signing them *baisers tendres* or just *amour*. He was considerate, his manners impeccable. He always held the door and offered me his jacket when it was cold. He bought me thoughtful presents: a silver chain-link Hermès bracelet, a beautiful antique frame, and a bottle of my favorite perfume, Eau d'Hadrien. If love is about timing, then Hervé arrived as a kind of balm when Parisian exactitude and indifference were chafing my soul. My French dream, the illusion I held on to about my place in Paris, had been drowning; Hervé saved it.

One night the phone woke me up well past midnight. It was Will. A call I dreaded. When we had said goodbye in New York in late August, we had agreed that we would see other people, but the reality of that happening never occurred to us. Now he was calling to see if everything was okay; he hadn't heard from me in several weeks. I took a deep breath and told him about Hervé, blurting out the facts in quick, nervous spurts. Long silences weighed down the line, interrupted by his terse questions and my apologetic answers. I tried to minimize my emotions, play down the affair to protect Will's feelings. A part of me wasn't ready to lose his affection and I didn't want to hurt him. "It's not serious." But Will knew me, and he could hear the lie in my halting voice.

He was angry and heartbroken and proud. How could this happen when we had such a great time together in New York? I tried to explain that I hadn't been looking for someone, it just happened. I told him I was unsure if it was love. But just as quickly I thought, *How can you not know?* Maybe it wouldn't last, but who even considers the longevity of love in its first blush?

"There will always be a part of me in you." He kept saying it, over and over again. He was right: We had fallen in love so young, and so much of our connection had formed us. And yet my response to the fear and pain of knowing that I had broken a deep bond was to move too quickly, too brusquely. Naïvely, I thought the best way to handle such sorrow was with a clean break, scorched earth. I was too young and self-involved to see that the guilt welling up inside me would not be temporary. With Will, it was indelible guilt.

Not only was my relationship with Will shattered, but my friendships were changed, too. Stéphane was furious that I had taken up with his best friend and vowed never to speak to either of us again. Nikki had been transferred to Geneva, where she was in charge of opening yet another Ralph Lauren store and didn't have much time to keep in touch. The few times I saw Hélène, she would ask me if it was true I was dating someone from La Rochelle, her eyes widening with shock. *"C'est vrai?"* It made no sense to her that I would come all the way to Paris only to fall in love with some *plouc* from the provinces.

I loved Hervé *because* he was from the provinces. He was down-to-earth, not like the flashy polo players at Chez Miocque and not insular like François's bourgeois family. He was just the companion I had longed for on those lonely summer nights in Paris. He introduced me to the France that is a world apart from Paris, another country, sending me tickets to meet him in different cities. One weekend it was Cannes, where we holed up in a tacky hotel while rain drenched La Croisette. Another time we took the train down to the Pays Basque and skied at a funky resort in the Pyrénées called Gourette.

About six months into our affair, I met Hervé in Toulouse and we drove to Carcassonne and over the Spanish border to Catalonia, to the tiny fishing ports of Cadaqués and Roses, where Salvador Dalí had lived and painted. It was broiling hot but such a relief to be out of Paris, away from the lonely streets of holiday weekends. We drove north up the rocky coast in the sweltering heat, windows down, through Portbou and back over the border, through charming run-down beach towns like Banyuls-sur-Mer and Collioure, where the Fauvists painted the chunky medieval lighthouse in the 1930s.

As we drove, I tried to imagine what life must be like in a village where everyone knows your name, where families return for generations. It seemed comforting and eternal in a way, so different from life in a chaotic, competitive city like New York. We listened to French classics on cassettes Hervé had made—Serge Gainsbourg, Jacques Dutronc, and Michel Fugain. Charles Trenet singing *"Douce France."* We sang along, laughing at my off-key singing. I can still hear the dulcet sound of Trenet's voice: *"Douce France, cher pays de mon enfance."* This was *douce France*: Soft France, tender France. Small-town France.

In the late spring Hervé invited me to meet his parents in Redon. I took the train from the Gare d'Austerlitz and arrived late in the evening in Nantes. Hervé picked me up in his secondhand Deux Chevaux—one of those weird-looking French cars with plastic flaps for windows. They lived in a house with an enormous gate, on a hill in the nice part of town. His mother, Joelle, a nervous housewife who treasured her son, was waiting up for us.

"Salut, Hervé," she whispered as she opened the back door. *"Bonjour, Kate."* She embraced me warmly, *les bises* on each cheek. She was skinny in the way French women are, wiry and short, with a shock of red hair.

"Entrez, entrez, I have some dinner ready. You must be starving after such a long trip." Her husband, Jacques, had already retired to bed. She took our coats and ushered us into the dining room, where a table was set with plates of fresh langoustines, homemade mayonnaise, and flutes of champagne.

It was the first of many carefully prepared meals we would share together—Joelle always taking such joy in choosing food and dishes that Hervé liked. The way she looked at Hervé and spoke so softly and affectionately to him was poignant, almost heartbreaking, in the way that a mother's fierce love of her only son can be. She wanted him to be happy, and so she worked hard to make me feel welcome.

The place was impeccably neat and sort of tacky, with faux-marble tiles on the floors and leatherette couches. We slept in the same bed, which made me self-conscious. Was the wedding already being planned? When Hervé and I weren't in bed, we were sipping champagne aperitifs and feasting on Joelle's elaborate meals. Jacques would appear only at lunch, opening a bottle of wine or champagne well before noon and retiring two bottles later for a nap. Joelle was curious about my life in

New York and my family. She showered me with gifts—tins filled with butter cookies, scarves, a sapphire ring she wanted me to have. It was overwhelming but also comforting to know that she cared.

"Elle t'adore," Hervé told me as we waited for the train at the station in Nantes. She loves you. He beamed, excited that the weekend had been such a success. "I hope you will come back again. Maman will be waiting for you."

Soon I was taking the train almost every Friday evening out to Nantes to meet Hervé. We would go to their beach house in Penthièvre, a spit of land joining Carnac to the peninsula of Quiberon. Joelle liked to say the beach house was her escape. She often said she could stand in front of the big picture window in the living room all day and watch the tide come in and go out. She would take the Quiberon "cure," walking along the Côte Sauvage—the rocky cliffs along the ocean—inhaling big gulps of the cold salty air. Hervé and I would walk along the coast, too, the wind slapping our faces with sprays of seawater.

One weekend I hitched a ride out to Quiberon with Virginie and Alex. In France, every weekend in May is a long weekend, with an additional *pont*—or day off. Hervé wanted to introduce me to his best friend, a quiet military type called Jean-Marc. His girlfriend, Christel, came from a liberal upper-middle-class family, a strata of society known as *Les Bobos,* or Bourgeois-bohème. Christel and her two sisters,

Domitille and Angelique, stayed at their grandmother's near Virginie's house on the Pointe Churchill. They were all part of a *bande* of friends who summered in Carnac and had known one another since they were seven. There were others in the group, including Florence— a fitting model with an aquiline nose—who worked for the couturier Christian Lacroix, and her boyfriend, François-Henri, the son of another local businessman who would later build a company called PPR and eventually become one of the ruling czars of the French luxury business.

We drove up to Domitille and Christel's grandmother's house in Hervé's Deux Chevaux that Saturday afternoon. The girls were lounging on a sofa in the living room, making plans to meet up with the *bande* later that evening at a nearby nightclub called Les Chandelles.

"You are *très province* for an *Américaine!*" Jean-Marc introduced himself. He was blond and blue-eyed, with a warm smile. The women looked me up and down, bemused by the idea that Hervé would bring an American girlfriend to their home.

"I'm sure in *l'Amérique* you do not have to drive around in shitty cars like that one." Jean-Marc pointed to the Deux Chevaux.

"It is typical of *la France profonde*." Christel tried to explain in broken English that they weren't used to seeing Americans in Carnac, a resort frequented by old French families, not foreigners.

"Too funny to see you getting out of such an old car, *très vieille famille*." She smiled. "Carnac is not so *branchée*, you know."

It seemed hip to me, or at least Domitille and Christel seemed hip. Domitille was a stylist's assistant, arranging fashion shoots for an editor at French *Elle*. She and her boyfriend, Gilles, lived in a loft in Montparnasse. She carried a beat-up Hermès bag that she'd bought in the flea market and wore oversized cashmere V-neck sweaters and skinny jeans with Repetto ballet slippers. She dabbed perfume on her wrists when she went out. I had never met anyone who was so exact about the way they cuffed their jeans or applied lipstick. She had that taut French discipline. I was in awe of her confidence.

They all spoke quickly and in slang that afternoon in Carnac, but they were kind to *La Grosse Américaine.* They invited me to dinners and parties in Paris. They offered me rides to Carnac on weekends and taught me to surf on a boogie board. I didn't know much about Jane Birkin and Serge Gainsbourg, and they didn't care much for Bruce Springsteen. But we were all the same age and we shared that universal need to belong to something larger than ourselves.

Hervé and his family and friends made me feel welcome in Brittany, but every once in a while I would feel a pang of recognition that somehow this scenario wasn't forever. I remember standing with Hervé in the living room in Penthièvre one morning, looking west into the Atlantic oblivion, the angry waves crashing on the long, desolate beach. "Look! I think I can see the Statue of Liberty!" he said. "There's New York City over there. It's not that far away."

Oh, but it was, it was. Or at least it felt that way. I thought of my dad's letter. *Five thousand miles is nothing.* I thought of my friends on the other side of that wide, wild ocean. What would they be doing on this sunny morning in late May? Would they already be lying around a pool at some rental in the Hamptons? I thought of Will teeing off at the Greenwich golf club or my mother rushing out to buy more Elizabeth Arden

face cream at Bergdorf's. What would they think of me here, standing on this tacky faux-marble floor in this strange French house?

But who was the stranger here? When I appeared in the picture frame, in front of that window facing the sea, I must have thrown Joelle for a loop. I didn't fit into the wild landscape of Carnac and Quiberon, dotted with the Celtic menhir stones that dated back to prehistoric times. I was probably as odd and mysterious to her as those five-thousand-year-old monoliths jutting out of the adjacent fields. In this provincial seaside resort, Joelle must have envisioned someone completely different keeping her son company in their Breton cottage, hugging the savage landscape.

Sometimes when she would flutter around me, offering salted caramels and buttered biscuits, I would catch Joelle stealing glances at me with a quizzical look in her eye. Was she trying to imagine what future her son had with this American girl? Did our transatlantic love story make any sense to her? Did she hope to make me feel at home in her home, or hope her son would come to his senses and find a local girl, a doe from a nearby forest?

Douce France

by Charles Trenet

Sweet France
Dear country of my childhood
Cradled in tender insouciance
I have kept you in my heart
My village with the bell tower and with noble houses
Where children of my age
Have shared my joy
Yes, I love you
And I give you this poem
Yes, I love you
In good times and in bad

I have known landscapes
And these wonderful suns
On distant journeys
Far away under other skies
But how much I prefer
My blue sky, my horizon
My main road and my river
My meadow and my house.

CHAPTER SEVEN

In the Forest of Brocéliande

We left for the Rallye Bretagne just before dawn on a Saturday morning, speeding north through the rugged Breton landscape toward Rennes in Hervé's Deux Chevaux. Hervé was dressed in a stiff-collared white broadcloth shirt that made him sit up very straight as we bounced along. The brass button on his tie was embossed with the head of a wild boar. In the backseat, next to his blue velvet frock coat, lay his trumpet and six long knives wrapped in a leather pouch.

La France profonde. We were a million miles from the refinements of Paris, speeding into the forest of Brocéliande, a twenty-five-square-mile tract of ancient beech and oak trees reputed to have once been the haunt of King Arthur and his knights. The land was the natural habitat of the wild boar, the creature embossed on Hervé's tiepin, and Hervé that morning would be joining some sixty of his

fellow Bretons on a wild-boar hunt. What I was chasing was a story—a magazine assignment I could not have gotten if Hervé, nearly a year into our romance, had not wanted to introduce me to one of the great passions of his life.

Around midmorning we came to a clearing near a lake called Étang du Pas du Houx. Mist was lifting off the water. Men opened the back of a big truck, and five dozen frenzied dogs—English and French foxhounds—came spilling down a wooden ramp. They milled around, waiting for the trumpet blast that would set them off in search of a scent. Some of the hunters were on horses, patting their mounts and reining them in; the rest were on foot, trumpets slung over their shoulders, blue velvet frock coats buttoned up, boots gleaming in the morning light.

And then a blast of a horn and the cued hounds were off, noses to the ground, yapping furiously as they scrambled into the woods. Hervé would normally be running with the other hunters, but because he was looking after me, we followed as best we could in the Deux Chevaux. Sometimes we paralleled the progress on paved roads; sometimes we careened over dirt tracks in the forest, the rusty car jouncing and swaying and bashing through branches. Hervé would cut the motor and hop up on the doorframe, peering through binoculars and listening for trumpets and hounds. He could tell from the pitch of the barking that they were on the trail of their quarry. Every once in a while we would glimpse a flash of blue velvet as horsemen bounded through shafts of light or across distant fields. Oh, the elegance of those horsemen! It was as if King Arthur were still riding in the woods with a retinue of knights. I could see how Coco Chanel, who had come to the Rallye Bretagne with her lover, the Duke of Westminster, back in the 1920s, would have been inspired. The blue coats with the broadcloth shirts were the epitome of French sophistication and timelessness. The French breathed so much vitality into their traditions. They lived in the past as easily as in the present. I could see how for Hervé the *chasse à courre* was a way of ennobling his own roots, of connecting the dull provincial town and the dreary business of a souvenir factory to the poetry of Brittany's medieval past, its castles and aristocrats and a nobility surely the rival of any found in Paris.

Hours passed, and we chased the hunt as tirelessly as the hunters chased the boar. Sometimes we jumped out of the car and ran through the woods to get closer to the action. My Nike sneakers were soaked through to the socks. I scribbled in a spiral notebook. The shadows of a late October afternoon lengthened. At around 4:00 P.M., as the trumpet fanfare echoed in the woods, Hervé shut the ignition to listen for the call that signaled that the boar had been cornered—or "taken," as they say in the language of the *rallye*. The hunters had been going for more than six hours, over hills, through thickets, even across a lake. At one point in the afternoon we had spotted Hervé's friend Patrick, one of the *boutons*—or hunters on the team—and a stockbroker on the Paris Bourse, wading into le Pas du Houx. He was pushing a small dinghy, while two other *boutons* paddled furiously to catch up with a boar on the other side. But by the time they had climbed back out of the boat and thrown the paddles ashore, the boar had escaped to a nearby field. We drove over a rough forest track around the lake and arrived just as a ring of hunters in blue were closing in. I was glad we were far enough away not to see the kill.

The executioner with the knife was Georges de Jacquelin, the seventy-five-year-old master of the Rallye Bretagne, whom Hervé had taken me to meet the day before. De Jacquelin had devoted his life to the hunt. He gave us a tour of the Château Le Val Henri, where his family had lived for nine centuries. Every wall was lined with stag heads and boar heads, trophies from centuries of hunting. In front of one ferocious-looking boar, he bowed his head in respect and whispered, "This one, mademoiselle, killed my dear father." Over his shoulder I could see Hervé chuckling, lifting his hand to his mouth.

Hervé rushed forward to join the end of the hunt, leaving me on the outside, looking in. For a moment, I thought of Will back in Connecticut, probably pulling the head cover off his three wood on his morning round of golf at the country club in Greenwich.

Before the hunters butchered the boar and distributed the meat to local farmers, in accord with tradition, the *boutons* recapped the events of the afternoon, raising their horns to blow a series of bracing and sometimes melancholy fanfares in honor of the hounds, the land, hunters come and gone. Something in the songs seemed to celebrate the survival of the tradition itself. But the effort to blow their horns after the long day left each hunter winded and panting. Still, all the hunters wore resplendent coats and shirts—barely marked by a splatter of mud or sweat—except for Patrick, whose pants were soaked from his trip through the lake. There was a moment of silence when all the hunters lifted their eyes and prayed for the spirit of the slaughtered boar, whose corpse was off to the side in a grassy field. De Jacquelin moved to the center of the crowd, holding one of the boar's feet, still bloody. He looked at me across the crowd and smiled, his pink cheeks flush with pride. I was startled when Hervé nudged me forward. Did I want to be a part of this? I found myself walking into the center of the ring of hunters in my muddy Nike sneakers, with no idea what I was expected to say or do—oh, that first tee at the country club in Greenwich was a cinch compared to this! Then, moved by some impulse, I found myself unaccountably bowing to Monsieur de Jacquelin, like a courtesan in a Japanese teahouse. Hervé beamed with pride as the grand old man of Brittany handed me the freshly severed foot of a wild Breton boar, wrapped in a kitchen towel.

CHAPTER EIGHT

L'Entretien

Only the French could invent seamless stockings that stay up with a rubber sticky band that grips the upper thigh. Dim Ups, as they were called, hit the market in the late eighties, with a splashy ad in the cinema featuring a pair of mile-long legs swishing from side to side like windshield wipers. For just a few francs, you, too, could feel like Catherine Deneuve in *Belle de Jour*. I bought several pairs at Monoprix and wore them almost every day, replacing the nubby black tights that had become a mainstay of my Parisian uniform.

So on the bitterly cold January morning of my job interview with Dennis Thim, the Paris bureau chief of Fairchild Publications, I slipped a pair of black dotted-swiss Dim Ups under my red plaid miniskirt and put on a pair of black pointy-toed pumps. I was no Catherine Deneuve, but I was a long way from my banker friends marching down Park Avenue in their Reebok sneakers.

To stay in France and keep my Paris dream going, I needed working papers and a full-time job. I'd had enough of sitting at my kitchen counter typing out *Met Home* memos and chasing aloof architects for interviews. My friends back home were announcing engagements, law school graduations, and job promotions. They were moving on and moving up. I'd started scanning the English-language employment classifieds in the *Trib*. One ad described a position as a features writer for an American publication. The only requisites were a working knowledge of French and some freelance experience. Bingo. I sent in my résumé and clips, not knowing the opening was in the Paris bureau of *Women's Wear Daily,* the fashion-industry bible.

Coincidentally, it turned out that John Fairchild, the big boss at *Women's Wear Daily,* had read my story about the Rallye Bretagne in *European Travel & Life* on a flight home from a Christmas holiday in Klosters. He loved the details of the hunt and the rituals of the swaggering, aristocratic hunt master, Georges de Jacquelin. It was exactly the kind of story he expected to read in *M* magazine, his latest creation, a glossy men's magazine.

I was oblivious to all this when I rode the tiny mirrored elevator to the second-floor offices of Fairchild Publications on the rue d'Aguesseau, tucked behind the Hermès shop on the elegant Faubourg Saint-Honoré in the 8th arrondissement. Quickly, I checked my look: professional and very French. Big dangly pearl earrings and a rust-colored peacoat bought on sale at A.P.C., near the Luxembourg Gardens. My hair was pulled back in a puffy black velvet bow. By now I had the BCBG thing down pat.

The Fairchild offices were brand new, equipped with the kind of crunchy wall-to-wall carpet and sleek glass-topped desks you might find in a Manhattan skyscraper. The usual French formalities were conspicuously absent—no rude secretaries or the deadening sense of indifference so typical of French bureaucracy. Telex machines nattered away, reporters barked into telephone receivers, a receptionist darted up and down from her desk, and the switchboard sounded off incessantly. And then there was Dennis, the bureau chief. He entered the reception area as if he were walking onstage, with exaggerated steps, a swoop of his long camel-hair coat, a shock of blond hair dipping over one eye. Dennis was much younger than I'd expected—perhaps not even thirty—and he had the handsome, chiseled face and suave sophistication of a talk-show host or even a movie star.

"Are you Katherine? Welcome to Fairchild!" He greeted me with a big flashy smile, his eyes darting from my earrings down to my scuffed black pumps. I had cobbled together what I thought was a fashionable look. But as Dennis shark-eyed me, I realized "fashionable" was a relative term in this office. My coat and hairstyle and miniskirt told Dennis more than anything in my résumé. Dim Ups alone could not propel me from preppy New Yorker to Parisian sophisticate.

"You can throw that over there." Dennis motioned to a spindly coat rack behind the receptionist's desk and beckoned me to follow him back to his office, at the end of the loft-like space. He ignored the reporters at each desk we passed. They were hunched over computers or reclining in their swivel chairs, cradling phone receivers between shoulder and neck, their eyes tracking me suspiciously. We settled into his small office, which was dominated by a huge glass-topped desk. The walls were filled with framed covers of *M* magazine, and his desk was cluttered with photos of him with various Parisian luminaries. I recognized Karl Lagerfeld peeking out from behind a black fan. My stockings caught on the caning of the chair as I sat down.

"So what brings you to Paris?" he asked as he scanned my curriculum vitae. Before I could answer, the intercom buzzed and Dennis excused himself with a floppy wave of his hand meant to say, "Stay right there while I take this call."

"*Irene,*" he purred into the receiver a seductive half whisper worthy of Anouk Aimée. "I was calling because . . . Oh, did you hear that Pierre Cardin . . . No? Okay, because Mr. Fairchild is coming on the fifteenth. . . . Okay. *Je t'embrasse.*"

He hung up the phone quickly and bolted out of his chair and stuck his head out of the office.

"Claire, get me a reservation at L'Espadon for four on the fifteenth. And tell Gloria."

He settled back in his chair and continued his review of my CV.

"Oh, do you know Ben Brantley?" he asked cautiously, referring to the former Paris bureau chief who would eventually become the chief theater critic at *The New York Times.* "You know who Marie-Hélène de Rothschild is, right?" He flipped around the social map a mile a minute, sprinkling names here and there: Pierre Cardin, the Costes brothers, Irene Amic, the wife of some big L'Oréal executive. I didn't know any of these people. He was testing me, trying to place me, to figure out who had sent me. His scattered attention and high-powered connections baffled me. I was way out of my league. What could I possibly add to this group?

"Well, here at Fairchild," Dennis continued, coyly tilting his head and smiling, "we have to come up with lots of ideas. Do you have any good ideas?" He leaned into the desk like a school kid, suddenly delighted by the possibility that he might finagle a few good scoops out of a witless job candidate.

I had a lot of ideas, none of them very original. They were ideas culled from French magazines like *Décoration Internationale* and *Art de Vivre.* As the Paris stringer for *Met Home,* I'd been mired in the slow-moving world of decorators and furniture designers. To me, a Paris scoop meant landing an interview with a radical and little-known architect like Jean Nouvel or touring the Rungis fish market with the food critic Colman Andrews. The fast-paced fashion world was not my beat, but I was eager to please Dennis. Something about his boyish charm and his Cheshire-cat grin seduced me. He was smart and tricky, but he also had a warm, knowing look in his eye that revealed an old soul.

"Claire! Claire! Claire de Lune!" Dennis shrieked, abruptly stabbing the intercom button on his phone. A wiry, bespectacled French woman appeared in his doorway.

"Yes, Dennis?" Claire was clearly familiar with these outbursts.

"Where are those new issues of *M* magazine with Rocky on the cover?"

Claire disappeared for a nanosecond and returned silently with a magazine bearing the image of Sylvester Stallone. Dennis held it up and explained that he was looking to fill the position of feature writer for *M.* Some of the stories would also appear in *W,* the company's flagship publication. Although Dennis had written a lot for *M,* he seemed more interested in contributing to the society pages of *W* and *Women's Wear Daily.* He spoke of parties he'd attended and celebrities he'd met. He fired off another round of who's who, launching a string of names as aristocratic-sounding as a necklace of South Sea pearls: Laure de Beauvau-Craon, Joy de Rohan Chabot, Hélène de Yougoslavie. I nodded and smiled. Who on earth were these people?

"So Mr. Fairchild read your story in *European Travel and Life,* about the hunt in Brittany," Dennis said matter-of-factly, riffling around in his desk.

"Really?" I blushed, suddenly boosted by a strange mix of pride and disbelief.

"He loves that kind of story. That's exactly what he wants in *M* magazine. Now, how did you find those people in Brittany?"

Keeping the details vague, I explained that my friends had invited me on the hunt. Dennis instantly lit up, imagining I was some sort of society girl with connections in the international jet set. He desperately needed a writer who could cover the esoteric tastes and high-society whims of the boss.

"Well, obviously you have connections." Dennis jumped up from his desk again. "And, frankly, that puts you ahead of everyone else in this office. We're not going to ask you to write about SKU's and charge-backs," he laughed, swiping a shock of blond hair off his face.

I nodded, as if I knew exactly what he meant.

"We have enough people covering fashion, but we need someone who can cover the rest of the world, if you know what I mean." Leaning in, he winced slightly. "*You* know, the *gauche caviar,* the society queens, those aristos hiding out in their ridiculous châteaux!

"And the fact of the matter is, Katherine," he continued, drawing out the first syllable of my name for added emphasis, "you have to speak French to get to these people! How did you learn to speak French?" He raised an eyebrow and gave me a long, sideways look, pursing his lips. "Do you have a French *lover?*"

Yes, I did have a French boyfriend, I said. Dennis seemed satisfied by my response, as if I'd rattled off the VIP-reservations number at Maxim's.

"So, why don't you come up with a letter from Paris?" He thumbed impatiently through his Filofax. "Send me a list of the new hot places to go and things to do."

And, with that, Dennis leaped up from his desk and stalked out of his office. I rose gingerly from my chair and—*zut!*—felt my Dim Ups snag. There goes that job. I grabbed my bag and walked awkwardly to the front desk, trying to keep the run from sprinting down my leg. By the time I reached the reception area, Dennis was already perusing a stack of messages and snooping in the receptionist's top drawer.

"Okay, *merci,*" he said, handing over my coat. "We'll be in touch."

Out on the Faubourg Saint-Honoré, it was getting dark. Raindrops sprinkled the wide gray paving stones. The gold trim around the vitrines of the Chloé boutique glistened in the light of the Art Deco streetlamps. Shopkeepers in three-piece suits and bow ties were locking up their swanky storefronts for the night. I clacked down the sidewalk toward the Élysée Palace, still reeling from the whirlwind interview. Cops in bulletproof vests and helmets stood guard in front of every corner, waiting for what? Paris had been quiet since the previous summer, no bombs. But in the wake of the terrible Lockerbie bombing that had killed 259 people aboard Pan Am Flight 103 in late December, the specter of terrorism loomed once more.

Taxis idled in the rush-hour traffic. Along the avenue Matignon, the pristine gallery windows overflowed with eighteenth-century commodes and torchères; these were the kinds of places where Dennis's society people shopped. I thought about Dennis and his bizarre bursts of energy, his gossipy rant. Who were these people he was talking about? Who was Irene Amic? And how would I ever track down Pierre Cardin? I knew Paris well. I could pick out the best vacherin at any cheese shop, rattle off the sale dates at Robert Clergerie and Dorothée Bis, and teach someone how

Chloé

prie *Madame BETTS*

d'assister à la Collection Printemps-Eté 19

to dance Le Rock. But I'd never been to most of the places he mentioned, and I didn't have the chutzpah to call Marie-Hélène de Rothschild and ask her where she bought her underwear.

By the time I crossed the Pont Alexandre III, with its gilded warrior horses charging ahead toward Les Invalides, the rain was coming down in heavy drops. Taking cover under the chestnut trees on the Esplanade des Invalides, I wondered what it would be like to work with someone so manic, in a business where I had no real footing. Dennis didn't strike me as particularly loyal, but there was something touching about him. He was smart and funny. If I could keep up with Dennis, I would learn a lot. His relentless pace and endless quest for more information and details about the world of Paris fashion intrigued me. I wanted to get further inside that life, but I had no formal fashion education. Chargebacks and SKU's sounded like something you would memorize for a chemistry final at Princeton. I buzzed myself into my building and trudged up the dirty staircase to the third floor. When I got to the landing, I could hear the old man across the hall sliding open the peephole in his door. I unlocked my door and slammed it behind me, disgusted by the French and their strange voyeuristic habits.

I pulled my Canon typewriter off the shelf and began typing a list of ideas for a "Letter from Paris":

- Bonetti and Garouste's new Bastille shop.
- Jean Nouvel's Institut du Monde Arabe building.
- A new Saint-Germain hotel called La Villa.
- A Latin Quarter bistro called La Rotisserie.

Dennis called two days later and offered me the job: features writer at *M* magazine and *W*, the elitist society bimonthly that brought John Fairchild's famous "In and Out" decrees into the living rooms of the international jet set. Mostly I would be covering new chefs, restaurants, actors, shops, and anything else that struck the boss's fancy. Occasionally there would be society parties to cover, as well as fashion reviews during the collections. It sounded overwhelming and fun.

"What kind of salary are you looking for?" I hadn't thought about salary. Caught off guard, I asked Dennis if I could get back to him within an hour.

Quickly, I called the *Trib* to ask my godmother's boyfriend for advice. Bob was skeptical about Fairchild. The reporters there had a reputation for being difficult, bitchy, superficial, and scrappy. Fairchild himself wasn't well liked, either, given his history of picking favorites, casting people "in" and "out." If there was a tradition of gentlemanly journalism in Paris—the expat descendants of Malcolm Cowley and Ernest Hemingway—Fairchild had no place in that pantheon of intellects, nor did he aspire to one. He was a sharp, somewhat devious newspaper reporter with a businessman's reflexes.

"Take whatever number comes to mind and double it!" Bob instructed. It was my first lesson in salary negotiation. At the time, twenty thousand dollars was the going rate for entry-level jobs in the publishing business. Forty thousand dollars seemed impossibly high, especially for someone with no credentials.

"Well, you won't get it if you don't ask for it," Bob said, losing patience.

When I called Dennis back and spat out the frightful number, he didn't miss a beat. "Not a problem."

I agreed to start the very next day.

CHAPTER NINE

5, Rue d'Aguesseau

When I arrived at the Fairchild offices at 9:00 A.M., Dennis was flipping through the receptionist's drawer, searching for a Doliprane, the French equivalent of Tylenol.

"Oh, hi." Dennis looked at me blankly, as if he had never seen me before. "Oh, *yes*, Katherine, yes. Come in and let me show you to your desk." He slammed the receptionist's drawer shut and pointed to a big empty desk against the windows on the far side of the room, between Claire de Lune and a fashion reporter named Elizabeth, who was on the phone, speaking French with a slow drawl. She smiled and waved. Dennis patted the computer on my desk.

"You know how to work one of these, right?" He chuckled and disappeared into his office, shutting the door. *Um, sure.* The truth of the matter was that the only time I had ever used a word processor was in college, and computers like these were a mystery to me.

I was on my own. I had to figure out who was who and introduce myself. There were several reporters in the office: a reporter who worked for the menswear weekly *Daily News Record,* a business reporter, and a housewares reporter who worked for a trade rag called *Home Furnishings*

Daily. Elizabeth introduced me to a photographer named Philippe. He was a frumpy, exhausted-looking middle-aged French guy who worked exclusively for Fairchild.

"You'll be working together *a lot,*" Elizabeth said, with a knowing glance at Philippe. It didn't take long to realize that photographers were the only employees who ranked lower in the Fairchild hierarchy than reporters. They were responsible for loading up all the equipment—lights, cameras, lenses, tripods—and hustling to far-flung destinations or nearby couture salons at a moment's notice. Then they had to endure the humiliation of being told how to frame a shot. The editors and reporters were responsible for the copy and the photos. On that morning, Philippe and Elizabeth were reviewing film from a preview at Christian Lacroix, the young couturier from Arles who had made a splash in French and American fashion magazines with his kaleidoscopic prints and pouf dresses. Elizabeth and Philippe had forgotten to shoot color film on one of the outfits, and they were bracing themselves for a dressing-down from the New York editors.

After showing me how to turn on the computer and giving me a few pointers on the phone system, Elizabeth began methodically calling press attachés to get more precise information about the fabrics used for the three Lacroix gowns they had photographed.

"Le shantung est de Bucol?" she asked. *"Radzimir, Gandini. Et la guipure est de Jacky Tex?"*

This was a whole new language. Elizabeth sounded impressive rattling off obscure technical terms with such ease. Later, I understood that she was Dennis's secret weapon when it came to fashion: She could identify any embroidery or stitch, the name of the cut of a sleeve, the weave of a fabric, even the mill where the fabric was woven. She was passionate about fashion. She sewed her own clothing and dreamed of one day becoming a designer, but she lacked the social dexterity necessary to navigate a Parisian party. So Dennis took on that part of the job and left all the fashion details to Elizabeth.

Dennis was a product of an area known as the Five Towns on Long Island, and he spoke, even in French, with a distinct nasal twang. *"Kaaaaaatherine,"* he would say, sitting behind his desk, fidgeting with his phone or flipping through the pile of magazines and newspapers he frantically surveyed every morning—*L'Express, Time, Le Figaro, Libération,* and the *Herald Tribune.* He aspired to five-star hotels and limousines, but he never forgot his roots and his Irish Catholic upbringing. In conversation he would often refer to his many sisters and one brother or slyly drop the fact that he had graduated with honors from Columbia University.

At Fairchild, Dennis had wangled the unthinkable: switching from ad sales at *M* magazine to the editorial side of *Women's Wear Daily.* He'd been hired when the former bureau chief had supposedly suffered some kind of breakdown. At least Dennis liked to call it that. He told a story about his predecessor hiding behind his desk, trembling in a moment of crisis. He was replaced temporarily by a woman who had a lot of flair with words but not with people. Nobody liked to admit it, but Fairchild Publications was a boys' club, and the editors who made it into the inner circle, Mr. Fairchild's favorites, were all men. When Dennis came along, Fairchild supposedly fired the female "acting" bureau chief in the elevator while on his way out to lunch with Dennis. "This is Dennis," Fairchild said to her. "He's replacing you."

Dennis thought the whole thing was amusing. He behaved outrageously to mask the discomfort he felt when editorial types would snub him, assuming he was just a lucky ad salesman who had charmed his way into the top spot. He was not a natural writer, but he was a natural talker. He spent hours on the phone gossiping with anyone who had a morsel of information to share. His writing sounded like his garrulous conversations, which Mr. Fairchild encouraged.

Dennis loved show tunes. In the midst of a crisis he would burst into song: *"Kids! I don't know what's wrong with these kids today!"* Or he would bellow: *"It's a hard-knock life—for us!"* as he swooshed through the office on his way back from lunch with a society-party planner or some ex–Madame Claude girl—the famous French call girls—who had lucked into an aristocratic marriage, complete with château.

Another favorite was the crowd-pleaser from *Pippin: "Rivers belong where they can ramble, eagles belong where they can fly."* Dennis was definitely an eagle. He flew high, full throttle, determined to soar.

Society matrons loved Dennis. And nothing thrilled him more than their morning phone calls to divulge a delicious bit of gossip from a dinner party the previous evening. You knew the conversation was getting juicy when Dennis lowered his voice to a whisper or closed his office door.

Dennis made it clear from day one that I would not be covering fashion but, rather, all of the other subjects that piqued Mr. Fairchild's interest—things like five-star hotels, Michelin-starred chefs, classical musicians, potato farmers, bookbinders, and any other purveyor of taste who might come along. Mr. Fairchild was interested in the best of the best—whether it was the best bread or the best facial or the best secretary. He recognized that the people who bought expensive designer clothing also wanted to buy the châteaux and the five-star hotel rooms. Mr. Fairchild understood what many more-serious publishers refused to acknowledge: that clothes come with certain accessories—not just handbags but houses, furniture, vacations, and boats. The accessories you bought revealed the associations and groups you identified with, where you belonged. He was a sociologist in the sense that he understood that fashion is tribal: It's not about who you are but where you belong.

My first assignment was to write about a very expensive brand of bottled water called Chateldon, which was once the favorite water of Louis XIV and was now served at the Ritz. Mr. Fairchild had heard from one of his cronies—was it Emanuel Ungaro or Hélène Rochas?—that it was absolutely the best water on earth. Dennis barked at me to find out more about it, write it up.

Was he kidding? I sat at my desk, contemplating exactly how one goes about finding more information on *recherché* vintage water. As I stared at my computer screen, I felt a silent presence several feet away from me. I looked up and found Mr. Fairchild staring down at me, hands thrust deep in his pockets, his head tilted back as if to question this imposter who had suddenly landed in his office.

"Hello; nice to meet you." He offered his hand while looking distractedly over my left shoulder. Was there someone more interesting behind me? He had a shock of white hair and menacing blue eyes, and wore an impeccable tweed blazer with a bright-blue silk handkerchief tucked into the breast pocket. Shiny brown John Lobb shoes peeked out from under cuffed gray flannel pants. He was WASPy and worldly, an unusual combination that he owed to the years he'd worked in Paris for his family's publishing company after graduating from Princeton. He had been dispatched to Paris to work for the newspaper his grandfather had founded in 1910; the trade rag reported on the haute couture showings so Seventh Avenue garmentos and big department stores like Bonwit Teller and Lord & Taylor could copy the outfits and sell them to American women at a fraction of the price.

In terms of glamour, Seventh Avenue was the opposite of the Paris fashion world. As the editorial director of the sleepy paper, Fairchild would pull all sorts of hijinks to earn respect from the snobby French press attachés. He met and interviewed Coco Chanel and Cristóbal Balenciaga. When couturiers would not allow him access to their collections, he worked around their embargoes, interviewing seamstresses or dispatching stylish staff members to pose as potential clients. When he was banned from couture shows, he stationed a photographer in a building across the street, with instructions to shoot with a telephoto lens. As a young reporter, Mr. Fairchild made a habit of sneaking into couture showings when press was not allowed, and later he would expect the same kind of cunning from his staff. Recognizing the connection between fashion and society, Mr. Fairchild launched *W* magazine in the 1970s and transformed his family's humble publication into the fashion industry's most powerful mouthpiece.

Although Fairchild Publications was based in New York City, the company had bureaus in London, Milan, Paris, and Washington, D.C. Paris was Mr. Fairchild's favorite place. He would show up in the Paris offices several times a year, to cover the haute couture shows or the ready-to-wear collections. He and his wife would stay at the Ritz and he would wander in and out of the office, sometimes taking part in previews with designers he liked or assigning stories on people and places that interested him. He even occasionally composed headlines and leads to reviews of fashion shows.

Mr. Fairchild was a reporter at heart, but he maintained an air of detachment that was unmistakably WASPy. Given my own roots, I was not intimidated by him. In fact, he seemed vaguely familiar to me, in the way that he didn't pander or even feign interest unless he liked someone. He made snap judgments about people; everyone who worked for him knew this. In the office, he usually communicated with only Dennis or one of his two trusted deputies from New York, who accompanied him to the shows. He once instructed Dennis not to promote a colleague because he didn't like the sound of her voice. She was energetic and good at her job, but that didn't matter.

I assumed, because Mr. Fairchild deigned to speak to me, that he was giving me a chance on that first day. I also knew that he liked the fact that I spoke French fluently. He recognized a fellow Francophile—and a fellow Princetonian. He never mentioned it, but I knew he knew I went there, too. Like it or not, I was a member of his tribe.

"Are you working on the story about Chateldon?" he asked, pacing in front of my desk. "Call the manager of the restaurant at the Ritz. He'll tell you all about it." With that he pivoted on his heel, stalked into Dennis's office, and closed the door.

When Mr. Fairchild was in town, Dennis would surrender his private office to the boss and hover around Claire de Lune, barking orders at her and anyone who came within earshot. He would assign Mr. Fairchild's kooky story ideas to each of us in an urgent, need-it-by-yesterday tone. There was no time for discussion. We were expected to just get it. And get on it.

I tracked down the manager of the Ritz within a few hours. He described the water to me as one of the finest vintages because of its clarity or its mountain drain-off or something that made no sense. Philippe and I hustled over to the Ritz restaurant and spent an hour shooting the glass bottle from every angle. It appeared in *M* magazine under the rubric "What's Hot in Paris." A dispatch from Hanoi this was not.

The treatise on Chateldon must have been a success in the New York office, because in quick succession I was assigned to write about a potato farmer in the Île-de-France region, an antique-books dealer in Chartres, and a family of polo-playing vintners in Bordeaux. At the end of my first week, I found myself at a table for two at L'Arpège, a Left Bank restaurant whose chef, Alain Passard, would become France's first three-star Michelin chef to focus on vegetarian haute cuisine. Hervé came with me, and we marveled at our luck as we sampled portions of lobster grilled in sweet-and-sour rosemary sauce, monkfish stuffed with mussels, and mille-feuille with orange confit and lemon sorbet. Passard, also a Breton, sat with us for a while and talked about his career trajectory: from the university town of Rennes to the kitchens of Gaston Boyer, a three-star Michelin chef in Reims, then on to Brussels, and finally to his own place on the rue de Varenne.

We toasted one another with glasses of an eighty-year-old Savoie. Hervé smiled proudly, happy to be in the presence of a fellow Breton. He whispered romantically to me, reaching across the table for my hand, but I was too busy taking notes on the wines—a vin du pays from Jura, another from Cahors—and on the trend for serving Loire Valley Bourgueil cold. Passard, a genial thirty-two-year-old with an open face and big blue eyes, darted back and forth from the kitchen, filling us in on the ingredients of our meal and offering his favorite recipes: bread baked in beer, lamb grilled with almond butter, and an unusual *amuse-bouche* of fromage blanc, chives, and maple syrup. I scribbled down every word in my notebook, hoping to publish the recipes alongside my story.

Back at the office, I regaled Dennis and Elizabeth with blow-by-blow descriptions of every delicious dish.

"You seem to like the food beat. And so does Mr. Fairchild," said Dennis.

It was true. Ever since Bibiane had shared her arsenal of secret recipes for blanquette de veau and tarte à l'oignon, I had grown keen on the idea of learning to cook like a *Parisienne,* following Bibiane's instructions, as well as those in Patricia Wells's book, *The Food Lover's Guide to Paris.* "*C'est tellement facile,*" Bibiane would say. She marveled at the way a stick of butter or a generous pinch of salt could make or break a recipe. Her kitchen was always stocked with the necessary ingredients—never too much: fresh eggs, a baguette, and a round of cheese to make a gooey omelet, or bitter chives and a head of sweet Bibb lettuce for a simple salad. I never could strike the right balance between vinegar and oil to achieve both the sweet and sour flavor of Bibiane's vinaigrette.

Food was an easy way to learn about French tradition, to feel like I belonged. Shopping every Wednesday on the rue Cler, a market street near my apartment, I became a regular at the butcher and the cheese shop. You know you're a New Yorker when the dry cleaner remembers your name. In Paris, it's that moment when the poissonier or the boulangère recognizes you and smiles.

On another assignment, I met Lionel Poilâne in his family's bakery on the rue du Cherche-Midi. His father had opened the place during the war. We stood in front of the hot brick oven in the back room, and Poilâne—with his stringy hair cut in a kind of Elizabethan-style bob—recounted how his father had saved his business during the war by trading his country bread—or miche, as it is called—for paintings of the miche by the impoverished artists in the neighborhood. Lionel had continued the tradition, later crafting an entire chandelier out of bread for Salvador Dalí.

The next day, on Dennis's orders, I booked a ticket to fly to Zurich to interview the watchmakers at IWC. The assignments came fast and furious. I traveled to Saint-Cyr to interview the military students of France's equivalent to West Point (Mr. Fairchild was obsessed with their uniforms). A week later, I was on a train back to the Loire Valley to write

about the *attelage* carriage races at a château called Le Fresne. My life was accelerating; I was rushing from story to story with little time to spare in the evenings or on weekends. At night I left the office later and later, only returning home after covering a party or attending a dinner. Hervé left messages on my answering machine, to say good night. He was proud of me and of my success at work. He recognized that my happiness brought us closer, even if it meant fewer trips to the forest of Brocéliande and fewer kir royales or plates of fresh langoustines in Quiberon.

CHAPTER TEN

The Daily Metamorphosis
of Exterior Things

E verywhere you go in Paris, every question you ask, every favor,
phone call, post-office visit, the answer is always the same: *Non.*
Ce n'est pas possible.
Désolé.
Il n'est pas là.
Il n'est pas disponible pour l'instant.
Veuillez rappeler plus tard.

These are just the entry hurdles you have to surmount to get someone on the phone or get a reservation, call a taxi, find a hotel room. In
France, people show their power by saying no. In America they show it
by saying yes—getting things done, giving people access. The French
have a meticulous code in business that allows them to sound incredibly
helpful and generous and courteous while basically telling you to get
lost. They deliver this dismissive news with the most mellifluous voice
imaginable; the more melodious and beautiful the delivery, the less ac-
commodating the message. Simple sentences such as *Je suis désolée, madame,* are delivered in a soprano worthy of opening night at the Paris
Opera.

Mr. Fairchild dealt with this fake politesse by speaking perfect French with a flat, gruff voice. And all of his lieutenants, including Dennis, copied his intonations. We all answered the phone the way he did, with a honking American accent, and always in English: "Hello, FAIR-child," we would bark into the receiver. It set us apart.

Working in Paris was hard. But I had nothing to compare it to, since I'd never had a real job—apart from summer internships and salesgirl jobs—in New York. The pace at Fairchild was relentless, even though email and common use of the Internet were still five years away. If "computer age" appeared in the same sentence as "fashion," it referred to the industrial programming big companies used to track merchandise or performance. Copy was filed on a telex machine. Push the "send" button too many times, and the machine would *rat-a-tat-tat* until dawn, sending and resending text for hours. Dennis had a habit of losing his patience with the telex. If it didn't jump to attention the first time he pushed "send," he would absently push the button over and over again. The editors in New York would call and scream at us about how their machines were going berserk. There was a fax machine, too, which was considered modern. It was used almost exclusively to send designers' sketches to New York on deadline. The originals were put in the "pouch," a rudimentary system that might have been an early model for FedEx. Photos, film, and sketches were placed in a black rubber pouch, which was couriered to the airport late at night and placed on the Concorde, bound for New York. It was the only way to get anything across the Atlantic in less than twelve hours.

Working at Fairchild Publications in those days was like being an emergency-room medic, on call 24/7. We were constantly on the lookout for scoops. "What's new?" "What's new?" "What's new?" We operated on the adrenaline of fear. My Filofax was riddled with endless lists of story ideas and random quotes. We were always on deadline; stories were always needed yesterday. The only real luxury we had was the time difference between New York and Paris and the fact that we were so far away. When editors called from New York asking for a story, a page-one photo, or a gossip item for the next day's paper, we could ignore their calls for a few hours. Of course, we were expected to produce as much copy as possible, but if we didn't have anything good, or if Dennis wasn't feeling up to it, or if he was pissed off at an editor, he would ignore them.

"Don't pick up the phone!" he would scream at Claire de Lune, jumping up from his desk and scrambling out of his office.

More often than not, the assignments came directly from Mr. Fairchild. He loved lists, any kind of lists. He had made *W* magazine a must-read with his famous "In and Out" list, which seemingly arbitrarily cast socialites, restaurants, cars, cities, watches, and people in one month and out the next. Another favorite list was "What Tempts Them Most," basically an itemized shopping list of the rich and famous, long before *Us Weekly* and *InStyle*. We were always calling up socialites and actresses and asking them what they were buying or which designers they were wearing ("Who Wears Who?"). We asked them anything—what they wore, where they shopped, how they cooked. We were charting the social structures of the French through their exterior presentation, in much the same way that Manet and Monet had expressed these structures in their late-nineteenth-century paintings—what Baudelaire called "the daily metamorphosis of exterior things."

I would often wonder if this was really what it meant to be a journalist. The stories Mr. Fairchild assigned were a far cry from subjects like the Tet Offensive, the fall of Saigon, and the rest of the material we had studied in Gloria Emerson's journalism course in college. I didn't have as much confidence in the fashion beat, but I was fluent in the codes and customs of Paris. I could deliver authentic Paris.

Early in my tenure, Mr. Fairchild instructed Dennis to come up with a list of "The People Who Make Paris Paris." As much as Paris is architecturally beautiful, it is the people—the characters—who give the city its vitality. But Mr. Fairchild did not want an obvious list; he liked to mix it up. He liked famous faces and men in uniforms,

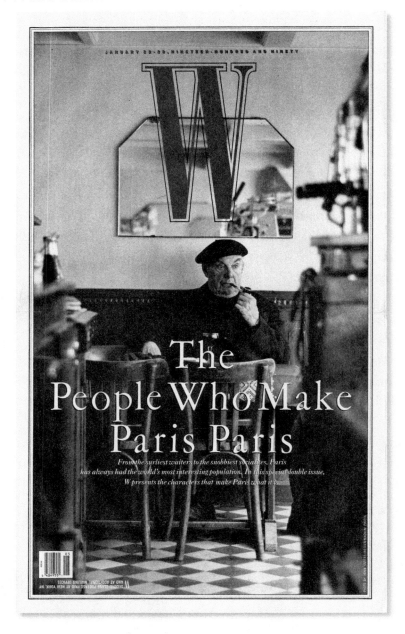

workers and society people. If we photographed a magnificent château, he wanted to see the staff in full uniform, posed on the grand staircase.

So we canvassed our sources and came up with a master list. We photographed obvious people like Karl Lagerfeld, and less-obvious ones like Juliette Mathieu, a coiffeuse who was known among a discreet circle of insiders for preventing baldness. Her clients included Isabelle Adjani and Yves Saint Laurent.

Mr. Fairchild had the wacky idea to photograph Lagerfeld at McDonald's. Lagerfeld had recently taken over the House of Chanel, and the fact that he was German irked the French. Mr. Fairchild liked to poke fun at Lagerfeld, referring to him as the Kaiser and photographing him with a Big Mac and a Diet Coke.

Many of Mr. Fairchild's best ideas were culled from dinners the previous evening with friends, people like Emanuel Ungaro and Doris Brynner, an ex-wife of the late Yul. We photographed Jean-François, the rude waiter at the café La Palette in the rue de Seine, and Janette Mahler, the secretary who had occupied the desk opposite Hubert de Givenchy for thirty-eight years. They had known each other since he was a twenty-three-year-old apprentice at Schiaparelli and she was a salesgirl. We photographed the *ouvreuses*—or usherettes—at the Théâtre du Palais-Royal, who were outfitted in the chambermaid's uniform created for the original 1963 stage version of *La Cage Aux Folles*. Then there was the taxi driver, the president's wife, the academic, and the *oenologue*. We photographed the philosopher Bernard-Henri Lévy and the photographer Jean-Paul Goude. And we tracked down an obscure silk-stocking mender, Annie Daviet, who had inherited her parents' shop on the rue Tronchet, a booming business in the 1950s when women wore stockings every day.

In many ways I think back on these idiosyncratic assignments and stories and wonder why we went to such lengths to cater to Mr. Fairchild's whims. I was too young and too new to question them. Dennis made me feel as if I had to keep going, keep delivering the goods, like a bear on a ball. "You're a smart girl," he would say, "you can do this. You went to Princeton." And I felt obliged to help him, to make the Paris office look good. We were all in it together. I also felt proud. *Yes, I can do this. I can write about bottled water, potato roots, philosophers, secretaries, and polo players.*

What was harder to swallow was the bitchiness. In the name of not tolerating egos, Mr. Fairchild would sometimes cruelly belittle people. He ran a feature called "SIPs"—Self-Important People, a withering counterpoint to VIPs. He coined the phrase "fashion victim," and he encouraged everyone who worked for him to write with the same irreverent flair. He admonished us to grab the reader. Tell it like it is. But, in Fairchild terms, "telling it like it is" could take on theatrical proportions. If it was raining hard in Paris, it was raining *chats et chiens* or Paris was a swamp. If a meal at a three-star restaurant was served warm instead of hot, the chef did not know how to light his stove. He once found a pubic hair in the bathtub in his room at the Crillon and swore off the hotel forever. *Out.* He had a penchant for drama—creating it, mimicking it, and puncturing it.

Mr. Fairchild had high expectations of every reporter. Nothing was out of bounds. If something was going on in London—if the Duchess of York was acting up, wearing black leather YSL to a children's charity—Fairchild would call James Fallon, the London bureau chief, and order him to get a quote from the queen. Fallon, as diligent and thorough a reporter as any I've ever met, complied, dutifully calling Buckingham Palace. Mr. Fairchild masterminded rivalries and indulged in public spats with designers like Geoffrey Beene, Azzedine Alaïa, and Jean Paul Gaultier. He was not intimidated by anyone. At a couture show on a sweltering hot day in July, he told Anna Wintour, the newly appointed editor of American *Vogue,* that she looked like a cucumber in her Azzedine Alaïa knit dress. He thought this was hilarious because she took herself too seriously. From then on, he referred to Wintour as "the cuke."

Society matrons were Fairchild's favorite targets, and he used his party coverage on the "Eye" page to skewer them. No one irritated him more than Marie-Hélène de Rothschild, one of the richest women in France and also a great tastemaker. She was known as Paris's supreme hostess, having thrown some of the most lavish and memorable balls in all of Europe in the 1970s. The Surrealist Ball featured a cake in the shape of a life-sized naked woman served on a platter of sugar. At Roth-schild's Proust Ball, Cecil Beaton photographed guests like Princess Grace and Audrey Hepburn. Rothschild was from a wealthy Dutch family and had been educated in New York, but she was imperious and powerful.

My first "Eye" assignment was to help cover a charity ball the Baron-ess de Rothschild hosted at the Paris Opera Ballet. It was the social event of the season, billed as a birthday party–cum–gala for Rudolf Nureyev and held in the grand halls of the Palais Garnier. Society gran-dees had spent months planning their gowns and hairstyles, buying tick-ets for tables, and flying in friends from all over the world to watch Sylvie Guillem dance Nureyev's version of *The Sleeping Beauty*. But, at the last minute, the dancers threatened to strike.

Dennis and I and several other reporters were dispatched to the opera, notebooks in hand, photographers in tow. We stood at the en-trance as society ladies filed by in extravagant confections of lace and taffeta, each dress more exquisite than the last. Dennis knew most of these women and shouted their names at me. "Go ask her who made her dress!" he screamed. "Lynn Wyatt! Susan Gutfreund!"

I was mortified, dressed in a plain black suit, like some kind of vol-unteer usher at a Broadway theater, begging them to reveal the names of the couturiers who dressed them. They all obliged.

Minutes before the curtain was to go up, a voice on the PA system announced that the ballet would not go on. The dancers were on strike. But the ball had to go on. Rothschild, devastated, took a "let them eat cake" kind of stance. It was too late to turn back her guests, but they had nowhere to go in the opera house. Women dressed in millions of dollars' worth of diamonds from Cartier, emeralds from Harry Winston, and $100,000 Christian Lacroix gowns sashayed aimlessly through bow-laden balconies decorated to look like an enchanted forest. One guest fainted. A waiter fell. The food was served cold. The former budget minister Alain Juppé was swigging Veuve Clicquot rosé directly from the bottle. I never dreamed that I would see this Paris up close—the char-acters, the drama, and the grandeur—but I was smitten by it in a way that even I couldn't understand. It was so far beyond any extravagance I had ever imagined, and to have that kind of access and keyhole view was intoxicating. For the first time, I understood why Dennis cared so much about succeeding at Fairchild Publications.

The next morning, Mr. Fairchild marveled at the way Rothschild had handled such a fiasco. He couldn't believe that she hadn't canceled it. He had a bit of the *soixante-huitard* in him, too, defending the French right to strike, to toss a paving stone into the social abyss. From his room at the Ritz, he started calling party guests who'd witnessed it, vacuuming up details from the ill-fated gala and feeding them to Dennis for the story. He was on a mission to put Marie-Hélène de Rothschild in her place. She had made the grave mistake of saying, with a definitive hauteur, that she didn't do things "*too badly.*" Mr. Fairchild went ballistic. The story was ruthless. We were instructed to use fake names for sources.

The next day the headline in *Women's Wear Daily* read: ROTHSCHILD BURNS WHILE SLEEPING BEAUTIES STRIKE.

Radio silence.

The phones went dead. No socialites called to curry favor. No gossip was confided. The Sleeping Beauty Ball was a breaking point between *Women's Wear Daily* and French society. A devastated Marie-Hélène pulled rank, demanding loyalty from her subjects. Dennis spent hours on the phone, cooing into the receiver, trying to win back his favorite socialites. But Rothschild had lowered the boom. *Women's Wear Daily* was banned from her parties and any party she had any hand in organizing. Mr. Fairchild didn't care; in fact, he seemed rather amused by the impact of his coverage. But Dennis understood that if we didn't get invitations to parties, the Paris office coverage would suffer and so would we. So he worked his charm for months and eventually finagled his way back into favor.

I had never written anything intentionally malicious or gossipy. It was new for me to be on the lookout for something negative about someone. Although nobody had bylines on gossip items in *Women's Wear,* the experience of reporting and writing about the Sleeping Beauty Ball left me feeling uncomfortable, like some sort of traitor or, worse, an insurgent among royals. When I expressed my queasiness to

Dennis, he dismissed me with a wave of his hand. "You'll get over it; they're all so full of themselves, anyway," he said. But how could I write nasty things undercover, an accomplice to Fairchild's scathing wit, and then expect to be invited back, to dine at their tables or to ride in their *attelage* carriages?

I didn't get over it. At four o'clock in the afternoon, when the "Eye" desk in New York would call for scoops, I let my phone ring. I was too naïve to navigate these shark-infested waters. Dennis had taught me the tricks of the trade—how to read reservation lists at maître d' desks upside down, how to eavesdrop while carrying on a conversation (well, actually, my mother taught me that), but I didn't know what to do with all this information. Gossip was (and still is) the currency of fashion and publishing, but I had yet to learn how to manage it. Mr. Fairchild managed it by couching gossip in his own brand of oddball humor. I wasn't that clever.

More than just moxie and wit, Fairchild's style of reporting required sophistication. Working in the Paris office of *Women's Wear Daily* was a lesson in the aesthetics of everyday life, a subject Mr. Fairchild found endlessly fascinating. Watch the French, he would tell us. Eat their food, sit in their cafés, visit their ateliers and their salons, and learn about the art of living. Discover their sense of civilization through the details. Breathe it.

"Run through the lavender fields!" he barked at me once when I asked him what exactly I should be doing on assignment in Provence. *Just go!*

Usually, the sources of his most impassioned ideas were personal, drawn from his travels, his passions, or his real estate interests (we had a joke in the office that an assignment in Provence meant he wanted to sell his house there). James Fallon, the London bureau chief, was once dispatched to Dresden with orders to find the hotel with "the wonderful string quartet in the lobby." Fallon spent five days searching every hotel in the city. Finally he found a lone flutist in a hotel bar. "That's it! That's the one!" Fairchild exclaimed, shocked that Fallon had delivered. Dresden was still under Communist rule, and the hotel lobby was dilapidated and dirty. The photos were hardly glamorous. The story never ran.

"You never know where the next story will come from!" Fairchild would exclaim. Even if Dresden seemed like a stretch, we had to go. We were instructed to dig deeper, always. Mr. Fairchild was a reporter above all else.

The *bizutage*—or hazing—was never easy. If you didn't deliver what Mr. Fairchild wanted, there was hell to pay. Or, worse, you would be frozen out, which meant the story assignments ceased. Invitations dried up; even small talk and conversation came to a halt. You were persona non grata. The prospect of a Fairchild freeze-out kept us on our toes. We jumped at any and all requests.

After a few months I started to wonder why I was jumping so high, especially at the cost of my social life. Sure, Mr. Fairchild had impressive journalistic skills. He had all of Paris's designers eating out of his hand, but what was my place at that table? I didn't pause long enough to search for the answer; I was too consumed by work and ambition to contemplate the hollowness of it all, the abyss in the middle of the vanity fair. My mother questioned my attraction to this world of couture clothes and titles and over-the-top parties. "Aren't those people terribly bitchy?" she asked me on the phone one evening as I was describing a drama at the office. "Are you sure you want to do that?"

Yes, I did feel sure. Success was within reach. I knew I was on my way up at Fairchild, and that gave me enormous confidence. And I felt indebted to Dennis. I wanted him to like me and depend on me. I wanted to deliver for him.

My French friends questioned my relentless work ethic. When Bibiane and Antoine invited us to dinner parties, as they often did, Hervé would show up alone and I'd arrive an hour or two late, stammering with excuses about the office, the assignments, an interview that ran late. *Désolée, désolée.*

"*Allez, allez, on se calme!*" Antoine would say, clucking and shaking his head. "You work *comme une folle*, a crazy person. You have to enjoy more."

"She is a superstar!" Bibiane would exclaim, beaming with pride.

"She goes in the big hotels and fancy restaurants! She knows Isabelle Adjani!" But on other occasions, when it was just the two of us, Bibiane would caution me to pay more attention to my friends and my family.

"Come to Normandy *chez mes parents,*" she would say. "Take a weekend, or come in August for a month."

"Now you are the one who is *folle,*" I told her, picturing the look on Dennis's face if I asked him for a month off.

CHAPTER ELEVEN

Follow the Money

One Sunday morning in early May, Mr. Fairchild called Dennis at home to tell him he had heard there was big news at Dior. The couture house had been bought several years earlier by Bernard Arnault, the scion of a real estate family who planned to build a luxury conglomerate with the Dior name. People couldn't envision such a thing. The word "luxury" was rarely used in tandem with "fashion," and the word "brand" referred to Crest and Coca-Cola, not clothing labels.

"What if Marc Bohan is out?" Dennis screamed down the line at me. I fumbled around, looking for my alarm clock. What in God's name was he talking about? What time was it? I had stayed up late the night before, at a costume party for Domitille's twenty-fifth birthday. "Come as an American icon," she had written on the invitation. I had gone as Marilyn, in blue shantung pedal pushers and a beaded top I found in the fashion closet at work. Domitille wore a fishnet dress and a platinum wig, her best Tina Turner. Gilles was Elvis. Hervé had found a Rasta wig and a yellow, green, and red knit cap. He was Bob Marley. Now he was lying beside me in bed, sound asleep. I wrenched myself upright and stumbled out into the living room. The shutters were still open—I must have forgotten to close them the night before—and the early-morning sun blasted the room with harsh light. Where was my notebook? A piece of paper? I rummaged through my handbag as Dennis fired off orders. Too much wine at Domitille's party; my head was pounding.

"Who is the new designer?" I asked, picking glitter flakes off my eyelids. I didn't cover the fashion beat, but I had been in the office long enough to know that Marc Bohan had been the designer at Dior for thirty years and he was one of Mr. Fairchild's best friends. Who could possibly replace him?

"That's what we have to figure out," Dennis snapped, irritated by my nonchalance.

"Why do I have to figure it out?" I asked. "I don't know anyone at Dior."

"Because we *all* have to figure it out. *Capish?* We are all in this to-gether." He hung up.

"Who is that?" Hervé had followed me into the living room, dressed only in boxer shorts, squinting in the sun.

"I think I might have to go to the office; I'm sorry."

He kissed me and pulled at my hand to come back to bed. Sundays in France were sacred days, reserved for *la grasse matinée*—or sleeping in. Long romantic interludes in bed with a lover were followed by church, the flea market, family luncheon—the *déjeuner de dimanche à domicile*—or a walk in the park. Offices were dark, stores were shuttered, even baker-ies closed at noon, once Parisians had stocked up on their daily supply of baguettes.

The phone rang again. I wanted to let it ring, to climb back into bed with Hervé. But I knew it was Dennis and, dutifully, I answered. He was panicked, barking orders and cursing co-workers who weren't picking up their phones. The business reporter who had sources inside Arnault's company, Financière Agache, was nowhere to be found. Ian was an Irish lad, and he liked to carouse on Saturday nights and spent a little too much time recounting his epic pub crawls in the office on Monday mornings. Sunday was not a working day for Ian, either. But he was such a talented reporter he could call in stories from his barstool. Even if he didn't show up, Ian would get the scoop. That fact irked Dennis.

"Surely Ian has this covered," I said, gently reminding Dennis that Dior wasn't my beat.

"You better get in here, Katherine, right now! We need all the help we can get." Dennis had no time to waste. "Everyone has to get to the office and work the phones. I'm sorry, but this is a major story."

He was right; Paris was in the midst of a couture boom. Valentino was moving his haute couture show from Rome to Paris to boost his prestige and advance sales of fragrance and ready-to-wear. Yves Saint Laurent was preparing to list shares on the Paris Bourse—a first for a fashion house. And a new generation of investors was buying up dusty French brands and renovating them with young talent. Arnault was leading the pack.

I dressed quickly and kissed Hervé. He was leaving for La Rochelle that afternoon; I didn't know when I'd be back.

"Probably not in time to take you to the station."

"I'll call you."

"Je t'aime."

"Moi aussi."

I rushed to the taxi stand on the corner of boulevard de la Tour Maubourg and rue de Grenelle. At the office, the overhead lights were still off, but as I stepped through the door I could hear Dennis yelling. A business reporter named Jeff was already at his desk, the telephone wedged in the crook of his neck. He nodded his head toward Dennis's door and rolled his eyes.

"Call Irene Amic!"

Amic's husband was a bigwig at L'Oréal and might have had some information on the Dior deal.

"Call Beatrice Bongibault!" Bongibault was the managing director of Dior, a crisp blond taskmaster, considered an Arnault favorite.

The London bureau was roused; the Milan office was on it. Soon we were all dialing for details, stabbing our phones in the hope that a call would be answered, that someone would have a tip, a detail, a *soupçon* of information. One reporter called a fabric manufacturer in Lyon who had worked with Dior for years, weaving custom orders of duchesse satin. Another called a hairstylist who was friends with an assistant in the Dior studio. Dennis dialed the Dior PR office over and over again.

Ian was still at large.

As the minutes ticked by, Dennis became more and more agitated, pacing in and out of his office.

"Claire! Call Fallon in London! What the hell is he doing? Someone in London makes hats for Dior!" Dennis was not going to let this Dior news bring him down. He knew how much Mr. Fairchild cared about getting the story first—and getting every last detail. It was part the Fairchild ethos—and also Dennis's five-alarm personality—to call in every reporter when a major scoop was at hand. Whatever emergency he was facing was our problem, too.

At noon, confirmation came from Milan: Gianfranco Ferré had been named design director at Dior.

"Fuck!" Dennis screamed. "How the hell are we supposed to know about Ferré?" I assumed Mr. Fairchild and Ian knew about Ferré. And Ferré was based in Milan.

"So the Milan office will write the story?" I asked hopefully, packing my things and getting ready to go home, back to Hervé.

"Get a grip!" Dennis shrieked. "I don't know if you noticed, but the House of Christian Dior is located in Paris, France!"

No, the Milan office would not take the credit for the Dior news. Dennis made sure that the Paris office would handle the story and file all the follow-up stories, flood the zone.

When I got home at around ten o'clock that night, I called Hervé in La Rochelle.

"I'm sorry." I felt guilty and far away, still preoccupied by the adrenaline and excitement of the day.

"Ce n'est pas grave, Kate." He was sympathetic to a point. "But I don't know why you have to work so much. Can't somebody else do these stories once in a while?"

I tried to explain that everybody in the office was working this hard. None of it made sense to Hervé. He warned me, "Don't let them take advantage of you." I didn't know how to explain to him—or perhaps I didn't want him to know—about the ambition propelling me. I knew my relationship was suffering, but I had set my course.

If special punishment is reserved for those who pull a fade on Sunday mornings, Dennis made sure the ongoing Dior story was Ian's problem. He would have to keep on it, getting reactions from retailers, reactions from fragrance distributors, and reactions from society clients. For the next few days, Mr. Fairchild parked himself on the corner of Ian's desk, swinging his foot and shaking his head and saying, over and over again, "You've got to follow the money."

CHAPTER TWELVE

Flâneurs

Balzac wrote that Paris is a place where one wants to walk, *flâner*. *Flâneurs* were devoted to "the gastronomy of the eye." They strolled the streets of Paris, taking in the architecture, the crowds, the culture and fashions of the cafés. Impressionist paintings depict the Parisian *flâneurs* turned out in shiny black top hats or beribboned straw bonnets. *Flâneurs* today are not dressed as elaborately, but they are just as hungry for the sights of Paris, and May is their prime month, the time when they come out to strut their finery, to see and to be seen. *M'as-tu-vu.*

Everywhere you look, you can see the pride Parisians take in their

Buvette des Marionnettes
jardin du Luxembourg
(entrée côté rue Guynemer 75006 Paris)

crêperie   saladerie
                salon de thé

Téléphone   ouvert toute l'année
01 43 26 33 04   *(l'été, terrasse ombragée)*

Buvette des Marionnettes

appearance: When spring comes, young women doff their winter coats and revel in bare legs, miniskirts, and snug tweed jackets. Pint-sized girls frolic in the Luxembourg Gardens in smocked Liberty print dresses and red leather Mary Janes. Sunbathers, joggers, tourists, and fashion photographers emerge from the winter *grisaille* to congregate along the banks of the Seine. In the spring of 1989, Paris appeared pristine and fresh, too. The façades of official buildings had been cleaned in preparation for the bicentennial celebrations. The new I. M. Pei pyramid at the Louvre glistened in the midday sun. Mitterrand's *grands projets* were in full bloom.

Compared to my college friends back in New York, I had high-fashion hauteur. But surrounded by the exotic orchids of the fashion world, I felt like a common dandelion. So many impeccable *flâneurs,* so many larger-than-life personalities. And me in my unfashionable *micmac* of plain-Jane peacoats, leggings, and those slightly tacky jet-set pumps. The other editors—the fancy ones from American *Vogue,* like Carlyne Cerf de Dudzeele, André Leon Talley, and Polly Mellen—floated through the fashion shows in the Louvre's Cour Carrée in head-to-toe Versace prints, Chanel tweeds, or long duchesse satin capes. They would flick wrists of chunky gold watches and charm bracelets around as they smoked and barked fashion dictates into the crowd. *"Magnifique!" "Génial!" "J'adore!"* At Fairchild we were encouraged to tone it down. We were reporters, not *flâneurs.* We were expected to not call attention to ourselves.

Still, this was Paris, and I arrived each morning at work in what Dennis called my air-hostess suit—a navy-blue double-breasted mini-skirted Lolita Lempicka I'd bought on sale. I knew I needed an upgrade, but Versace and Chanel seemed like a reach, certainly not the uniform of a newspaper reporter.

On Saturday mornings I would drag Hervé out to the rue de Sèvres to shop at Le Bon Marché. Later we would make the rounds in the streets around the rue de Grenelle, dropping in to buy cardigans at Agnès B. and pencil skirts at Kenzo and Loft. In the nearly two years since I had moved out of the Deschamps' apartment, many of the family-owned antiques shops and working-class cafés had been replaced by slick designer shops. A Stephane Kélian shoe boutique opened next door to Bibiane and Antoine's building. I would drop in to try on the designer's woven leather pumps, bracing myself against the rude Parisian salesgirls. At Robert Clergerie on the rue du Cherche-Midi, I ignored their disdainful looks and well-rehearsed exhaustion as they descended one more time to the basement for another pair of shoes in my size. The parting gesture was always the same: an exaggerated sigh followed by an eye roll or a lifted eyebrow. Hervé, sensing the tension, would nervously nudge me to a quick decision. He could get lost for hours in any flea market, digging around in grubby stalls for the perfect treasure, but shopping in Saint-Germain was arduous. He had no interest in becoming an urban *flâneur*. He wore his finery in the forest.

"*Prends les deux*. Take them both," he would say, just to hasten an exit from the cramped boutique.

Afterward we would stop for lunch at the Bar de la Croix Rouge, where long-legged Left Bank *minettes* mingled with taxi drivers in the early morning on a terrace under a leafy chestnut tree. By noon the place was a mob scene of *flâneurs:* over-tanned garmentos in washed denim cradling miniature Pomeranians, and preppy students from the nearby Sciences Po, Paris's prestigious political institute. We ordered neat tartines on Poilâne toast with slices of rare roast beef and tiny cornichons. The waiter would sway from side to side, steering through the

crowd with plates held high before he landed them on the zinc-topped table with a flourish: *"Assiette Saint-Germain!"*

We would meet Domitille and Gilles and Christel and Jean-Marc for dinner at a trendy place called Coffee Parisien. They loved the bistro's cheeseburgers. Anything American appealed to young Parisian *flâneurs*. Domitille was always in search of the perfect vintage Levi's denim jacket or the right pair of Converse sneakers. She wore an oversized menswear jacket and ripped jeans, which was radical for a French girl. She was into tight T-shirts and minimal makeup. Her hair was cropped short. If I arrived at lunch with a new purchase—a new handbag, say—she would inspect it carefully and shake her head. If I held up something she didn't like, she would wince, as if in pain. "I would never carry a new one, *jamais*," she lectured me, shaking her head. "You have to buy vintage, in the flea market."

I was impressed by how precise Domitille and Christel were on matters of style. They knew exactly what they liked and what they could not bear. If they bought something new—which they rarely did—they wore it with pride, as if it was something they had waited for their whole lives. They laughed when I splurged on clothing, incredulous at my over-stuffed shopping bags. My spending seemed inversely proportionate to my lack of taste and self-knowledge. Uncertain what looked right, I bought a little of everything.

Domitille and Christel had no doubts when it came to fashion. They knew exactly what looked good; their instinct seemed uniquely French. It surfaced in every gesture, every flourish of their style—jeans crisply creased, a button-down shirt with the cuffs rolled up just so.

The sisters shared an apartment above Poujauran's bakery, and after parties or late nights at clubs, they would crawl home at dawn, sneaking by Jean-Luc's trays of freshly baked croissants and canalés, filching a few when they were still too hot to hold and tossing them in their handbags. Domitille painted the walls of their tiny apartment black and bought leather club chairs at the Porte de Vanves market. She obsessed over the color of her faded linen sheets and the size of the armholes in her T-shirts. At a time when everyone else was wearing stonewashed jeans, she wore hers unwashed, the color of real indigo. It seemed strange to me that a couple of French girls who looked and acted like the French singer and actress Françoise Hardy would have such reverence for Americana. Little did I know that Domitille and Christel were ahead of the curve, harbingers of a trend that would unfold in the following decade, when young designers from all over the world would embrace a less fussy, more minimal style. This pared-down look, a repudiation of

Claude Montana's elaborately tailored jackets or Christian Lacroix's heavily embroidered poufs, was percolating up from the streets of Paris, from young men and women drawn to the unfettered ease of American style. For Domitille and Christel, appearance wasn't so much a fashion statement as a part of their regimen. It was almost like table manners to them: They had to have the right coat and the right jeans. Taste was not a choice; it was their way of life.

"Go to the flea market to buy vintage handbags—only Hermès! The real thing!" they said, sprinkling every conversation with delicately placed words of advice. I listened; I followed. I bought T-shirts a size too small, in the children's department at Bon Marché; I found the blackest opaque tights money could buy, and I stopped wearing socks with sneakers. I bought beauty products at the pharmacy, like Embryolisse to remove makeup. "But why are you even wearing makeup?" Domitille asked. "Only old ladies wear foundation!" Some style habits were harder to break. Makeup was one of them, especially the pots of Terracotta powder. Manicures? *Jamais.* A true Parisian knows how to care for her nails, keeping them short and square and only occasionally applying a few coats of red polish.

I was invited to a Chanel sample sale in the suburb of Pantin, an industrial area northeast of the city, where several fashion and beauty companies stocked inventory in giant warehouses. The train stopped several blocks away, and I walked in the early-morning rain one Saturday to the vast industrial hangar. Two discreet black signs with double C's and arrows pointed me to a side door, where a line of fashion editors and Chanel employees waited. When the doors opened, we all rushed to a table stacked with cardboard boxes and plunged our hands into piles of gold-chain belts and cameo earrings and big pearl clip-ons embossed with double C's. I picked out an orange tweed jacket that fit me perfectly. It was an odd color, not one I would normally choose, but I was desperate to own something, anything, by Chanel. I wanted to appear French, even if I looked like a slice of cantaloupe.

Domitille stared in disbelief at the color of my jacket and shook her head at the idea that I would wear something with a logo on it.

"*À chacun son goût,*" she would say. To each his own. The underlying message of this phrase, I came to understand, was: If you don't have taste—or if you are not true to yourself in your style—you are clueless or, even worse, low class. It may have been Chanel, but the color wasn't me, and Domitille knew that. I had yet to figure it out. Wear Chanel when you can afford to buy it in the color that suits you (or you can find it at the flea market). That is the essence of style.

One rainy afternoon I ran into Antoine's tall, elegant friend from Versailles, Virginie, along the Faubourg Saint-Honoré, near my office. I had forgotten an umbrella, so I was taking cover under a café awning. Anticipating summer, I had picked out a pair of bright white jeans and wore them with a navy-blue jacket, a kind of crisp sailor look I thought perfectly mimicked some of the girls I'd seen in the streets of Saint-Germain. Virginie stared at me in disbelief. *"Tu portes du blanc un jour de pluie?"* You're wearing white on a rainy day? Her eyes widened as if she had witnessed a profound lapse of common sense. Looking down at my white jeans, now spattered by the sudden downpour, I realized I'd committed yet another faux pas.

Hervé had been talking about moving to Paris, and in mid-May he called to announce that his employer had finally agreed to transfer him from La Rochelle. He had been commuting every weekend to Paris, so it felt as if we already lived together. But he wanted to look for a bigger place in my neighborhood, move in together. The idea felt grown-up and real, as if we were starting our adult lives. Another step closer to becoming French, my Paris dream.

Standing on line at Poujauran one morning, I overheard an aristocratic-looking young woman talking to Jean-Luc about a one-bedroom apartment she had just bought as an investment. She wondered if she could post a "For Rent" notice in his bakery. I introduced myself and explained what I was looking for. "Keep in mind that it needs some new paint," she said, "but I can take you over there this afternoon."

We met in front of the building at number 3, rue Ernest Psichari.

"You can call me Madame de Rohan." She tucked her short brown hair behind her ears and tugged absently on the silk scarf around her neck. The street, which was lined with 1930s-style brick buildings, was hidden behind a small passage that gave onto the rue de Grenelle. It was quiet, with very few pedestrians or cars, just the occasional concierge opening a heavy glass door to receive the mailman.

Madame de Rohan explained that she had purchased the apartment as an investment, for her two young children when they were old enough to live on their own. She had spent her whole life in the neighborhood and wanted to keep her family together in the 7th arrondissement. I told her about my job and how I had come to Paris and lived with the Deschamps family. She seemed impressed with my French and mentioned several times that she wanted a *locataire* who would stay awhile—but not forever.

"How long will you be staying in Paris?" Madame de Rohan asked politely as we followed a plush red carpet up the elegant circular staircase to the second floor. The front door was glossy mahogany, Art Deco style. It shut behind us with a heavy *click*.

How long would I stay? The question vexed me as I gazed out a large bay window in the living room onto a riot of cherry blossoms in the street below. Would I stay long enough to appreciate these smooth parquet floors glistening in the sunlight? Long enough to entertain friends over countless dinners? The wide porcelain sink in the kitchen looked big enough to accommodate dishes for three parties at once. Oh, and the fireplace in the bedroom worked, Madame de Rohan explained. What was my future here? Six months, a year? Two years of falling asleep by the light of a fire on a cold, damp Paris night? Two years seemed too long to fathom. But the apartment felt like a home. I could see myself throwing open the kitchen window every morning and listening to the birds chirping in the garden below. Civilized, that was it. I felt grown up as I walked from room to room.

"I plan to stay in Paris indefinitely," I told Madame de Rohan. But as the words spilled out, they surprised me. *Indefinitely? Really, Kate?* It was my mother's voice.

I signed the lease the next day.

Hervé's father's construction crew would come to Paris to paint the place. They could put up wallpaper, too. We sat on the terrace of our favorite café on the boulevard de la Tour-Maubourg and planned out a schedule for work on the apartment. We could move in by early June. Hervé had bought a big Art Deco bed at the auction house Hôtel Drouot and arranged to ship some of his furniture from La Rochelle. We went to IKEA and picked out a dining table, some shelves, and a Formica kitchen table. A kitchen table! How grown-up it seemed to have a proper kitchen in Paris. I imagined the dinner parties we would host and the cooking I could do, using Bibiane's recipes. We sipped kir royales and toasted our luck at finding our apartment, our luck at finding each other.

"*Je t'aime.*" Hervé raised his glass.

In that moment, I loved him, too. "*Moi aussi.*" Whatever I was saying back to him, I was also saying to Paris. It was Paris itself and my realization that I was finally Parisian, really Parisian. More than just a lease and an apartment, I had a real kitchen, a kitchen table, a notebook full of recipes for coq au vin, a working fireplace, an Art Deco bed, and even the creased jeans Domitille had implored me to wear. I was in love, with Hervé and with Paris. But I couldn't see where my love for Paris ended and my desire for Hervé began. I couldn't separate my experience of one without the other. The romance of my boyfriend enhanced the city, and the beauty of Paris cast a golden light on Hervé.

A few weeks later my mother came for a visit. On a Saturday morning Hervé rented a car and drove us out to Giverny, Monet's home. We picnicked among buttercups and tall grass beside a small river near the artist's house. My mother was charmed by Hervé's effort to speak English, the way he made reservations at restaurants and brought her a gift of Breton butter cookies from his mother. She was charmed by his *galanterie française*. As I stood on the famous bridge, looking over the pristine water lilies floating in the pond below, I thought, *Where else in the world can you live in a painting?*

On the way home, we stopped at Versailles and toured the king's apartments. The palace was packed with tourists. We had to fight our way back through the crush of people and escape to the gardens, which were every bit as grand, with their elaborate topiaries and long processions of fountains. Later that evening, back in Paris, I took my mother to one of the bistros I had written about in *W* magazine, and we ordered tasting menus with cooked apple caramel for dessert. My mother looked so beautiful sitting on the velvet banquette, her wide eyes and warm smile glowing in the light of the bistro lamps.

The next day I took her to the Louvre to see I. M. Pei's glass pyramid. There was a Le Pen rally inside the Tuileries Garden; a bunch of right-wing protestors, wearing armbands and buzz cuts and impassioned faces, were chanting in unison. They were complaining about something having to do with multicultural Paris: the Algerian grocers, the African chambermaids, and the Portuguese concierges. "Get over it!" my mother said, dismissing the right-wingers, amazed at how quickly Paris was changing, becoming a true global village.

I took a few days off from work and we went shopping. We set off to walk my favorite route, two American *flâneurs* in Paris, traversing the Place de la Concorde, the Seine, winding through Saint-Germain on backstreets like the rue de Bourgogne and the rue Barbet de Jouy and up the boulevard Raspail. I wanted to buy linens and curtains for the apartment, so we ducked into a home-furnishings shop and I picked out gray-and-white-striped wallpaper for the front hall and a lavender color for the bedroom. It took forever to get the salesgirl's attention. As we waited, my mother became more and more exasperated. I was finalizing my order, marking down the exact measurements, when suddenly my mother burst into tears.

"What's wrong?" I asked, but I knew exactly what was wrong. All those afternoons on café terraces, toasting with kir royales and walking along the Seine, eating in our favorite bistros or admiring Monet's water lilies, my mother had been hiding her dismay.

"I don't want you to stay here forever," she said, blotting her tears with a Kleenex, a smear of mascara on her porcelain cheek.

I wanted to comfort her, to wipe away her fear that I would be forever beholden to a country and a city that were not mine. But I couldn't promise to come back to New York. Paris was not a dream anymore; it was my home.

CHAPTER THIRTEEN

Le Bizutage

By the end of the summer of 1989, I was consumed by work and travel, zigzagging across Europe in high-speed trains, rental cars, and overbooked flights. I lost track of the friends I had made during my first years in France. Nikki had moved to Dublin for six months to launch Polo Ralph Lauren. Hélène and Stéphane faded from my agenda. Dinners that had once filled my calendar every weekend were replaced by perfume launches, lingerie trade shows, and last-minute assignments. With every dispatch the bar was set higher: Deadlines got tighter, story ideas got more esoteric, and the lessons in European aesthetics and culture came faster and faster. Could I fly to Baden-Baden, hug the trees in the arboretum, and be home to file the story the following morning? Find the best Chinese restaurant in Gordes? Interview some guy in Brest who had just circumnavigated the globe in a sailboat? Did I know anything about sailing? My answer was never *no*.

Dennis sent me to Madrid to report a story on the city's racy society ladies. I met Generalissimo Franco's granddaughter and partied late into the night with a group of countesses who lived in the Puerta de Hierro section of town, in gated compounds patrolled by armed guards and

rottweilers. Dinner was called at midnight, and everyone danced fla-
menco on the tables until 5:00 A.M. They were *flâneuses* in their own
homes, dressed in sexy little cocktail dresses that stopped just below the
pubic bone. They stomped their stiletto heels on the tables and clapped
their hands, shimmying their bare brown shoulders. At 1:00 A.M. a waiter
in white tie brought around a tray of steaming baked potatoes and a
huge silver bowl of Beluga caviar, which was served with a ladle.

One August morning a few weeks later I was dispatched to Provence
with little notice. Mr. Fairchild wanted me to have lunch with Jeane
Kirkpatrick, the former U.S. ambassador to the United Nations. She and
her husband had a house in Les Baux, a place where they escaped every
summer to get away from the stress of Washington.

"Get in the kitchen with her!" Fairchild thundered down the line.
"She's a great cook! Just don't discuss politics!"

Don't discuss politics with the first female ambassador to the United
Nations? Don't discuss politics with one of Washington's best diplo-
matic negotiators at a time when the president of the United States was
in talks to tear down the Berlin Wall? It seemed strange, but I took my
assignment literally.

I booked a flight for Philippe and myself, and that afternoon we
were sitting on the terrace of Villa Regalido in Fontvieille, discussing
the quality of French tomatoes versus Catalan tomatoes with a famously
cranky political powerhouse. Tomatoes and cheese, it turned out, had
inspired Jeane Kirkpatrick to buy a place in Provence.

Kirkpatrick, an obsessive cook, revealed her personal way of infiltrat-
ing the French culture as a foreigner. She would go to the market in
Arles or Saint-Rémy or Maussane every day and buy produce. Going to
the market helped her feel at home in France. "Just to stand next to
other ladies smelling the melons," she said. "It's an event, and you par-
ticipate; for an hour or two you take part in French culture."

Like Mr. Fairchild, Kirkpatrick had studied the French and the sense
of measure in their culture: She admired their ability to lay down certain
laws and their determination to obtain a level of excellence, which we

didn't have in America. It was evident even in their cooking—especially in their cooking. We ate roasted lamb en croûte and eggplant ragù. We strolled through Saint-Rémy's open-air market. And she gave me her favorite recipe for salad, based on the one from the restaurant where we had lunch. It was easy, she said, but it was all in the ingredients: fresh basil, tomatoes, and chèvre.

I had never interviewed anybody like Jeane Kirkpatrick. Sweating in the August sun, I tried to look relaxed and sound smart. How could I possibly sound smart about tomatoes? Thanks to Bibiane, I could cook, but I'd never cooked with someone who had Secret Service cars purring outside her farmhouse. And yet the assignment was so typical of Fairchild, so essential and absurd.

I returned to Paris, giddy with success. Fairchild demanded to see the film immediately, as he often did. It took a few days to process, and when it finally arrived in the office, we all gathered around the light box, armed with loupes to look at the slides. For a few moments, five of us jostled for position around the small light box, bending down in turn and nervously guiding the loupes over the slide sheets.

Suddenly Mr. Fairchild plunked his loupe down on the desk, swiveled on his heel, and marched away. He didn't say a word or even look back. How could he find fault with our intrepid work? An hour later Dennis called me into his office.

"Why did you shoot Jeane Kirkpatrick in the market?" he asked.

Fairchild was furious. He couldn't believe we hadn't photographed her in her garden. I thought of the Secret Service. How could I ask her to pose in her garden? Normally I would have blamed Philippe, but it was my responsibility to get the best photo possible.

"Get her on the phone and get back down there," Dennis screamed. How could I ask the ambassador to pose again? It was the kind of phone call I dreaded.

The next day, Philippe and I took the train back down to Aix. The photo of Kirkpatrick in her garden appeared the following week on the cover of *W.*

FRANCE:SO SEDUCTIVE

Jeane Kirkpatrick at ease

KIRKPATRICK ON: Poland

"Poland is providing the first test as to whether various moves toward non-Communist dominated governments can work in the Eastern-bloc countries. Gorbachev has indicated, but never really come out and said, that he would support this. We are now moving toward one of many crisis moments in the Eastern bloc. It's hard to overestimate the importance of this."

Bush And The Hostages

"I was dismayed by his initial reaction. I think it was very confused. I was dismayed by his comments on the Israeli captive, Sheikh Obeid, and by the incredible suggestion of moral equivalence between this Israeli captive and Col. Higgins. I was shocked that they said such things. His administration has been much too reluctant to speak out on Syria's role in most terrorist acts in the last decade. In a world where there is no international authority on terrorist actions, I think it is the job of the U.S. to take the strong role on this issue. But we have to do it consistently. Reagan was on a right tack when he targeted Libya. I didn't think so then, but I do now. He took good, strong, clear measures."

The French Bicentennial

"I know Mitterrand and he is a very French man. And he is a man of the left. I think the Bicentennial was his way of personally commemorating a French Leftist institution. I think you have to remember that. And don't forget, the French are the greatest propagandists in the world."

A tough negotiator at
the market in St. Remy

My mother called and left a message: "Congratulations! That's the kind of writing I like to see." I was brimming with pride, even though I knew deep down that in Fairchild's world, a story about Jeane Kirkpatrick didn't really rate, because it wasn't about fashion.

Several weeks later we were sent to a small spa town south of Hanover, Germany, called Bad Driburg. We landed in Hanover very late at night in a freakish thunderstorm. Rain lashed our car. The sky lit up with bolts of lightning as Philippe drove slowly through a forest outside the city. Nervous about the horrible road conditions, I was a terrible backseat driver. Philippe kept shouting at me to calm down. Finally we came to a railroad crossing. The gate was down and we stopped. The minutes ticked by. The signal lights blinked on and off. It seemed like we were waiting forever there, in the middle of nowhere, in the middle of the night. No train came. Cars on the other side of the crossing weren't budging, either. We had to get to our hotel that night. We waited. The slow swish of the windshield wipers elevated my anxiety. I was tired. I'd worked for seven straight months with barely a day off. We debated what to do: Should we turn back? Or should we say a prayer and gun it across the tracks? Visions of bullet trains barreling out of the darkness and bearing down on our cheap rental car paralyzed me.

We were at a crossroads, and it felt ridiculously metaphorical.

Forty-five minutes later, the train thundered by and we crossed the tracks to the other side. But the anxiety and tension were seared into me. I didn't want to do this anymore, running hither and yon to capture esoteric moments in European culture. My French friends had given up on inviting me to dinner parties and weekends in Carnac. Hervé marveled at the hours I put in and the amount of traveling I did. He wondered why I never invited him along. Frustrated, I tried to explain myself: I was on a trajectory at Fairchild; didn't he see? I was ambitious. I wanted to write and get noticed.

That night, waiting to cross the train tracks outside Hanover, I knew that I could write forever about Madrid's society ladies, the newest thermal bath, or a political figure's tomato and basil salad and never get anywhere, because nobody read that stuff. And who on earth read *M* magazine? The stories that mattered were fashion stories. Fashion was the main event at Fairchild, and if I wanted to rise through the ranks, I had to write about fashion. Only fashion.

Jeane Kirkpatrick's Take on Her Favorite Dish at Oustau de Baumanière

D'Aubergines Baumanière

INGREDIENTS:

2 medium-sized eggplants
3 tablespoons olive oil
3 cups basic tomato sauce
A handful of fresh minced herbs—a mixture of basil, chervil, thyme, and Italian parsley
Salt and pepper to taste

PREPARATION:

Preheat oven to 400 degrees.

Prepare eggplants by peeling and cutting each one into thin slices. Brush them with olive oil and place on an oiled baking sheet. Roast until light brown on one side, five to ten minutes. Turn and roast until light brown on the other side. Check frequently.

Assemble by covering the bottom of a shallow five-cup baking dish with a thin layer of tomato sauce. Sprinkle with herbs and cover with a layer of eggplant slices. Season with salt and pepper. Continue until all ingredients are used, ending with a layer of tomato sauce.

Bake until crispy and bubbly, about 30 minutes.

CHAPTER FOURTEEN

Inside the Tabernacle

Hervé and I were sitting around at home, talking about going to the movies, when the phone rang that Saturday afternoon in January.

"Mr. Fairchild wants you to meet him at the office at four-thirty. You're going to a preview."

Click.

It was Claire de Lune, trying not to sound too exhausted. I nodded to Hervé, pointed to the phone, and cringed. Change in plans. The boss was calling and it was important, a preview. At previews, Fairchild reporters were privy to fashion trends and looks before they were presented to the press and buyers on the runway. Only Mr. Fairchild and his staff had that kind of access to designers and their inner sanctums. Dennis had noticed my ambition and he trusted me, so he sent me out on appointments at lesser houses, the ones nobody else wanted to cover. But this preview was different; it was with Mr. Fairchild.

When I got to the office, Dennis was frantically calling a radio taxi. A slew of editors had just arrived from New York to cover the haute couture shows, and the tension in the air was thick. They were demanding front-row seats, G7 taxis, and tables at Brasserie Lipp. Dennis looked exhausted.

"Katherine, you go with Mr. Fairchild," he said. "He likes you. Just make sure that damn photographer gets a cover. Do a good job and you'll go far in this company." As he strode back to his office, he looked over his shoulder and hissed at me under his breath. "It's Saint Laurent." The most important preview of the season.

Soon we were bouncing along the boulevard in a black Citroën taxi, the putrid fumes of Gauloises cigarettes filling the backseat as the driver careened around du Rond-Point, accelerated up the Champs-Élysées, and took a sharp left down avenue George V. It was late in the afternoon, that time of day the French call *entre chien et loup,* between dog and wolf, when one can't be distinguished from the other. It's the hour of metamorphosis, as Jean Genet wrote, when every being becomes something other than himself.

Mr. Fairchild, a jolly British photographer named James, and I were unlikely partners in crime. We spilled out onto the sidewalk in front of an austere limestone façade punctuated by stark white shutters and two black iron lanterns. To the left of the glass door, small brass letters spelled out the address: 5, AVENUE MARCEAU. The House of Yves Saint Laurent, the epicenter of Parisian style, a threshold only an elite few ever crossed.

Mr. Fairchild bounded up the carpeted steps, past a receiving line of neat potted plants. I followed, trying to remain inconspicuous, to adopt the French compactness in my movement. The last thing I wanted to do in the *maison* of France's greatest living couturier was to make a fool of myself. Oh, *La Grosse Américaine!* I felt the rush of my affectionate moniker come back to me. *Please don't trip. Please don't say something stupid.* Behind me, the photographer juggled three enormous suitcases stuffed with collapsible lights and heavy cameras.

A press attaché with a sleek chignon and perfectly drawn crimson lips greeted us at the top of the steps. She smiled demurely and motioned for us to enter a grand salon, *s'il vous plaît,* dipping her head in a demi-bow of practiced Gallic politesse.

Inside the hexagon-shaped salon, the sweet, velvety smell of Casablanca lilies and musky perfume enveloped us like smoke in a jazz club.

I took a deep breath. What was that perfume? Spicy and thick: Opium. There was something wild and untamed about the salon—the soaring ornate ceiling, immense windows, and voluptuous red jacquard settees. And yet the décor was so refined, the essence of French taste mixed with a stroke of exotic whimsy. An Oriental vase on a mantel spilled over with a tangle of large white lilies, their trumpet-shaped heads nodding. On either side of two massive mirrored doors, gilt cherub statues gazed down at the deep velvet sofa in the center of the room. Pressed white sheets were tucked neatly over the cushions, as if in a hospital examining room. Several wide-brimmed straw hats swathed in dotted-swiss tulle perched like parakeets atop wooden hat forms on a nearby table. Fuchsia. Turquoise. Daffodil. Their bright, eccentric colors popped out of the plush Second Empire décor as if to say, "Look at me." The detritus of a day of fittings was scattered about: pincushions, loose pins, and a giant pair of dressmaker's scissors.

On any other day, during any other week, this salon would have been a *cabine,* where society dames like Marie-Hélène de Rothschild and Paloma Picasso and actresses like Catherine Deneuve slipped into wispy chiffon evening gowns and supple silk-lined suits. But with the runway show only a few days away, the room had been transformed into a makeshift studio, or *cabine de mannequin,* where exotic models waited to be called upstairs to their fittings. They were not supermodels but fitting models, and they knew the drill. They would slip behind a screen and change into white housecoats, black silk stockings, and black patent-leather high-heeled pumps. They would apply the obligatory slash of red lipstick—every model had to wear red lipstick before presenting herself to Monsieur Saint Laurent—and twist their hair into a tight chignon. Couture fittings can take hours, and so the models would sprawl on spindly gold chairs, waiting their turn, their impossibly long legs stretched across the room like fallen branches.

We waited, too, for what seemed like an eternity, jazzed up with anticipation and excitement. I tried to contain my enthusiasm and act nonchalant. I caught my reflection in the gilt mirror. Between *chien* and *loup,* I looked more dog than wolf. My thick black stockings had taken too many turns in the industrial dryer at the *laverie.* And the cuffs of my coat, upon inspection, were a bit threadbare for an appointment in the 8th arrondissement. Even my hair, brushed back in a 1980s-style pompadour, was obviously not the hair of a French woman, not professionally coiffed. I was a mongrel among greyhounds.

I had been living in Paris for three-and-a-half years, long enough to know how nearly impossible it was for a foreigner to master the gestures and shrugs that make French style so effortless. I spoke like a Parisian, adding the necessary "uh" to the end of certain words to affect the local accent. I could even crack jokes in French. And, thanks to Hervé, I knew *la France profonde*. I knew the contours of each region—the savage coast of Brittany, the dry, fragrant lavender fields of Provence, and the bright-green foothills of the Pyrénées. And yet, you can have all the ingredients and still never master the recipe.

I fantasized about what would happen if I tried on one of Saint Laurent's bright, wacky hats. Or handled some of the couturier's artifacts lying around. The scissors—how heavy? I could fondle the bolts of brilliantly colored satin and glittering gold jacquard that were propped up in the corner, waiting to be brought into the studio. I could swipe a stroke of red lipstick across my mouth and wrap my hair up in a tight chignon.

No, not here, not inside the tabernacle, where so much thought had gone into each silk tassel on every velvet curtain. The books on the table placed just so, and every sketch on the wall in a proper gilt frame. Every detail was considered, every artifact infused with meaning. Would I ever care so much about such things? Saint Laurent had created more than just clothes; he'd created a powerful aesthetic. Saint Laurent and his *maison* were institutions, cultural treasures.

It was tempting to snoop around in that salon and read stray faxes, open doors, or leaf through sketches. But we were on our best behavior, stiff with self-consciousness and anticipation. I longed to plunge into one of the deep velvet sofas for a quick break. Fairchild reporters were never allowed to sit down. Mr. Fairchild thought everyone should always stand, like soldiers, ready to pounce on the smallest detail or eavesdrop on a whispered confidence. If we sat down, we might miss something. So we paced, nervously waiting our turn in the tabernacle.

A preview like this was a privilege. A first look at the upcoming couture collection was access writ large. Not many reporters ever made it past these doors or up the stairs to the third floor, where a sign on one door spelled out STUDIO in small letters. Very few would get to see the great master of French haute couture sitting at his small, plain desk— two sawhorses supporting a white laminated plank—a pencil held loosely in his fingers as he sketched. We had to be on our toes, taking notes on every spoken word and firing questions at anyone who would listen. We had to make sure the photographer got as many photos as possible. There was no time for small talk.

As we waited, Fairchild grilled me. Had I been to the bistro off the Place des Victoires where the sole meunière was filleted at the table and the cheese soufflé collapsed with the slightest touch of a cold fork?

Wide-eyed and irritated, he fired off questions as if he were cross-examining me in some crazy trial about savoir faire. If the answer was no, or even a too-faint yes, the defendant was dismissed with an eye roll and a shake of the head. Asleep at the wheel! Totally out of it! Once targeted as a barbarian or a dunce in Fairchild's court, redemption was almost impossible. Careers at Fairchild Publications rose and fell like the weightless soufflé at Chez Georges.

Before I could respond, the press attaché reappeared in the doorway with her perfect chignon and bright-red lips. Saved by the *belle*.

"Venez par ici," she signaled with another formal demi-bow, directing us up the stairs to the third-floor studio.

Opening the door to Saint Laurent's long, narrow, all-white studio was like walking in on someone in their bedroom during an intimate moment. We were disrupting a certain creative intimacy.

At the far end of the studio, Saint Laurent's small tribe was gathered like a coven around his modest desk. A wall of mirrors behind them created the optical effect of infinite rows of the long black granite-topped cutting tables that lined the room, elongating the distance between us. In single file, we followed the press attaché past these tables piled high with long bolts of magnificent silks from Lyon, guipure lace from Saint Gall, and rich gold-thread-flecked jacquards from the renowned Swiss fabric mill Abraham. Trays of gaudy gold and glass paste costume jewelry

were scattered across the desks like anthropological treasures. A stray steamer leaned against a wall of shelves filled with buttons, zippers, hook and eyes, ribbons, and random sewing essentials—what the French call the *manutention:* an archive of the extras that are used to sew hundreds of couture outfits.

Anne-Marie Muñoz, Saint Laurent's assistant who had worked with him since his days at Dior, was hunkered down over a desk. She looked straight out of a Goya painting, with her jet-black hair, deep-brown lipstick, and sad eyes rimmed in kohl. She was talking to Loulou de la Falaise, the eccentric accessories designer and muse, who was perched on the corner of her desk, gesticulating, a cigarette dangling between her fingers, decadently sprinkling chunks of ash on the white carpet below, more Toulouse-Lautrec than Goya.

It was Loulou who caught my eye first, with her perfect crop of tousled reddish hair floating above her sharp, square jaw. Her piercing blue eyes danced with trouble, and her deep, gravelly voice was rich with cigarettes and experience. Decked out in an emerald-green peasant blouse with a cascade of amber beads falling to her waist, she exuded every ounce of the self-possession we clumsy Americans lacked.

Saint Laurent's business partner, Pierre Bergé, popped up to greet us, slapping Mr. Fairchild on the back and barely nodding to the rest of us. Bergé was the shark-eyed Napoléon, the quintessential French patriarch, ignoring women when more-powerful men were present. Ever since Saint Laurent opened his couture house in 1962, Bergé had worked tirelessly to craft and manipulate the couturier's image. It was a lifelong task, which continued up to that very minute as Bergé answered Mr. Fairchild's questions about the business, the sales figures, and, of course, sotto voce, the couturier's health.

Paris was buzzing with stories of Saint Laurent's breakdowns, drug overdoses, and hospitalizations. He shattered his wrist while punching a wall. He fell down in his Marrakech villa. He checked into the American Hospital to detox. The rumors came around every few months like clockwork: Saint Laurent was drunk or drugged; Saint Laurent was in a mental asylum; Saint Laurent was dying. In the Paris bureau of Fairchild Publications, keeping track of every blip on Saint Laurent's proverbial cardiogram was a full-time job. Even those of us who didn't cover fashion lived in fear that something would happen to the king of fashion on a Sunday, when Dennis and the rest of us were off pillaging the flea market or, worse, sound asleep.

Getting scooped on Saint Laurent's news by *The New York Times* or the *Herald Tribune* was not an option. Mr. Fairchild had a special relationship with the couturier, dating back to the 1950s, when Saint Laurent had been an assistant at Dior. As a young reporter, Fairchild had had a hunch about Saint Laurent (fashion is all about hunches). He saw him as a rebel, breaking from the old tradition of couture. Fairchild liked to say that Saint Laurent's collections crackled. Years later, when the couturier's health was failing, when his fame had eaten him up, and the rumors were once again ricocheting around Paris that he was having a nervous breakdown, and when Bergé forbid anyone to see him, Mr. Fairchild would go to 5, avenue Marceau to check and see if Saint Laurent was still alive, waiting outside the door until Yves emerged, heading home with his beloved bulldog, Moujik.

Prior to my arrival at Fairchild, relations with the house of Saint Laurent had deteriorated. Bergé had banned Mr. Fairchild and his minions from Saint Laurent's shows because of what he thought was an inadequate review. Fairchild had scrambled to redeem himself and his staff, producing a leather-bound book of the many editorial pages devoted to Saint Laurent. But Bergé would have none of it. *Women's Wear Daily* was kept at bay for two years. Finally the ice broke. Saint Laurent recovered from his nervous breakdown, and Bergé summoned Mr. Fairchild.

As much as they fought and complained about each other—often bitterly—Bergé and Fairchild needed each other. In order to keep his multimillion-dollar global brand going, Bergé needed *Women's Wear Daily* to feature Saint Laurent on the cover of the newspaper and to rave about his collections, even when they weren't news anymore. In return, Mr. Fairchild needed Bergé to give him exclusive access to Saint Laurent. Access was Fairchild's currency.

In those days, before fashion became a business controlled by luxury groups and number crunchers, Paris fashion was its own fiefdom, a magical machine where trends emerged and were then disseminated by *Women's Wear Daily* to retailers and consumers around the world. Mr. Fairchild's power lay in his ability to access the designers first and to control and manipulate the information they gave him. If Saint Laurent or Emanuel Ungaro or Claude Montana lopped off hemlines and showed miniskirts, Mr. Fairchild would see it first in a preview and proclaim it on page one of *Women's Wear Daily:* PARIS SAYS SHORT! He pushed fashion in the direction he believed it should go.

Mr. Fairchild had a soft spot for Saint Laurent. Some would say he even had a kind of a crush on Saint Laurent, a fashion crush. Bergé knew this. What was not to love? Saint Laurent was a brilliant storyteller with a soaring imagination. He was sure of his success, always had been, since his early days growing up in Oran, Algeria, watching his mother in fittings with her dressmaker and telling his sisters what to wear. This confidence allowed him the freedom to dream: He would write and direct plays, using his sisters as actors. He would create dresses from scraps of fabric and entice his sisters into his fantasy world. Fashion for Saint Laurent was about drama and theater; the runway was where he'd tell his story.

Thanks to champions like Mr. Fairchild, Saint Laurent had been the reigning designer in the Paris fashion firmament for some time. But now it was clear that he was starting to age, worn down by the relentless rhythm of the business and disabled by nerves, drugs, and drink. But to Mr. Fairchild he was still Saint Laurent, the legend who blew up the conservative world of 1950s haute couture with beatnik motorcycle jackets and masculine tuxedos and iconic collections inspired by Masai warriors, Picasso, Braque, and the magnificent Ballets Russes. His couture shows were still breathtaking, even though they mostly rehashed his greatest hits—Le Smoking tuxedo pantsuit, a brilliant satin ball gown, a wisp of chiffon for an evening column—looks that had become hallmarks of Parisian chic.

At the end of each show, the barrel-chested couturier would stride unsteadily down the runway, gripping the arm of a model, the bride, and smiling his zigzaggy smile. To behold this old master in the twilight of his brilliant career was painful and poignant. And yet, no matter how drunk or drugged he appeared, Saint Laurent made you feel as if you were in the presence of greatness. The soaring notes of Puccini on the soundtrack, the bold painterly strokes of color, the gazelle-like models: He could still summon such emotion. He could tell a story of elegance and sex and exotica with fabric, inevitably leaving the devoted society matrons and jaded magazine editors in the front row in tears.

As we approached Saint Laurent in the studio that afternoon, he did not get up. He was sitting at his desk, nodding and smiling timidly behind his Coke-bottle-thick glasses, a cigarette dangling from the side of his mouth. Shaky, with a crooked smile that seemed to move horizontally across his face, Saint Laurent fixed his rheumy gaze on the fitting model's reflection in the mirror. She was swathed in a cloud of black-and-white silk chiffon, her arms awkwardly suspended in the air like wings. The *première d'atelier flou,* Madame Georgette, hovered over her, tugging nervously at a swatch of intricately pinned lace.

Mr. Fairchild had always warned us about the power that lurked in Saint Laurent's shyness. "He is stronger than an ox," Fairchild would say, "stronger than any of us!" And although the couturier didn't say much, he was taking it all in, sizing up each of us, one by one. And then he started to speak, haltingly, in a soft voice.

"*Il fait chaud* . . . New Orleans when it's too hot," he said, and the room went still.

"*Vous sentez le soleil.*" The sun. Hot. Yes, you could feel it, almost.

The model, dressed in a voluminous hoop skirt with a snug bolero and a wide-brimmed straw hat, sat down in a chair in front of the mirror, and, like an actress, she began to inhabit the role, to take direction from Saint Laurent. The photographer snapped away while the couturier told his story, bringing his sketches to life in the mirror.

He was difficult to understand, because he spoke so softly. Was she— the protagonist of his story—a grande dame, a Steel Magnolia, or a Scarlett O'Hara–style heroine from the antebellum South, sitting on the porch of her Greek Revival townhouse in the Garden District? Or maybe it was an eighteenth-century garden? Part of the effectiveness of his storytelling was a certain elusiveness. As you listened, you were free to fill in the story with your own imagination. He may have described the thick white columns fronting the porch, the rocking chair swaying slowly back and forth, and the stillness of the afternoon. Or maybe I imagined all that.

As Saint Laurent spoke, the model's head rolled back lazily and she slid down in her chair, as if she were wilting from the humidity. At one point she reached a long slender hand into the pocket of her skirt, pulled out a fan, and began waving it rhythmically away from her face. The temperature in the room seemed to rise.

I scribbled down every word, mesmerized by the weird and wonderful character in his double-breasted pin-striped suit—so formal, like a banker lunching at Taillevent, and yet so shy and childlike, telling a story about his model as if he were back in his childhood home, instructing his little sisters on how to dress, how to behave. In that moment, I understood Fairchild's obsession with Saint Laurent as a storyteller and with fashion as a carefully coded language that tells both an individual's story and a culture's broader history. You could dismiss fashion as something frivolous and ultimately irrelevant, but we all have to wear something, and what we wear says so much about who we are and how we see ourselves. Saint Laurent understood that.

Had Saint Laurent ever been to New Orleans? Was he describing a place he knew well? It was difficult to imagine him stumbling through the French Quarter with his lion-like mane of overdyed orange hair, the ever-present cigarette in his mouth.

Of course he had never been to New Orleans! When Saint Laurent traveled, he ventured as far as his home in Marrakech or his dacha in Normandy, and even those trips were less frequent now. Saint Laurent lived in his head, feeding his imagination with books piled high on his desk or crammed into the shelves along the studio walls: Watteau, Goya, Picasso, Frida Kahlo, Warhol, Lanvin, Fortuny, Seurat, Cassandre. Like the brilliant colors of the glittering satins and silk brocades scattered across the desks, these books illuminated his imagination; they gave him passage to distant cities and streets so he could describe their mysterious residents and characters as if they were intimate acquaintances, members of his family. Saint Laurent's true gift was his ability to give his fantasies a material life of their own.

He never actually described the dresses we had come to photograph, their fabrics, their shape, or their colors. He didn't tell us anything about the haute couture collection he was preparing. So many designers rattled off names of muses, colors, artists, all in an effort to associate their designs with worthier images and icons. But Saint Laurent told a simple story. He gave his clothes meaning by putting them in a context, a place in which he could evoke a woman's style, where she sat, why she wore a particular dress, how her hat kept the sun off her face and the lace bolero kept her cool. He understood better than anyone that style was not simply about appearance. Style was about gestures, experiences, and taste. Style was about context. Style told a story: It began with a time and a place.

"*C'est ça,*" Saint Laurent said, jutting his chin out for emphasis, snapping us out of our reverie. The story was over. The preview was done. Mr. Fairchild glanced at me with a look that said, "I hope you got all of that."

"Merci, Yves, c'est magnifique," Mr. Fairchild said, patting the couturier on the back. He turned on his heel and headed toward the door.

The photographer quickly gathered his things. No time to linger. We said our goodbyes, the press attaché ushered us downstairs, and we tumbled out onto the slippery black pavement, into the misty Paris evening. Back to the office, back to reality. Back to the keyboard, where I would sit and type while Mr. Fairchild composed a front-page story, a story for the Park Avenue socialites who would wear the look, the Neiman Marcus buyers who would buy the look, and the Seventh Avenue garmentos who would copy the look. Bylines never appeared on previews or fashion reviews, but when it was Saint Laurent, readers knew the author was more than likely to be Mr. Fairchild.

I was only in the studio at 5, avenue Marceau for half an hour, but that moment looms large. Watching the model's metamorphosis in the giant mirror, I was watching my own transformation. Three and a half years into my Paris *séjour,* I had yet to reflect on what I wanted to do with my life. Paris had been an escape, a dream, and then it had become a reality in which I was struggling to keep up, filing stories every day, asking questions about subjects of which I knew nothing, and familiarizing myself in an instant with a subculture or a society. I was learning to become a journalist.

I had come to Paris to lose myself in another culture, to imagine my own life far beyond the boundaries of New York City and Princeton. Saint Laurent was living proof that putting yourself in a foreign context—real or imaginary—is often the best way to see yourself more clearly. Everything about my life and my place in Paris crystallized that day in Saint Laurent's studio. I saw a masterfully articulated vision of French style, of the elements of style: the discipline, the imagination, the sophistication. I was so different from Saint Laurent's tribe. They were worldly and glamorous. They knew exactly who they were, how they wanted to live, what they liked and what they couldn't tolerate. I had been trying for so many months to calibrate my position in that city, to stake my identity on something that made sense, to say, "This is who I am." But I was still so naïve and unformed, so unsure of who I was and who I wanted to become.

That day, looking at my reflection in the mirror, I began to visualize her, the person I wanted to become. I saw the story I wanted to tell.

CHAPTER FIFTEEN

The Cour Carrée

In the late 1980s and early 1990s, the Cour Carrée of the Louvre was the citadel of fashion. Every March and October, three huge white tents went up inside the grand Renaissance courtyard. From nine in the morning until nine at night, photographers, buyers, magazine editors, journalists, trend forecasters, fabric manufacturers, and hangers-on poured in and out of the entrance just beneath Claude Perrault's famous pediment arch—the one built by Louis XIV during the ancien régime, before the royals decamped to Versailles. The façades had not yet been sandblasted; the sculptures tucked into alcoves and stacked one on top of another around the courtyard gazed down at the crowd like grimy angels, covered in a century of soot.

In just a few years, fashion's royals would also decamp, moving their tent village to a venue underneath I. M. Pei's great glass pyramid. During that time, fashion's hierarchy—a kind of caste system of its own—would also split apart, with the "royal" designers remaining in the established location and the revolutionary designers—insurgents from Japan, England, and the Netherlands—showing their collections in faraway warehouses and underground garages on the edge of the Périphérique. But in the spring of 1990, the Cour Carrée was where Paris fashion thrived.

Depending on which designers were showing in the tents—Sonia Rykiel, Emanuel Ungaro, Claude Montana—the ancient courtyard was either mobbed or empty. Between shows, fashion folk loitered in the archways of the colonnade, dispensing showroom addresses, discussing dinner reservations at Tong Yen, relaying updates on Yves Saint Laurent's health, and passing out Tylenol or Doliprane. Music boomed out of the tents; giraffe-like models glided around backstage with hot rollers in their hair and cigarettes between their fingers. The Reagan years were over, and the United States was headed into a gloomy recession, but American department-store buyers still climbed out of sleek black limos and picked their way across the paving stones in big-shouldered Bill Blass suits and spindly Manolo Blahnik stilettos. Burly runway photographers barreled through, grunting and shoving, the tripods and boxes of equipment strapped to their backs making them look like Sherpas on Everest.

Security was light, save for a group of good-looking young French guys known as the Cravate Rouge. If you hung around the tents long enough or pushed your way up against the metal barricades with a modicum of urgency, the Cravate Rouge would eventually recognize you, wink, and whisk you through without an invitation. When Claude Montana showed in the Cour Carrée, maneuvering around the Cravate Rouge guys wasn't as easy, because Montana hired his own security, an army of beefy former cops dressed in white hazmat suits, and entrée was only granted to those bearing oversized cobalt-blue invitations. The Hazmats lorded it over the crowd, holding the throng at bay in the courtyard and only opening the doors to the tent at the last minute.

Montana was a short, insecure Spaniard who strutted around in a leather bomber jacket and lip gloss. His strawberry-blond hair swirled around his head like cotton candy. He stalked Paris nightclubs with an entourage of platinum-blond women and burly bodyguards, all dressed in his sculpted jackets. With their pointed shoulder pads and tight leather pants, the group seemed both ridiculous and a little scary. Montana could cut a jacket with scalpel-like precision. American department-store buyers worshipped him. They called his style of tailoring money in the bank. He set trends *and* sold clothes, a trick most designers never master.

I once spent several hours circling a designer discount shop behind the opera, debating whether to spend my paycheck on a Montana jacket that was the intense blue of an Yves Klein painting. With its squared-off shoulders and scalloped hem, the jacket made me look like Jane Jetson, but I loved it and closed my eyes when I signed the credit-card slip. I had never owned such a trendy piece of designer clothing before—save for a neon-yellow-and-gray plaid Jean-Charles de Castelbajac coat my mother had given me for my twenty-first birthday. I felt powerful in that Montana jacket, as if I could command a table on the terrace at Café Costes or a booth at Le Palace.

Montana and Thierry Mugler were the twin kings of Paris fashion. They were both masters at cultivating hype, which limited the number of invitations to their shows. They made audiences wait for hours, further promoting an aggressive and icy indifference. Instead of prancing down the runway gleefully, their models paced slowly down a long, high podium, never smiling, never a hair out of place. It was fashion as a cold repudiation of femininity, or a cartoonlike spoof of it, depending on your point of view.

To get to the shows as fast as possible from the office, I hoofed it up and down the rue de Rivoli. Taxis were a luxury, or a last resort on a rainy day. After every show we had to scramble back to the rue d'Aguesseau to write up a review and send it to New York, which meant we were often late. Reporters  and editors wrote in groups, but at the important shows one reporter was always assigned to stand outside the tents and solicit reactions from department-store buyers. Dennis usually gave this story to a neophyte, which is how I got my first Claude Montana ticket.

It was March, and the designers were presenting collections that would be sold in stores the following fall. Several *Women's Wear Daily* editors were in town from New York to cover the shows. Fairchild had flown in from Klosters, and Patrick McCarthy, his executive editor and right hand, had come from New York with Etta Froio, another editor. Etta had worked at Fairchild longer than most of us had been alive. She oversaw the retail beat because she knew the key players. At the last minute, she decided to skip the Montana show so she could whip that day's copy into shape. I got her front-row seat next to Mr. Fairchild.

Dennis and I elbowed our way through the crowd in the Cour Carrée and skulked around before the show, chatting up CEOs, buyers, and other reporters. The buzz that season was all about whether Montana could cut it at Lanvin. He had been named the couturier at the fabled French house the season before and his first show had tanked. Suzy Menkes had written in the *Herald Tribune* that it looked like a graduating art student's efforts. More than any contemporary, Montana was poised to carry the baton of French couture, but his behavior—the nightclubbing, the rumors of drugs, the strange entourage—left people wondering whether his personal habits would keep him from holding on to such a high-profile job.

The lights dimmed. We took our seats. This was the most anticipated show of the season.

We waited. Twenty minutes. Thirty minutes.

Discussions of dinners the previous night petered out. Kal Ruttenstein, the fashion director at Bloomingdale's, fanned himself nervously. Mr. Fairchild tapped his foot and shook his head. A rumor buzzed through the front row: Montana was unhappy with the hair and had demanded the hairdresser re-coif every model. The press attaché hurried over to assure Mr. Fairchild that they were almost ready. Another fifteen minutes passed: Nobody dared leave.

Finally the lights went down. The music rose and a model wearing a sleek white suit appeared. She froze before pivoting on her heel and stalking down the runway toward us without a smile or so much as a blink of an eye. The music—the *thump, thump* of Verdi's Triumphal March from *Aida*—seemed to follow her, escalating as she got closer.

At the end of the runway, she stopped in front of us and jutted her hip out to the right, provocatively placing her hand on it. She raised her chin slowly, turning her head, offering a frozen profile. Her stiff white shantung jacket was perched above a skirt that seemed to undulate at the hem like a ring around Saturn.

The next models cantered forth faster: Yasmeen Ghauri, Christy Turlington, Gail Elliott, Carla Bruni. Each wore shiny stockings and matching satin shoes, their hair whipped up in elaborate meringue beehives. The palette of colors deepened, from ice blue to cobalt to plum. As Verdi engulfed the audience, I could see people pitched forward on the edge of their seats, transfixed by the perfection of the ice queens and Montana's glacial vision of grooming and tailoring. All except Mr. Fairchild, whose frown deepened as the music swelled. When the last model stalked away into the proscenium, the lights went down and Montana appeared arm in arm with a bride, a neat line of models marching behind him. No smiles; just a nod and he was gone.

Mr. Fairchild stared straight ahead for a few minutes, his arms crossed firmly over his chest, his shoulders hunched. Was he making some sort of decision about what he had just seen? I never really knew, but we all grew accustomed to these pauses. The entire fashion industry was tuned to Mr. Fairchild's reaction. If he sat there pensively after a show, he was undecided, still forming his reaction. If he leaped up and pivoted out of the tent, that could mean he liked it. He always said he knew a show was good when his feet tingled. To this day I'm not sure if he was kidding. The idea seemed so strange, but at the time I hoped to experience some feet-tingling of my own someday.

Before the last model had exited the podium, I clambered over Mr. Fairchild and Dennis and Patrick and dashed up the aisle, out of the tent. To be first out of the show was a *Women's Wear Daily* tradition. You had to get out quick to get the crowd's reaction, especially the retailers'. In those days we didn't line up backstage to heap false praise on the designer. (That dubious ritual would not begin until a decade later, when advertising began drying up and magazine editors began promising editorial coverage for ad pages.)

I stationed myself at the tent door, notebook open, ready to buttonhole the fashion directors of the big department stores: Ellin Saltzman of Saks, Andy Basile of Bergdorf Goodman, Joan Kaner of Macy's Northeast, and Kal Ruttenstein of Bloomingdale's. "What did you think of the show? Was it a good season? What is your open-to-buy?" I felt like a traffic crossing guard signaling the retailers as the crowd approached. They stood out in their double-breasted suits and perfectly coiffed hair.

The buyers hated answering on the spot. Their jobs depended on making margins; they didn't want to risk overstating their interests. They were also loath to reveal their newest discoveries, for fear a competitor would sweep in and nab an exclusive.

"Brilliant."

"Breathtaking."

"Directional."

They rushed out of the courtyard, off to feast on foie gras and French fries at L'Ami Louis or back to the office to review orders. Directional? Which direction?

If they didn't like the show they scuttled past, shaking their heads nervously, no reaction to this one. But from their broad smiles and enthusiastic quotes, it was clear the Montana show was a hit.

In hindsight, the direction we were headed in was obvious. There was only one direction. "Follow the money!" I was still too caught up in the fantasy of fashion, the thrill of getting dolled up in all the right labels and wearing them indifferently, like the fashion editors I sat next to—as if these beautiful clothes were just some old thing I'd thrown on, no big deal. I was naïve enough to think that fashion was interesting for its own sake, that Claude Montana's hemlines constituted important breaking news. It seemed inconceivable that someone of Montana's stature would eventually fritter away his talent and disappear entirely from the fashion scene, selling his name and retreating from the public eye, a casualty of a grueling industry that grinds people up in its relentless search for new product.

I rushed up the rue de Rivoli, pulsing with excitement from the show. I wanted to get back to the office before the big brass from New York filed the Montana review. By the time I arrived, Patrick was already seated at the telex machine, tapping out the review. I could tell from his twitching hands that he had loved the show.

"Katherine, what did you get from the retailers?" he barked, spotting me out of the corner of his eye.

I read through my notes out loud: "'Fabulous.' 'Major fashion moment.' 'Directional.'"

Mr. Fairchild grimaced. But Patrick kept going, pushing me to tell him more. "What was the open-to-buy at Bloomingdale's? Up how much?"

I was flustered, unsure of why I hadn't asked all the right business questions, but Dennis saved me, swooping out of his office with the correct numbers.

"If you thought Paris was hot, think again," Patrick read as he typed. "At Montana, the temperature was as cold as ice, but the fashion was on fire."

Watching Mr. Fairchild pace in and out of Dennis's office, taking phone calls and offering quotes from front-row regulars, I could tell he didn't think much of Montana's fashion, but he let Patrick flesh out the review. I wondered if it was because Patrick was the Fairchild favorite or because whoever was at the keyboard held the power to sway a review. Mr. Fairchild stalked around the office, barking out zingers and pirouetting when he reached the end of the room.

"Okay, Patrick, read it out loud now," he said, jangling the change in his pocket.

We sat quietly as Patrick went through the review, his words spilling out with gusto and excitement, as if it took physical movement to actually make the story better. Patrick was a pro at incorporating puns and writing catchy headlines. Mr. Fairchild had taught him how to tweak the designers and let them know he knew when they weren't delivering the goods. Patrick and Mr. Fairchild did this through their reviews and headlines. When the designers were bad, they were really bad. An Ungaro show was "like stumbling on a Carvel ice cream cake in the middle of the desert." When they were good, they were great: Romeo Gigli was the "Garibaldi of Fashion."

I had never written in a conversational tone before. My writing was formed on the trellis of college essays and research papers. Writing in a group forced me to loosen up. The only problem was that Mr. Fairchild didn't want reviews to sound like any of us. He wanted them to sound like him, or like the witty, irreverent, slightly ridiculous voice he had created for the paper. We were not hired to burst out in song with our own opinions. Only Patrick could get away with writing his opinion into a review.

The Montana review was over the top. The headline read: MONTANA's POWER PLAY. And the description of the show left no detail unexamined. The retailers' "directional" plaudits furthered the designer's cause. I felt proud, as if I'd had some kind of hand in swaying the opinion. But of course that was totally naïve. Patrick was enamored of Montana and would have written a positive review even if the show had more misses than hits.

In fact, it was axiomatic that no runway show was perfect. We were always instructed to find the dogs—or the "woof-woofs," as Mr. Fairchild called them. He loved a lead that deflated the pretension of Paris fashion. Stories would begin: "Yves Saint Laurent is full of beans!" or "Karl goes Krazy." He ridiculed writers who praised collections unequivocally. If someone suggested that a relatively unknown designer had sent out a brilliant collection, Mr. Fairchild would wince and snap, "You don't know anything about fashion!"

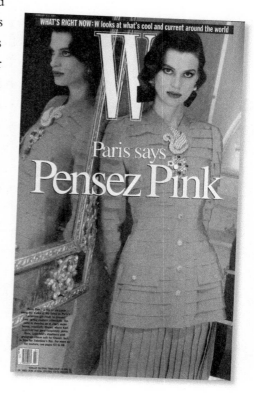

He admonished us always to see fashion in a larger context. To do that, we had to be fluent in the recent and the not-so-recent history of taste and style. Long is out; skirts are short! Paris was the capital of *la mode*. Every headline was

a pronouncement. PARIS SAYS PENSEZ PINK! PARIS SAYS PANTS! PARIS IS
LOOSE! We were always declaring the shape or length of the season. Last
season's pants are this season's miniskirts. It was a formula, and it set the
tone for the entire industry. I knew even as the review was being written
that Mr. Fairchild disliked Montana's clothes, but he recognized the designer's commercial appeal and gave him a pass—*money in the bank.*

From Patrick and Mr. Fairchild I learned how to write a lead and
review a fashion show, but the maven who tutored me in trends was Kal
Ruttenstein. He was the only retailer who dispensed "off-the-record"
information. Toward the end of the Paris fashion week, I would call him
at Le Meurice hotel and we would exchange gossip, new designer
names, showroom addresses, and opinions. Kal was a genius at spotting
trends. He would go to every show—at great effort, because he was
overweight—but he would also go to nightclubs and restaurants to see
what the kids were wearing. If he saw someone on the street or on the
terrace at a cool restaurant wearing gold lamé leggings and they looked
great, Kal would call a manufacturer in the Sentier—Paris's garment
district—and order three hundred pairs of those leggings. Whichever
trend Kal picked almost always sold out on the floor back at Bloomingdale's.

Kal had gone to college at Princeton, too, and we would often joke
about how unlikely it was that two Tigers had ended up in the *schmatte*
business. Maybe we got along because, without ever admitting it, we
both recognized that much of fashion was petty and ridiculous. "What
was that?" he would chuckle at the sight of some young designer's three-
sleeved jacket walking down the runway. "Katherine, maybe you should
get yourself one of those."

It was Kal who had told me about a group of young Belgian designers coming out of Antwerp, known as the Antwerp Six. They were
graduates of the city's fashion academy, and they had a raw, minimalist
aesthetic and an intellectual vibe. One guy in the group, Martin Margiela, was buying up vintage jeans, cutting them apart, and patching
them back together into coats and jackets. Unlike the camera-loving
designers showing in the Cour Carrée, Margiela refused to have his
picture taken. He wanted to remain unknown, an enigma. Margiela's

approach was intriguing, an indication that things were changing. Kal urged me to go to one of his shows in an underground garage.

"Just go," he said. "You'll see."

Kal didn't take any of it too seriously, but he loved the spectacle of fashion and the characters in it, and the money, of course. Kal was great at following the money. He understood the seasons and rhythms and cycles of fashion and how they played into and reflected larger cultural shifts. He saw fashion everywhere around him. He loved Broadway, and when *Rent* opened, he commissioned a raft of clothing inspired by the show and then hired the stars to sing at the store. When rap music took off, Kal ditched his suit and tie and made silver Nike sneakers and Juicy Couture sweat suits his uniform. He loved food and he loved discovering the latest restaurants. In Milan, he would always eat at the corner table at Bice, ordering the seasonal favorite, truffles, or artichokes— carciofi with grana.

Fifteen years later, when he died of cancer at age sixty-nine, Kal's memorial service was held at Carnegie Hall. He would have loved to know that the house was packed, standing room only. The stage was empty except for a pair of silver sneakers. The Princeton Footnotes, an a cappella group, sang his alma mater's song, "Old Nassau," and his boss, Michael Gould, the CEO of Bloomingdale's, called Kal a teacher at heart, a tutor to fashion's young. Gould also read a note that had been sent from the owners of Bice in Milan. "We will miss Kal in the season of the truffle," it said. And I thought, in that moment, that Kal had shown us all something so practical about such an impractical, ephemeral business. He never apologized for his love of fashion; rather, he used it to reach further and to expand life's feast.

After writing a few reviews and befriending retailers like Kal, I started to find my footing in fashion. I wanted to get better assignments, learn how to make my feet tingle, and win the boss's approval.

In many ways we were a dysfunctional family, all vying for approval from the aloof patriarch. Perhaps that explains my comfort level and confidence at Fairchild: I had the survival skills of a refugee from a broken home; I could handle remote patriarchs. At the office I recognized a pattern from my own family—namely, that of seeking approval by overachieving. When my parents divorced, my brother had rebelled, causing trouble and getting kicked out of school. I had taken the opposite tack, working as hard as I could. "What drives you?" my mother would ask. I didn't know the answer then, but I see now that I wanted to make my unhappy parents proud. And maybe, irrationally, I believed that my success would also make them happy. I had the yearning that every child of divorce has, to put the pieces back together.

Mr. Fairchild pitted staff members against one another, making it difficult for any of us to feel successful, but I was lucky. Mr. Fairchild told me early on that I reminded him of his daughter, and everything was family with Mr. Fairchild. He loved fashion families, like the Fendi sisters or the Ferragamos, and he loved to talk about family. Sauntering into the office, he would pass my desk and, out of the side of his mouth, whisper, "Katherine, you and Dennis are both blondes! Like brother and sister!"

In later years, after I had a few couture seasons under my belt and Karl Lagerfeld's private telephone number in my Filofax, Fairchild would make more-outrageous comments. He would suggest that I marry Patrick McCarthy. Everyone knew that Fairchild desperately wanted Patrick to have a wife and a family to go with his Anderson & Sheppard suits.

"It would be good for business," Fairchild would say, his ferocious white eyebrows dancing mischievously across his forehead. Was he joking? I never thought Patrick was the marrying kind.

I took advantage of my pet status at Fairchild. I disregarded many of my colleagues or pushed them aside, reaching for the best stories, the most bylines, the favored position. A few times I caught them whispering behind my back, gossiping about my cocky, bossy attitude. But I was too young to care, blinded by ambition. I was impatient with people who didn't speak French as well as I did or couldn't secure an interview with a designer. I bought into Mr. Fairchild's games and favoritism, because I wanted to succeed. Dennis had trained me well, and I believed him when he told me I would go far. Deep down I harbored thoughts that perhaps fashion wasn't a serious occupation, that it was something too frivolous to build a meaningful career on. And when these thoughts overwhelmed me, when I daydreamed about becoming a foreign correspondent, I would snap out of it quickly, reminded that fashion was now my ticket to the top.

CHAPTER SIXTEEN

29, Rue Cambon

"*Elle n'a pas de culotte.* She is not wearing underpants."

Oh, dear.

Even at a distance, I could see from the window of the van that the strips of fuchsia ribbon on the model's Chanel couture miniskirt were flapping in the wind like a car-wash brush. She hobbled across the cobblestones of the rue Royale, hands flailing above her head as she picked her way through the traffic.

"*Ce n'est pas très chic,*" the photographer's assistant whispered under her breath. Cars were honking and swerving. Pedestrians had stopped along the curb and in the crosswalk to gawk at this wild creature with long red Rita Hayworth hair fluttering in the wind like a flame. She lurched toward the Place de la Concorde.

"Flying by the seat of her pants," the photographer's assistant said, smiling. "Or not."

I laughed, but who was kidding whom? I was flying by the seat of my pants, too, throwing together fashion shoots in the middle of rush hour. *Women's Wear Daily* previews were scrappy business: last minute and low budget.

I scrambled out of the van, which was illegally parked in the cross-walk on the corner of the Faubourg Saint-Honoré. All I could think of was the lawsuits that would land on my desk if something happened to this kooky model. Had we taken enough insurance on the van? I'd checked the box for collision, but there was no box for rogue fashion models. I ran up the rue Royale between idling taxis. The photographer, a guileless American expat named Don, usually didn't lose his cool, but now he was pissed and sent his assistant back to get me.

Don was bent over, hands on knees, trying to catch his breath. He looked at me in disbelief.

"Where have *you* been?" he said.

Where had I been? Apart from gossiping in the back of the van, entranced by stories of society doyennes behaving badly, it seemed I'd been tumbling for months in fashion's relentless cycle. Winter had given way to spring, and now the cherry trees in the Tuileries were bursting with pink blossoms. The ready-to-wear shows of March had barely ended when we began booking previews for the summer couture collections, clothes for the following fall. How do you stay in the moment when you are always catapulting six months into the future, following fashion's commercial calendar, shooting winter outfits in the blazing hot sun or spring outfits in a blizzard of falling leaves? The only constant was the day of the week designated for each designer's show. In the office we called this fashion time: If it's Tuesday, this must be Chanel, we would say. Saturdays were for Montana; Wednesdays belonged to Saint Laurent.

Women's Wear Daily didn't have the budget to hire models, so we used fitting models from fashion houses. Sometimes we got better models for covers. On the phone the night before, the Chanel assistant had assured me they had booked someone good. Karl Lagerfeld

always chose models with personality, plucking them out of obscurity and shaping them into superstars. He had spotted the German Brigitte Bardot look-alike, Claudia Schiffer, and then the punkish, aristocratic Stella Tennant. Now he was betting on an up-and-comer from Easton, Pennsylvania, with alabaster skin and saucer-sized blue eyes. She had something different, a new attitude. Her name was Kristen McMenamy.

"Stop, *stop*! You don't have to run so far," I shouted, catching up to Kristen and grabbing her arm. She was trembling with nerves, like a frail deer.

"No, no, it's okay." She shook her arm loose. "Karl said to do whatever you asked to get a good picture." And with that she turned and cantered toward La Madeleine church, with Don, the hairstylist, and the makeup artist sprinting after her.

I recognized her wild-eyed determination to succeed. Never mind that she was flashing rush-hour pedestrians. She would take any risk to get the picture.

We had started the day at 29, rue Cambon, in the fourth-floor studio at Chanel, where Lagerfeld held court, sitting behind a half-moon-shaped desk, sketching, a Diet Coke in one hand and a Sharpie in the other. Karl knew how to sell clothes: He knew how to play the press. He made himself accessible, especially to young reporters.

"Miss Betts." He would always greet me in the same fashion, peering over his dark glasses as I pushed open the door marked MADEMOISELLE— Coco Chanel's original sign—and marched toward his desk. "What's new?"

The rap music was so loud I could barely hear him. It didn't matter. Karl already had his answer.

"Built-in stretch," he said, picking up a swatch of denim and pulling it apart with his fingers, then tossing it back onto his desk. "It's the most important thing in fashion." He held up a tweed jacket and stretched the seams apart. An assistant in spiky heels and black leggings presented a pair of stretch denim jeans. "Clothes that can move," Karl declared. *"Incroyable, non?"*

I sat down next to him and scribbled this idea in my reporter's notebook. All around us, assistants and models and tailors and seamstresses glided by, carrying trays piled high with quilted handbags and gold-buckled belts and ropes of pearls. They shepherded chiffon dresses covered in pins and sheaths of sketches back and forth—from the desks around the room, to Karl's desk, to a wall at the far end of the room pinned with a patchwork of fabric swatches.

"*Katherine!*" "*Katherine!*" The studio assistants shrieked over the blasting beat of A Tribe Called Quest or Salt 'n Pepa or whichever rapper they were *dingue* for at that moment.

"*Regarde! Regarde!*" They scooped up chunky gold-chain necklaces and plate-sized gold belt buckles inspired by the rappers whose music they were playing. Paris street fashion was moving to this new, raw, urban beat, and the studio assistants were clocking every look. They wore ripped jeans and wifebeater tank tops with high, chunky heels. They pinned neon-colored plastic camellias to elastic headbands. *Bêtes de la mode.* Fashion freaks. They knew how to push a look just far enough so people would notice—and copy. Karl surrounded himself with these *branchée* girls; it was a secret to his success.

He loved to tell the story of how, in the 1960s, Coco Chanel had made the mistake of saying men didn't like miniskirts. Karl was not going to make the same mistakes Coco Chanel had made by dismissing the hallmarks of younger generations; he embraced them and appropriated their style.

Compared to other Parisian design studios, where the mood was always reverential and hush-hush, the Chanel studio felt like a chaotic party. The maestro of the mayhem was Karl's studio director, a handsome designer named Gilles who came from a BCBG French family and had great taste. Gilles was cultured and energetic. He ran the studio for Karl and treated the assistants like schoolchildren.

"Karl would like you to do this," Gilles would whisper, or, "Karl would like to offer you a Chanel suit." Karl this. Karl that. The room revolved around the designer and his whims, but always with a buoyant sense of mischief and fun. Gilles hired his young nieces, Victoire and Mathilde, and dressed them in tweed jackets and platform shoes. He would smile affectionately and talk about a favorite intern who had worked for him, a teenager from California named Sofia Coppola. "*Elle est géniale!"* he would say. "She is *très intelligente* and very into fashion, crazy for fashion."

The studio assistants were the ones who really got it. They understood that to be in fashion, to be in the moment, you had to be ahead of the curve, to be willing to risk the unknown, to be slightly uncomfortable. Presumably they had told Karl to hire Kristen McMenamy because she was not like the other models. She was raw and quirky and androgynous. She personified the change we were all chasing. *What's new? What's new?*

I was always on the prowl for fashion news, looking for inspiration while walking around Paris, watching the *branchée* girls shopping in Les Halles and pasting Polaroids from fashion shoots and previews into my week-at-a-glance calendar. My desk became a mood board, with tear sheets from French *Elle* shoved under the glass top along with postcards bearing the images of 1950s photographers like Willy Maywald and Henry Clarke. I had become fascinated with the formality of Paris at that time: a model in a black Dior dress, one hand firmly planted on her wide-brimmed hat, the other on her hip, thrust forward in a whoosh of fabric. I studied Ilse Bing's famous 1931 photograph of the couple sitting in a café at the Moulin Rouge, the guy's arm draped over the woman's shoulder. I wanted to recreate that sense of intimacy and sophistication in the cover shoots for *W*.

The photos came back from the lab the next morning. All of Kristen's quivering uncertainty and manic jumping around vanished on film. She was regal and authoritative in her porcelain beauty, her hair falling in voluptuous waves down the front of her jacket. We picked a frame of Kristen posed against a lamppost on the place de la Madeleine, hands on hips, gazing into the distance. The photo said it all: "Wear this." And we did. At a sample sale a few weeks later, I snapped up a similar pleated miniskirt and wore it with a tight black turtleneck and high, sexy black patent-leather pumps. My style was evolving in sync with my professional status. The more comfortable I was mingling with the trendy kids in the studio at Chanel, the more confident I became dressing like them, in a sophisticated manner, more like a *Parisienne*.

Things at Fairchild were changing. Elizabeth had resigned to finally pursue her dream of becoming a designer. She had gotten a job in the studio at Chanel. Dennis rarely came in to work. Nobody ever gave a clear explanation of what was going on, but we knew Dennis was sick. He spent weeks at a time in the hospital. When he appeared in the office, he was pale and gaunt in a way that I had never seen anyone look. In Paris, AIDS still carried all sorts of stigmas and fears. And in the Fairchild offices, the illness was a verboten topic. Dennis had told me he was sick, but he remained vague on the details and I didn't dare ask. It seemed as if he wanted more than anything for us to continue as if nothing was wrong, business as usual. On the rare occasions that Dennis did come in to work, I would venture into his office to tell him bits of gossip. He would smile and laugh, but he no longer had the energy to toss his blond hair back and burst into song.

Dennis's absence created a power vacuum that we all jockeyed to fill, currying favor with editors in New York, vying for Mr. Fairchild's attention, lingering an extra hour or two at the office. Patrick, Mr. Fairchild's deputy, asked me to organize the ready-to-wear and haute couture previews. I missed Dennis and his guidance, his big-brother directives, but I was also empowered by my new position. I was good at preserving a sense of order amid chaos, just bossy and arrogant enough to think that I could maintain the status quo until Dennis returned. Patrick rewarded me with a new title: fashion editor. My business cards were engraved, the size of small cocktail napkins. Bookers at modeling agencies courted me. Press attachés sent bouquets of roses every time they got the cover of *Women's Wear Daily*. I wore suits and high heels to work, feeling my way into a new sophistication. Even my handwriting became more stylized: I crossed sevens in the European style and wrote nines with a curvy tail. Yikes. Could I have been more pretentious? I was only twenty-six, for God's sake. And yet I felt an urgency to establish a foothold in the

Fairchild masthead and to earn the respect of both my bosses in New York and the designers down the street.

I started hanging out with friends who had more in common with my frenetic fashion life: Tanya had moved to Paris from Milan, where she had been studying at the Bocconi School of Management. She worked in the Barneys buying office and would get me tickets to Jean Paul Gaultier shows—one of the few houses where Fairchild did not have access. Gaultier had taken a bad review to heart and banished all Fairchild reporters forever. Still, Mr. Fairchild expected us to file reviews of his shows. With reason: They were some of the most theatrical fashion spectacles in Paris at that time, with models dressed in nun's habits perched on mechanical pillars that rose out of a vast runway filled with smoke. Tanya would leave an extra Gaultier ticket on the windowsill outside her Palais Royal office and I would pick it up after work, then sneak into the show, hoping none of the retailers spotted me.

At the time, I believed it was these kinds of connections and my Parisian savvy that got me pro-

moted to fashion editor. But the more likely reason was that I was willing to work until midnight five days a week. I'd go to any extreme to get a preview, including waiting for hours in Claude Montana's showroom until the designer would finally appear with his model. I hired Domitille to style shoots. We took two models and a photographer to Brittany to shoot resort wear and accessories. I called in bags and bags of clothing from the press offices at Chanel, Dior, Ungaro, and Yves Saint Laurent, as well as shoes, jewelry,

Philippe Model hats, Isabel Canovas gloves, and Dominique Aurientis straw bags. Domitille chose each outfit carefully, laying the clothes out on the floor with the accessories for each look.

"Mais, on n'a pas besoin! We don't need all of this stuff!" she exclaimed. She was not familiar with the panic-stricken more-is-more *quotidien* of Fairchild. She had the French discipline of selection: Less is more. When I suggested we bring along a gold-lamé Yves Saint Laurent dress, she wrinkled her nose. *"Trop vieux!"* Domitille was more interested in the clothes of a group of young up-and-coming designers: Martine Sitbon, Agnès B., and a young, relatively unknown Austrian guy named Helmut Lang, who, as far as I could tell, made T-shirts and jeans.

I covered the London shows, traveling over for the weekend and staying in a tiny room off Sloane Square. During the days James Fallon, the London bureau chief, and I would run from show to show, returning to the office to type up reviews. At night I hustled to nightclubs like Ormand's and Kinky Gerlinky, photographer in tow, to see what the kids were wearing. I didn't know much about the London scene, and Jim wasn't forthcoming with his sources, so I befriended bouncers at clubs and PR assistants and I scoured the listings in *Time Out.*

Dennis suggested I call an English woman who worked in the Chanel studio. "You know who I mean," he said on the phone one night before I left for London. "She's the one who sits in the corner. She's always talking on the phone. Reddish hair, *belle poitrine."* He wasn't sure she had a clue about what was going on in London, but she had a fancy pedigree, and Dennis liked that. Her name was Natasha; she was the youngest daughter of the historical novelist Antonia Fraser. Her father had been a Member of Parliament, and her stepfather was the playwright Harold Pinter.

In fact, Natasha did have a clue. She knew everybody in London, from Mick Jagger to Mark Birley to the Duchess of Devonshire. She might have even been related to the Duchess of Devonshire. She had escaped London as a teenager to live in Hollywood, where she assisted the legendary producer Sam Spiegel. Then she'd made her way to New York to work as an associate editor at *Interview* magazine. Finally, in Paris, she had landed a job at Chanel, designing fabrics. She wore tight corsets that showcased her porcelain *décolletage*. She spoke with a posh accent and arched one eyebrow when she didn't agree, drilling into you with her steel-blue eyes. She was connected. She was also obsessed with astrology.

"Darling, you are a Pisces and the moon is in Jupiter," she would whisper into the phone. She always had some quick planetary explanation for the inexplicable *petit mal*. She was a Pisces, too. We became fast friends.

Natasha suggested I look up her friend Rifat Özbek, a Turkish-born Brit who was the darling of the London fashion press. He made sexy bodysuits and tailored jackets with tribal patterns and paired them with ten-gallon hats that transformed the models into fun-house-mirror cowboys. Rifat introduced me to a young milliner named Philip Treacy, a graduate of the Royal College of Art. He was creating Rastafarian-style caps in a basement apartment in Chelsea. Treacy, a skinny, soft-spoken guy with a big shock of red hair, was part of a new generation of talented designers coming out of London's fashion schools.

"Forget about the runway shows in London," Mr. Fairchild said. "It's in the air, on the streets, in the clubs. Fashion is happening everywhere." And it was true. These eccentric English designers lived and breathed fashion. I would travel out to council flats in the suburbs, to sad, sordid apartments where these kids worked. I listened to them talk, some quite timidly, about their love of craft. One of them, a guy called John Galliano, who wore dreadlocks and boxer shorts printed with the Union Jack, told far-fetched stories in a soft whisper, explaining how his worn-away velvet dresses were the clothes of young prostitutes escaping from a bordello. He didn't have much money, but he had an extraordinary imagination and an ability to cut and tailor clothing. He also had his ear to the ground, like the kids in the studio at Chanel.

Inevitably, when I returned to Paris with my discoveries, the only person Mr. Fairchild wanted to hear about was the dowager designer Vivienne Westwood, godmother of punk. He liked her because she was irreverent and she could cut clothes. He considered her one of the ten best designers in the world. I always thought he was just saying that to be subversive, but in hindsight I think it was more about his discomfort with the advancement of a new generation in fashion. Saint Laurent had been Mr. Fairchild's big discovery, but now fashion was marching into the workforce with a new generation of empowered women. The moment of bright colors and frilly flowery looks that designers like Saint Laurent and Emanuel Ungaro and Christian Lacroix had made so popular in the mid-eighties had given way to a severe, sculpted silhouette of Montana, Mugler, and Alaïa. The flowers and frills had served socialites well—those women who married into steel and coal fortunes, hosted benefits, and enlisted walkers to escort them from the limo to lunch at La Grenouille. But the next generation of women needed something commanding as they fought their way into the proverbial boardroom. They needed armor—sharp shoulders, sleek silhouettes, bold colors. And now another cultural shift was emerging, coming from the streets.

On Kal Ruttenstein's advice, I trekked out to the far reaches of the 18th arrondissement one night to see a Martin Margiela show in a subterranean garage. Instead of models, he put his droopy denim skirts and inside-out jackets on friends and "real" women he'd found in the street. They wore kohl-rimmed eyes and long, dirty hair dotted with daisies. They walked quickly through the crowd in the dark. Suzy Menkes, the critic from the *Herald Tribune,* squinted as she tried to decipher her handwriting on her notebook. Men and women in white lab coats poured red wine into plastic cups and offered them to guests.

"This is a real fashion moment," Suzy whispered to me as the last model trudged by and she scribbled furiously in her notebook. I had recognized it, too, something new and disturbing and different. That was what a "fashion moment" was—that pause when you saw something you didn't recognize but longed to understand and embrace.

At the end of the show, we waited for the designer to take a bow, but he never did. It was a statement in defiance of the eighties' culture of *m'as-tu-vu*—see and be seen.

I went back to the office and tried to write a review, but I couldn't find the right words to describe the scene in the underground garage without sounding pejorative and negative. Margiela made me uncomfortable; the whole idea of his deconstructed clothes made me uncomfortable. The torn jeans and ragged hems were so antithetical to the craftsmanship and aesthetics of the haute couture. By ripping apart the seams and deconstructing the silhouette, Margiela was rejecting all of that carefully stitched glamour of the 1980s. His show repudiated the cult of the supermodel, the snobbery of the gilded salons at the Inter-Continental hotel where established designers like Saint Laurent showed. He mocked the whole notion of brands and logos, sewing blank white labels into his clothes.

It was exhilarating and confusing. How could I call "destroyed" clothes beautiful? Did fashion have to be beautiful by definition? Or was fashion's only imperative to reflect the moment—in this case the crumbling world economy? Perhaps this sense of discomfort Margiela engendered was what Mr. Fairchild meant when he talked about the tingling in his toes, that quickening you get when you see something new and intriguing and not entirely comprehensible. The shock of the new. Fashion reacts against itself to renew itself.

"We have to do more stories on young designers in *W,*" I wrote in my journal in the spring of 1990. I was determined to bring this new generation of designers into *W,* to somehow show the reader that Paris fashion wasn't all gilded salons and taffeta pouf dresses. It had taken almost a year to convince Dennis to let me go to Vienna to interview Helmut Lang, the Austrian designer, who had begun showing in Paris.

Helmut sent a big black Mercedes for me when I arrived at the airport and booked me a room at the Hotel Sacher. I walked over to his studio in Vienna's old textile district. The place was painted all white, like a gallery, with a cement floor and two turntables on a countertop. There were no Stockman mannequins for fitting patterns, no walls of sketches or trays of accessories. He had one assistant and a few artist friends who hung out in his studio, spinning vinyl.

I asked him for a sketch of the nylon dress we were shooting for the story. It was for the preview, I explained. He pulled out a plain notepad and drew a triangle and handed it to me. He said he wasn't interested in changing the shape or direction of fashion; he just wanted to suggest a mood with his clothes. At one of his Paris shows, he had sent out a model in only a pair of silver-sequined hot pants. He did not worship Yves Saint Laurent or Cristóbal Balenciaga, the way many of his peers did. His fashion idol was Levi Strauss. He only wore jeans.

How the hell was I going to sell this story to my old-school editors back in New York?

Lang had grown up in the mountains around Vienna and had become obsessed with casual American style at an early age, because to him it was exotic. There were no Levi's and T-shirts, so he made his own and opened a shop. He showed his clothes in Paris in an abandoned warehouse. He used fabrics that changed color when they touched the skin. His models wore very little makeup and walked quickly, staring straight ahead. He explained that he wanted to show fashion on a human scale. The critics massacred him, dismissing his minimalist attitude as too intellectual. His clothes didn't look expensive, and that threw them out of sync with the eighties' aesthetic.

In Vienna we drank vodka and ate apple strudel at a trendy restaurant called Salzamt. "I like to observe from afar," Helmut told me, crouched over a shot glass in the corner booth. "I call it doing my own thing." He had steely eyes. He liked the perspective of living in Vienna, far from the hot runway lights. "There's a different idea about beauty here," he explained. "You have to break what's beautiful to make it even more so."

I returned to Paris with a quickening feeling and convinced the New York editors to run the story in *W*. I was excited about this story but not sure how I would explain the imperative of this change, the importance of a white T-shirt with tiny armholes or the advantage of wearing rayon instead of silk taffeta.

A few days later I received an envelope in the mail with a return address marked "Private." Inside was an orange Post-it note with three X's on it and Helmut's signature. I felt giddy with a sense of achievement but also of belonging: I'd delivered on my first fashion hunch and I had also made a friend. I had found my tribe.

My efforts to champion a new generation of designers finally paid off when Patrick and Etta, the big bosses from the New York office, called me to say they would be promoting me to help run the bureau. They sent out a memo announcing that in addition to my reporting and writing duties I would take an "active role in directing the bureau's coverage and supervising correspondents." My title would be associate bureau chief. It was a big step up. Now I was overseeing five or six reporters who had more experience and tenure than I did. Amy Spindler, who covered menswear for *Daily News Record,* left a note on my desk: "You work incredibly hard; you deserve it." I was too proud and excited and

consumed by ambition to see the jealousies brewing. She would later tell Dennis that she had coveted my job and felt sidelined on the menswear beat. I knew she resented me, but I lacked the maturity and experience to see how resentment could fester and become vindictive.

To handle the additional work, Dennis sent an intern my way. Michelle was connected but confided to me that she had lied to get the meeting with Dennis, saying that some socialite had referred her. She was smart and wry and persistent with her story pitches. One day she came in with a stack of sketches and spread them across my desk. Her roommate had introduced her to an aspiring shoe designer named Christian. He was charismatic but lost. Michelle felt sorry for him. He was down on his luck. She wanted to help him.

"Can you just go and meet with him?" she pleaded, after I had glanced at the sketches and turned back to my computer. So many talented shoe designers filled the pages of *W*: Michel Perry, Rodolphe Menudier, Walter Steiger. They were crafting elegant satin pumps in quirky colors. The sketches Michelle showed me looked bizarre—long pointy shoes covered in tiny squiggles. But I felt bad for her and eventually agreed to a meeting.

Christian's office was a small space at the back of a decrepit courtyard on the rue Jean-Jacques Rousseau. The room had a low ceiling and was furnished with just two chairs and a desk covered in papers. Christian had a big smile and wore a straw boater, a pink seersucker suit, and black suspenders. He was buoyant and charming and alive with ideas, plucking the straw hat off his head as he described his shoes and the women he loved and his dream of creating something exotic with a secret twist.

"So what's the secret?" I asked, pushing him to give me more information, in the way I had been trained to always push designers for more.

"*Alors.*" He paused for effect, his eyes darting left to right, left to right. And then suddenly he grinned and sat up straight. "The shoes will be covered in fish skin. *Voilà.*"

"Fish skin?"

"Oui, oui, oui." He nodded and grabbed a blank piece of paper from a stack on his desk, quickly sketching out the profile of a long, narrow pump. *"C'est unique,* eh? Nobody has done this before."

I could tell he was grasping around, trying to justify his inelegant idea. He began drawing tiny little circles—scales, I guessed—on the shoe.

"This will be very different. Very special fish," he said. *"Exotique!"*

It was a terrible idea and I told him so, in the gentlest way possible. He shook his head and continued sketching, determined to convince me of his brilliance. I sat there for a while and listened to him talk about his job designing shoes for the dancers at the Folies Bergère and his love of dancing. He went dancing every night at Le Palace. It sounded like fun, dancing with Christian at Le Palace. I understood why Michelle intervened on his behalf; he was incredibly likable. I felt as if I'd known him for a long time.

"Let's have lunch!" he said suddenly, plopping the boater on his shiny pate. We walked up the rue Jean-Jacques Rousseau, stopping every few steps to greet a shop owner or poke our heads into a gallery. Christian knew everyone. At the corner bistro, we sat on a leather banquette and the waiter appeared, magically carrying two salads. Christian was a regular, *ami de la maison.*

I went back to the office and told Michelle her friend was great, really nice and funny, but his ideas were terrible. What could be more disgusting than fish scales on shoes? *Dégueulasse.* I couldn't remember his last name, so I looked back in my journal and there it was, written in my loopy French handwriting: "Louboutin." He had offered to make me a pair of shoes—fish scales and all. I had politely declined. *"Non, merci!"* Louboutin would get a small mention in a roundup we were doing on Paris accessory designers, and that would be enough. Did the world really need another shoe designer?

CHAPTER SEVENTEEN

Leaving the Station

All that day in the hot sun, I felt like I was in a Fragonard painting. The grande dame and tastemaker Philippine de Ganay had been showing a photographer and me around Château de Courances, a seventeenth-century château about an hour south of Paris. Karl Lagerfeld had once called it the most beautiful private home in France. In a tweed suit and an un-Fragonard-like pair of Ray-Ban sunglasses, the seventy-year-old chatelaine explained the provenance of her Louis XVI antiques and the sixteen natural sources for the château's famous water gardens, which were designed by André Le Nôtre, who also designed the gardens at Versailles. Her grandchildren liked to swim in them. As the photographer moved his tripod across the manicured lawns, the chatelaine pointed to rare plants in the Anglo-Japanese gardens. Three white swans glided across the *miroir,* a large reflecting pool behind the château. So many gardens, each like a private room, surrounded by clipped hedges and walls of climbing white roses. *Jardin à la français.*

Still in the reverie of that exalted realm, I returned to the apartment that evening to find Hervé vacuuming in his boxer shorts. The cold supper he had prepared hours before, of salad and slices of boiled ham, was on the table, getting colder. He didn't say a word. In recent weeks I had been coming home from the office later and later. The apartment was always spotless—the wide porcelain kitchen sink pristine, the living room sucked free of dust, the Art Deco bed claustrophobically crisp, made with hospital corners and perfectly fluffed pillows. Obsessive housekeeping had become a source of comfort for him.

I wasn't hungry. The apartment was stuffy. I collapsed into bed and kicked off the covers.

How much longer could I ignore the tension in the air? I didn't know why I couldn't talk to Hervé about what I was feeling—or wasn't feeling. His lack of curiosity irritated me. Here was the man who had opened the door for me to France, to adventure in a country I loved, the man who had created a home for me in the city of my dreams, and now he seemed content to shape that magical dream into a mere routine with his mundane chores. Was Paris overwhelming for him? He ran off every weekend to hunt with Georges de Jacquelin and the rest of the blue coats. I don't know precisely when it dawned on me that we no longer shared happiness, that I couldn't feign interest in the things that delighted him. Is that what it means to fall out of love? I clung to the side of the bed, trying to make sense of this tectonic shift in my heart.

The deeper I got into Fairchild Publications, the hungrier I was to travel, to learn, to explore. The sound of the vacuum cleaner began to evoke a kind of stifling, premature domesticity; I felt imprisoned by the wallpaper and began to dread dinner at eight. We had never talked about marriage. I had no illusions about living in a seventeenth-century châ-teau with Le Nôtre water gardens, but Fairchild had exposed me to a wider world, a world of money and glamour and possibility. I wanted something bigger—a bigger job, a more complex life, a career. The sim-ple French way of life I had once craved was now closing in on me. The passion I once felt for Hervé dwindled. *Le plaisir* vanished.

And yet, instead of telling Hervé how I felt, I said nothing. I was afraid of hurting him. I was also terrified of being alone again in Paris. When he reached for me in bed at night, murmuring, *"Mon cœur,"* I pretended to be asleep. I used deadlines and couture previews as excuses to skip romantic dinners at Au Petit Tonneau or the sacred *déjeuner de dimanche à domicile*—Sunday lunch with his family. I was young, and when you're young you don't look around, you look ahead. Escape was heartless, cruel, and easy. The assignments abroad piled up: Barcelona, Geneva, London, Baden-Baden. I pulled a fade on my French life.

In late May, after almost a year of silence, I got a phone call from Will. His confident, knowing voice was small and weak. His mother had died the night before, of renal cancer. She had been sick for five years and had fought her illness bravely. She was fifty-six. I had loved her, perhaps as much as I had loved her son. She had accepted me into her family as if I were one of her own. She was tough, funny, and outrageously confident. I told him I was sorry; I didn't know how to comfort him. The weight of his grief filled the silences in our conversation. I was overcome by a longing for my old life and the comfort of his family.

His sad voice awakened something in me. It filled me with a shameful sense of regret. Suddenly I felt a rush of love and affection for Will. But I had treated him so badly, dumping him without much of an explanation. Plagued by guilt, I was disgusted by my self-centered behavior. What was I doing in France, so far away from my family and friends, the people who needed me? Why was I clinging to families I barely knew, families I didn't want any part of? The shock of death shook me, forced me to look at my life and myself, to look at the hollowness that was inside me. It had nothing to do with love—falling out of love with Hervé or back in love with Will. The emptiness I felt was about France. Some part of me was letting go of my Paris dream.

I came home from work one night not long after Will's call, sat on the bed, and told Hervé it was over. I'd known it was over for months: It seemed so clear to me that we were not well matched. In the cab on the way home, I'd repeated my reasons over and over again in my head, arming myself with all sorts of rational ammunition. Hervé was satisfied with his job selling life insurance to old ladies in Paris. He didn't care about a career; the word "career" meant nothing to him. He cared about hunting and collecting knives and riding the angry waves at Quiberon. I was riding my own anger, steeling myself for what I feared would be a messy dialogue. I knew virtually nothing of breakups. Saying goodbye to Will had been a horrible experience, mangled by the distance between us and by my own abrupt, cold delivery. I hoped the French were more adept at handling love, or the end of love. I imagined all those Truffaut movies, with teary goodbyes on black-and-white Paris streets. Hervé had to know that I had changed, that I had been stringing him along out of weakness, not love. Maybe he was hoping it would pass, or maybe he had a lover to fill in the emptiness, or maybe he was afraid of being alone, too.

"*Je ne veux plus, Hervé.* . . . I don't want to be with you anymore." I tried to say it softly, gingerly, but fear and sadness, and then a tinge of anger, rose in my chest.

"*Quoi?* Kate, what's wrong?" He took my arm and pulled me closer, but I resisted. I didn't want to be pulled back in.

"*Je ne t'aime plus.*"

"Why? Why can't we try to work it out? I love you; I don't want to lose you." He burst into tears.

"*Je suis désolée.*" I was crying, too, reaching for him but not wanting him. "*On est trop différent.* We are too different. You're French and I'm American. It's too hard to understand each other." It was an excuse— one that would come back to haunt me. I thought it was an easy rationale, a way of not acknowledging the fact that I didn't love him anymore. But it turned out to be the truth, and a much deeper one than I could have known in that moment. What made him exotic and alluring repelled me. I didn't know anything about love or how to tell someone I had loved that my once helium-filled heart was now deflated, my heart felt empty now. A better person would have empathized; the heartless careerist only felt contempt. Was it the WASP-bred gift for dispassion? Or the French art of *froideur*?

"I don't give a shit about France!" he said, his face twisting with sorrow. "If you want to be with your family, I will go with you. I can learn English."

I shook my head, astonished that he couldn't see how far our paths had diverged. How could he not have known it wasn't working? Didn't he see the signs?

He buried his head in the duvet and sobbed.

Oh, that big Art Deco bed! Once it was our happy nest, and now it was more like Géricault's *Raft of the Medusa*. As Hervé cried, I stared out the window at the same streetlamp I'd stared at while lying in bed on Sunday mornings, in better times, when we would linger in our bliss together. I was desperate for the scene to end, stunned by my own indifference but certain that something inside me had died.

We slept in the same bed that night, each of us clinging to the farthest edge. While we slept, Hervé had surrendered. In the morning, he announced that he would move out, to a friend's apartment on the boulevard Montparnasse. His efficiency made me wonder if, after tears and drama, the French Cartesian pragmatism kicks in and does the work of disassembling what love put together.

"*Ça sera mieux pour toi.*" It will be better for you, he said. I had been cruel, while he was still considering what was best for me. As I asserted my selfish prerogative, he became magnanimous. A lump rose up in my throat as I watched him pack his hunting books and antique knives and neatly fold his Lacoste shirts.

"You can have all the sheets and towels," he offered. "I don't need them." In the living room he left two dark squares on the wall, where he had removed the pen-and-ink drawings he bought in the Clignancourt flea market.

The next day I called Nikki and told her about the breakup.

"I'm not surprised," she said. "You were kind of mismatched, hey?"

Bibiane agreed, in a more practical fashion. "*Mais,* Kate, you were never going to marry Hervé! *Non, pas possible.*" Had it been so painfully obvious to everyone but me?

Natasha blamed the stars, of course. "Darling," she whispered into the phone, "Pisces and Scorpio. I mean, the sex is great, but that's about it."

A few days later I left for Saint-Tropez to do a story for *Women's Wear Daily* on what trendy French sun worshippers were wearing. Mr. Fairchild called Saint-Tropez the Gallic Fort Lauderdale. In the month of May, when every weekend is extended by a national holiday, retailers and trend spotters would follow the *flâneurs* south to the glamorous fishing port in hopes of spotting the next Bardot or, at least, gathering ideas for new denim washes and T-shirt colors. For three days I walked up and down

the rocky beach with a photographer in tow, shooting strangers in overdyed cutoff denim shorts, thong bikinis, and little else. The sun was broiling, but it was a relief to be away from Paris, away from the desolation of my empty apartment.

Over the next few weeks, Hervé and I talked on the phone and had dinner a few times, trying to hold on to some kind of connection. We met at a little Korean yakitori place in Montparnasse.

"How is work?" I asked.

"*Ça va.* You?"

"*Ça va.*"

"I went to Quiberon last weekend. Maman asked about you. She sends her love."

I smiled at the memory of Joelle, her house on the ocean, the plates of fresh langoustines.

Then August came and the city emptied out. The stress of fashion shoots and previews and endless deadlines exhausted me. I was looking forward to a vacation back home in New York City, but I still had a few weeks in Paris to endure. Paris, when there's nobody there, when the street outside my bedroom window was so quiet I could hear the buzzer on the door across the street and the rustling of leaves on the cherry tree in the courtyard. The air in the apartment was still. Hervé had left his hunting jacket in the hall closet. I pulled it off the hanger and tried it on, catching a whiff of his spicy Hermès eau de cologne on the collar. A flood of memories rushed back, visions of the glorious autumn afternoon riding through the Breton forest in Hervé's Deux Chevaux. It seemed so far away, as if it had happened to someone else. I took a box of photos down from the closet shelf and shuffled through pictures of me standing on a stone wall in Saint-Émilion, peering through binoculars; Hervé squinting in the bright summer sun, holding his surfboard. Quiberon? Long Island? Maybe it was a trip we had taken with Virginie and Alex to California, driving up the Pacific Coast Highway with two surfboards roped to the roof, looking for a good spot in Rincon. It had only been last summer.

I called him a few nights later.

"*Salut, ça va?*" He sounded buoyant, not sad. He was in a good mood after another long weekend in Quiberon with Jean-Marc and Christel, surrounded by his *bande* of friends.

"*Tu me manques.*" I broke down and told him I missed him. I couldn't help myself. My life was suddenly nothing but work. The pressures and politics of the office left me yearning for the carefree days of our first summer together, the long drives to Brittany and weekends exploring new towns and laughing over dinner at far-flung seaside restaurants—*au bord de la mer.* I had gone back to our neighborhood spot, Au Petit Tonneau, a few times with Sandy and Bob, but it wasn't the same.

I found myself telling Hervé how lonely I had been. He invited me to come

to Brittany for the weekend. *"Viens.* I'll meet you in Rennes and we can drive up to Dinard or Saint-Malo."

Is there a term in French slang for the brief recurrence of love? It's like a week of Indian summer after the debut of autumn's chill.

I surprised myself by saying yes. In the Gare Montparnasse, boarding the train to Rennes, I weighed my doubts against the prospect of another weekend alone, waiting for the sun to set so the apartment would cool. I had tried to relieve my loneliness by shopping. On Saturdays I would go to the rue Cler to buy cheese and fruit, or to Les Halles to check the sales. It was comforting to be in a crowded store, among strangers, among people. But on Sundays, when everything was closed, the day dragged on forever.

Hervé met me on the platform at the station and we exchanged *les bises,* the formal kiss on each cheek. There was a new formality to our posture. I felt myself reaching for his hand and then quickly pulling back. I longed for affection, his affection, the familiar *douceur* of his eyes and his hands.

We drove to Dinard, on the northern coast opposite Saint-Malo. We walked along the ramparts of the old fortified town and admired the spectacular Belle Époque villas built by shipping merchants, who would escape to the cliffside resort in the summers. We found a spot on the crowded beach to unfold our towels. The sun was hot. When I tried to broach the subject of our breakup, he pushed it away.

"Non, let's not talk about that now," he said, turning away. "Let's just enjoy this day." He went swimming several times. I buried my face in Kitty Kelley's biography of Jackie Onassis, lost in someone else's tragic love story. I had broken Hervé's heart; he was still mystified by my decision but too proud to ask again for any logical explanation. Is there such a thing when the heart wants what it wants?

At night we ate mussels and drank rosé on a charming slate terrace overlooking the sea. I was so melancholy I could hardly speak, but we tried to laugh about our differences, *La Grosse Américaine* and the small Frenchman. We were once so close. Even now there was something comforting about his kindness.

"Do you mind if we share a room?" He was still such a gentleman. I didn't mind. All day I had harbored this fantasy that we would fall into bed together, fall back into the passion we had known. But whatever sexual charge there had once been between us was gone. After a few minutes, Hervé switched off the light and fell asleep.

The next day we drove back to Rennes. It was late afternoon, and Hervé parked the Deux Chevaux at the edge of the station lot. We walked slowly as he rubbed my back affectionately.

"You're so quiet. Are you going to be okay?" The sun was roasting the metal roof above the platform. The heat seemed to slow everything down. Several metal luggage carts crowded the waiting area by the ticket kiosk. There was nobody behind the counter so I bought a ticket from the machine and shoved it into my small straw bag. I felt untethered, like a vagabond with nowhere to go. I would be returning to France from New York in two weeks, but something felt final in this goodbye. We kissed, once on each cheek, and hugged, and then I stepped up into the second-class car.

There were only four passengers seated near me. One complained about the broken air-conditioning. It was so hot, my legs stuck to the cracked brown leatherette seat. It was August and all of us on the rusty train were going the wrong way, heading back to Paris while all the Parisians were streaming out.

The car lurched out of the desolate station. Hervé was still standing on the platform, smiling, his hands in his pockets. As I waved goodbye, tears spilled down my cheeks. I began to sob. It seemed to me that I wasn't breaking up with Hervé, I was breaking up with France. Or France was leaving me—receding like the figure of Hervé on the platform, growing smaller until he vanished around the bend. Every little fishing port we'd visited together was bidding me goodbye, every restaurant with paper tablecloths, every medieval rampart vista, every rocky jetty reaching into the deep-green sea. Goodbye to the Brittany forests we had driven through, chasing stag or boar or some elusive story we had both imagined about our life together. I would never stand in front of Joelle's window, straining to see my homeland across the wild Atlantic. Yes, I had broken Hervé's heart, but France had broken mine.

For all the hours of the ride home, I cried. The conductor came through to punch our tickets. I'd forgotten to validate mine back in the station at Rennes. He didn't notice. He didn't notice my wet face, either. Perhaps I was just another pathetic casualty of French *amour*.

I took a taxi from the Gare Montparnasse to the rue Ernest Psichari. The street was dark. The apartment—our apartment, my apartment now—was hot and quiet. I walked from room to room, trying to find my place in it. I swept my hand across the gray-and-white wallpaper and remembered picking it out with my mother that day on the boulevard Raspail, when she burst into tears, fearing I'd never come home. She needn't have worried. I slipped a cassette Hervé had given me into the boom box, and Michel Fugain crooned softly: *"C'est une belle histoire."* The light on the answering machine was blinking. My mother had called. And Tanya. And Bibiane: *"Salut, ma biche, ça va?"*

As the machine played on, beeping and blurting out familiar voices, I wandered from room to room, past the mirror above the fireplace, past the kitchen window that looked out at the cherry tree in the garden— every wall and corner so familiar, but it didn't feel like home anymore.

For days I couldn't shake the melancholy. I dragged my feet at work, absently calling press attachés at Chanel and Ungaro and Isabel Canovas to ask for handbags, wallets, and shoes to be sent over for shoots. The office was quiet; no show tunes or telex tapping. Dennis was gone—on vacation or in the hospital? I wasn't sure. I hid in the bathroom when tears welled up. I interviewed Gianfranco Ferré about his first year at Dior. We talked about the difference between couture and ready-to-wear. It was a big story, but my heart wasn't in it. I interviewed Bernard Arnault and Beatrice Bongibault, the managing director of Dior, and the fragrance guy Maurice Roger. I interviewed Rose Marie Bravo, the CEO of I. Magnin, who said that they had sold several hundred thousand dollars' worth of Dior merchandise at a trunk show. "Ferré has made Dior glamorous and very nineties." All the blah-blah-blah of the business that had once seemed so important and interesting was now just noise.

Domitille had gone to her grandmother's house in Carnac for the month, but Gilles was still in town. He took me out to a café in Saint-

Germain. "You shouldn't be so sad; it's *les vacances!*" He tried to cheer me up, but tears were all I was good for.

Later that night, Hervé's mother, Joelle, called to say goodbye and *bonnes vacances.*

"Maybe Hervé and I shouldn't have broken up," I ventured. "I wish we could make this work." I was sure she would agree and encourage me to marry Hervé and become her daughter-in-law.

"Non, non, je ne pense pas." Her voice was firm, shockingly frank, perhaps even exasperated by my fickle affections. "You are too different. You're American and you have different values; you imagine a different life."

Her quiet resolve only made me clutch the fantasy more tightly. Why was I pleading to be her daughter-in-law when I had spurned her beloved son three months ago?

"I feel like I'm breaking up with France," I said. "I'll never find anyone here who understands me."

"Kate," she said softly. "*Vas retrouver ta famille.* Go find your family."

CHAPTER EIGHTEEN

3, Rue Ernest Psichari

The spring haute couture shows were only days away when the United States invaded Iraq in mid-January 1991. Paris was far removed from the violence and chaos of Baghdad, but fear quickly seeped into the city. Police in blue bulletproof vests patrolled street corners. Guard dogs circled hotel lobbies. Doormen at the Plaza Athénée waved handheld metal detectors over nervous guests. Restaurants and shops were empty. American clients and buyers canceled their trips. Designers holed up in their ateliers and followed

the news of the war on radios and miniature TVs tucked into the bolts of fabric and mounds of silk roses.

Some moved swiftly to acknowledge a changed agenda. Balmain and Mila Schön canceled their shows. Gianni Versace called off a party at the Ritz, and Dior postponed a reception in their avenue Montaigne salon. Up on the fourth floor at Chanel, Karl Lagerfeld abandoned a batch of black ostrich-feather boas he had planned to use in the show when someone pointed out that they looked like the oil-covered birds floundering around blown-up wells in the Persian Gulf. Jean-Louis Scherrer dedicated his collection to peace. Instead of the typical bouquet, the final model in a bridal gown carried a dove and an olive branch.

For others, though, it was business as usual. Yes, they said, it may be frivolous to care about extravagant jewels, or the feather embroidery on a dress, or a jacket that had taken four tailors three hundred hours to sew, but to cancel the shows would be playing into Saddam Hussein's hands. Or something.

"We must go on," Emanuel Ungaro said at a preview when asked what he thought of American buyers canceling their trips to Paris. "If we stop now, we're just succumbing to the psychology of fear." I thought of Antoine and Bibiane when I'd first moved to Paris amid the terrorist bombings back in September 1986. "We are *fataliste,*" Antoine had said, exhibiting pure French *sangfroid.* The show must go on.

At the office, I'd adopted a bit of that *sangfroid* myself and was fretting about the usual crises that arise during the week of couture previews. Would model Karen Mulder be available for our Claude Montana preview? Would Karl Lagerfeld pose at the Café de Flore with a hot dog in his mouth?

On the night the United States air campaign against Baghdad began, my friend Tom called from Moscow. I was lying on my couch watching CNN on the portable television Hervé had left behind. Tom was a producer for ABC News; he had covered the Iraq invasion of Kuwait and the fall of Communism; he had covered the famine in Somalia. We were in the same group of friends at Princeton and had shared the ambition of becoming a foreign correspondent. I listened to him talk as the surreal fireworks of "shock and awe" exploded on my tiny TV screen, and I wondered how our paths had diverged so sharply.

It wasn't just that the war or his work covering the major news stories of the time seemed so far away from the cosseted world of Paris fashion. It was also that I could suddenly see the choices I'd made as someone like Tom might see them. Tom had gone to dangerous places and produced stories from the front lines of world events, while I was producing stories on bottled water at the Ritz or the importance of stretch denim. He confessed that at times he, too, felt lonely and far from home, but, unlike me, he was braced by a clear sense of purpose; no one could doubt the value of what he did.

What was I doing? What was the value of chasing fashion trends and following superficial mercenaries who were devoted to little more than hemlines and bottom lines? How much energy had I spent rationalizing the frivolity of fashion? I must have seemed to him an awful fool. I had come to Paris to expand my world, to understand another culture in the intimate way you can only when you immerse yourself in it. But somehow my world had gotten smaller.

Of course, sooner or later anyone who loves fashion will have to defend a passion that to many people seems silly and self-indulgent. When Paris was in the middle of a war of its own fifty years earlier, when Bibiane's mother was stashing suitcases of silver in the garden and waking up to the sound of German boots on her parquet floor, French fashion went dormant. Fabrics were rationed; twenty-five thousand people in the couture industry were out of work. And yet the spirit of it never went away; it's commonplace in wartime for lipstick sales to go up. When nylon stockings weren't available, French women drew stocking seams on the back of their legs with eyeliner pencils. The couturier Lucien Lelong said during World War II, "The more French women remain elegant, the more our country will show foreigners that it is not afraid of the future."

There's nothing frivolous about the power of fashion to provide fantasy and escape from the grimness of hard times. When Christian Dior opened his house in February 1947, the femininity of his New Look silhouette (nipped-in waists, yards of luxurious fabric) was considered a blessed repudiation of the austerity of the war years. And I couldn't argue with what fashion had given me: a chance to cultivate an aesthetic, a chance to travel and explore. It exposed me to intensely driven and creative people like Karl Lagerfeld and Christian Lacroix. It had taken me as deeply into France as I could imagine. I was dreaming in French now, churning the inflections and reflexive verbs and impossible pronunciations through my subconscious. I dropped the *r* in *quatre* and pushed back the *u* in *feuille*. The subtle distinction between *dessous* and *dessus* was second nature.

But after I said goodbye to Tom and hung up the phone, I padded around my apartment in the dark. The light from the streetlamp filled the living room with an eerie glow. I felt the grim weight of what was playing out on my little television, and doubt cast a shadow on my Paris life. I felt like I did five years earlier, wondering what the future had in store, what I believed in, questioning what really mattered to me— except that now, with bracing clarity, I could see that Paris was a place I could never really call my home.

Several weeks earlier I had flown back to New York for the Christmas holidays. A few days after I returned, I went to the Condé Nast building—then on Madison Avenue—and took the elevator to the thirteenth floor. My friend Natasha at Chanel had arranged for me to have an interview with Anna Wintour, the editor of American *Vogue*. Whatever misgivings I had about the fashion world were overshadowed by the prestige of American *Vogue*.

Anna Wintour's assistant greeted me at the reception area. She had a soft Southern accent and wore a blouse with a Peter Pan collar, flat shoes, and a pair of gray flannel pants. She introduced me to an editor named Lesley, who was in charge of a section of the magazine called "Vogue's View." Lesley was wrapped in a black cashmere shawl, her hair pulled back in a ponytail. She wore flat shoes and looked more like a college student than a *Vogue* editor. I felt self-conscious, towering over her in my slick black patent-leather heels. When she turned, I noticed she was very pregnant and remembered that Anna was looking for someone to replace Lesley when she went on maternity leave.

"Anna would like you to meet with Lesley first," the assistant said.

I followed Lesley down the long gray corridor, peeking through glass panels that lined the hallway and revealed pristine inner offices. Young assistants dressed in cardigans and pleated skirts bent over their phones, talking earnestly. Doors were shut and the corridor was quiet, like a library. I didn't see any men, except a bald guy with round spectacles who waved at me when we passed. "Oh, that's Billy Norwich," Lesley said. "You know, the gossip guy from the *Post*." *Oh yes, of course,* I nodded. Lesley ushered me into her office, waving to a chair opposite her desk piled high with papers and books and magazines. I sat nervously, contemplating my fashion choice of sheer black stockings and a tight black miniskirt. My outfit seemed wrong for a Midtown office, too Parisian. Where were all the flamboyant *Vogue* editors I sat next to in Paris at the shows? I expected them to pop out of doors, flinging their Chanel bags and Versace coats. I was expecting *Funny Face,* with Fred Astaire dancing across an elaborate office set, not a generic Midtown office with industrial carpeting.

"So you work at *Women's Wear*?" Lesley said, plunking down into her chair while studying my résumé. She had also worked at *Women's Wear,* for many years. We exchanged the usual pleasantries about former bosses and the dreaded daily deadlines. Had I worked with Patrick? Yes. Did I actually write any stories or just work as an assistant? I explained that I had recently been appointed associate bureau chief. She nodded unenthusiastically, folded her arms across her big belly, pursed her lips, and concluded that my experience wasn't right for *Vogue.*

"At *Women's Wear* you probably do a lot of different things," she said, speaking like a kindergarten teacher. "Here at *Vogue,* each editor does only one thing. It's like playing the piano with two hands versus playing one note over and over with one finger. Or, if you think of a typewriter keyboard, then here at *Vogue* each person just types one key." She tapped her desk with her index finger, waiting for my response. I had no response. It was a strange analogy, but what did I know? No, she shook her head. "Sorry, I'm not sure what Anna had in mind."

I gathered up my coat and said goodbye. I felt confused and dumb for even thinking that I could be a good candidate for *Vogue.*

I walked quickly down the hall, hoping to find the reception area and get out of there as quickly as possible. As I turned the corner and headed toward the elevators, Anna appeared. She looked surprised.

"Where are you going?" she asked, glancing at the coat slung over my arm. When I told her about my interview with Lesley, she pulled me into her office.

"That's rubbish. She'll be gone soon, anyway. Sit down." She motioned to a spindly metal chair poised in front of a huge black desk decorated with a vase of giant amaryllis.

We talked about Paris, and she asked about my favorite designers and the differences between French fashion and American fashion. I told her about Karl and Gilles and my friends in the studio at Chanel, how I had met Natasha. I told her about my interview in Vienna with Helmut Lang. I was interested in writing a story about how American design was influencing European fashion. She liked that idea but thought it was perhaps a stretch to say that American designers could be successful in Paris.

A week later, Anna had called with a job offer. It was unclear whether I would be replacing Lesley or just filling in temporarily, so I tossed and turned for a few nights, struggling with the logic and morality of accepting someone's job while they were on maternity leave. It seemed risky to give up my position at Fairchild for what might be a temporary gig in New York. Finally, I summoned the courage to call Anna and turn down the job. My hand shook as I held the receiver and dialed the number. I wanted to go back to writing, I explained. The responsibility of managing so many people at Fairchild had pulled me away from doing what I really loved.

"Yes, yes, I understand," she said. "Of course."

"If a writing position comes up, I hope you'll keep me in mind," I offered. That was unlikely. Any writing position would go to those who worked their way up through the ranks at *Vogue*. I didn't know much about *Vogue,* but it would be a way out of Fairchild, a ticket home.

Mr. Fairchild's response to the war in Iraq was to press on, full speed ahead. He had convinced Capital Cities, the owners of Fairchild Publications, that the time was right to launch a European issue of *W* magazine, translated into four languages. He sent one of his lieutenants over from New York, a guy called Kevin, a Fairchild lifer and the former editor of *M* magazine. Kevin was perfectly nice, but he didn't speak a word of French and had a snobby attitude. There's a nasty French slang expression for people who reach too high: *Il pète plus haut que son cul.* He farts higher than his asshole. For the reporters who had worked hard to earn the confidence of sources and to forge connections in the French fashion business, Kevin's posture was insulting.

The office was suddenly filled with translators rewriting headlines like PARIS SAYS PENSEZ PINK in German and art directors ripping up layouts and booking photo shoots. The assignments tripled. Dennis would appear infrequently in the office, too ill to clock the long hours the launch of *W Europe* required. Without Dennis to steer the ship, I was promoted to fashion editor of *W Europe*. The promotion came with a lot of extra work and no extra pay.

Yves Saint Laurent's shows were always the last on the calendar, wrapping up ten days of back-to-back collections. No matter which party or club or dinner you attended the night before, if you had an invitation to a Saint Laurent show—always a plain white card printed with black script—you were expected in your seat at the InterContinental hotel at 11:00 A.M. sharp.

Once the fashion tribe was seated and hushed, the gigantic chandeliers would brighten, the first notes of Verdi or Puccini would sound, and a model would emerge from behind a proscenium of fresh foliage and stride confidently toward the end of the runway, red lips and tight chignon perfectly arranged, long limbs reaching forward, coat or jacket swinging.

On that day in March, we had all been waiting to see Saint Laurent take his bow at the end of his show. He had been in the hospital again, but rumor had it he was back in action. The anticipation in the salon of the InterContinental was palpable. As the last model exited in a puff of billowing taffeta, there he was, wobbly, grimacing painfully, gripping the arm of his bride. It was not a great show. How could it have been? The master was not in the house. He had been absent, sick, distracted. But the reaction was always the same: The audience applauded loudly; the front row of society ladies jumped to their feet. We sat, glued to our chairs, never allowed to stand.

After the show, a group of us huddled on the sidewalk outside the InterContinental—Mr. Fairchild, Kevin, Patrick, and myself—to discuss the review. Everyone had a different opinion—or at least I had a very strong opinion about what we'd just seen on the runway. The show was a bomb. I suggested we say as much.

"No, Katherine, here's what you're going to write," Mr. Fairchild said, and then he rattled off the lead to the review as he wanted it. "Go back to the office and type that up. We're going to go have lunch at the Ritz."

We're going to go have lunch at the Ritz. The phrase reverberated in my head with a cheesy echo effect, like a bad horror movie, as I ran down the rue de Rivoli, back to the office. The blatant rejection stunned me. Perhaps I did not deserve to be invited to lunch, but the subtext of the dismissal was devastating: You will never be a member of this club. You will never be good enough. I had poured myself into my job. I believed that my contribution mattered. I wanted desperately to belong—to a culture, to a company, to a fashion tribe. I had been excluded from the boys' club before, but this time it really hurt.

When I reached the office, I sat down at the telex machine and typed out a review—my review, in my voice, my opinion. I didn't think twice; I pushed "send." Ellen, the New York editor responsible for handling all the reviews, called immediately to make sure she had gotten the right version.

"Usually our Saint Laurent reviews aren't this negative," she said.

"Yup, that's it," I said. I was still burning with resentment.

When Mr. Fairchild returned from lunch and read the printed playback of the review, he was furious. Kevin called me into his office and, without looking me in the eye, began in his namby-pamby condescending tone, "Katherine, you know you don't have the authority to write the reviews around here."

He was right: Mr. Fairchild's opinion reigned supreme. My opinion mattered only in so much as it informed someone like Kevin or Patrick. I was powerless. I raged inside that night as I left the office, cursing Kevin under my breath, cursing Mr. Fairchild, cursing myself for buying into the whole system.

The next day *Women's Wear Daily* ran a photo from Saint Laurent's show on the cover. There he was, gripping his bride, beaming nervously at the end of the runway as his usual *brochette* of admirers and clients leaped to their feet. The review was a rave.

I left the office late that mild March evening and walked home across the Pont Alexandre III, talking aloud to calm myself down. I needed this job. Even though I hated them now, I didn't want them to hate me. But in my mind I kept crafting insincere letters of apology to

Kevin: Dear Asshole, Sorry I wrote what I believe. That's what they taught me to do in school.

As I unlocked the door to my apartment, I saw the light on the answering machine in the front hall blinking. I pushed the button to play back the messages.

"Kate. It's Anna Wintour."

CHAPTER NINETEEN

Saying Goodbye

"You wicked witch," Mr. Fairchild barked across the office. I was sitting at my desk, calmly trying to collect myself after informing Kevin that I had accepted a job at American *Vogue,* a fashion-writer position.

Every leave-taking is fraught with tension, but departures at Fairchild always played out with operatic drama. Kevin wondered why I didn't want to stay at the company and transfer to the New York office. A good answer eluded me. What I wanted to say was that I was done with the whole around-the-clock on-call demands and the patriarchal bullshit, the politics, and Mr. Fairchild's bizarre whims. Instead, I simply told him that I wanted to work at *Vogue,* which was also true.

"I'll never speak to you again, but it's the smartest decision you've ever made," Mr. Fairchild said, sidling up alongside my desk as he always did.

He kept his promise. For several years he didn't speak to me. He and Patrick would avert their eyes, cutting me dead when I climbed over their knees to get to my seat at fashion shows. Friends at Paris couture houses delighted in telling me that my former colleagues at *Women's Wear Daily* were spreading the rumor that I was washing the dishes at *Vogue,* demoted to a caption writer.

I began packing up my Paris life immediately. After another trip back to New York for more interviews at *Vogue* I had accepted Anna's offer. Now it was mid-May, and the chestnut trees were bursting with white flowers. Tulips lined the beds in the Luxembourg Gardens. At night, the enormous Ferris wheel in the Foire du Trône amusement park lit up the Tuileries. May was the worst time to leave, but Anna had asked if I could start by Memorial Day weekend, and I had agreed. French employment law required a minimum of three months' notice, Kevin insisted. Luckily, Fairchild Publications was an American company. We had been preparing the third issue of *W Europe,* and my agenda was filled with accessories photo shoots and appointments at Chanel, Robert Clergerie, and Yves Saint Laurent. I suggested to Kevin and Patrick that they hire Natasha to replace me, and she was named the Paris Arts and People editor.

Dennis was too weak to come in to the office to say goodbye, but he called me a few times, pretending he had work-related business to discuss.

"So, how's it going?" His voice on the other end of the line sounded the same, but the usual urgency was gone. He was doing his best to make this conversation like every other conversation we'd ever had, but now there was no talk of the future and no questions about why I was leaving. Dennis knew better than anyone about the high burnout rate at Fairchild Publications.

"Well, I'm sure I'll see you before you go." He didn't linger on the phone. I guessed he was too tired. I wanted to see him before I left, to thank him for all he had done for me, but I felt awkward. I couldn't invite myself over to his apartment. I didn't even know if he was in his apartment. I had the sinking feeling that I wouldn't have a chance to say goodbye.

Two guys from Desbordes *déménageurs* knocked on the door at nine o'clock one morning, with giant rolls of bubble wrap and sheaths of brown kraft paper to pack up my things for the move back to New York. I closed my bank account and returned the telephone to a little post office on the rue Lecourbe.

Hervé and I met for dinner at an Italian place on the rue du Cherche-Midi. We ordered a bottle of chilled Brouilly and reminisced about our hunting escapades in the forest of Brocéliande. Hervé's eyes welled up with tears. Even though we'd said our goodbyes already in so many ways, it was still strange to imagine that I might never see him again. I pushed the thought away. It was too sad, too final.

"Promise me you'll keep in touch," he said as we parted ways on the boulevard Raspail. "Don't forget about your French friends. Don't forget us when you are back in the concrete jungle."

Saying goodbye to Bibiane and Antoine was even more difficult. For Bibiane, who had taught me so much, Paris was not just a phase. She was not moving on to another job, to another set of friends, another rental deposit. Paris was her life. Wherever I was going after Paris, she would still be here. She would still be shopping the *soldes* on the rue de Sèvres and buying frozen chocolate cake at Picard Surgelés. She would still be complaining about Antoine's music, she would still be shimmying the frying pan full of potatoes over her stove, and she would still be dressing up in ridiculous outfits for the costume parties she always hosted on her anniversary.

A few days before I left, Bibiane invited me for dinner. She had big news—*des grandes nouvelles*—she said excitedly on the phone. What could she mean? With Bibiane, "news" could be something as pedestrian as a long-lost recipe for flourless chocolate cake ("only one hundred calories, *tu imagines?*"). Or maybe she and Antoine were moving to another country, too, an exotic locale like Thailand or Egypt. That had always been a dream of hers.

Sitting on the floor around the big square coffee table in Bibiane's living room, we reminisced about all the dinners and parties and people we had known in that room. How we smoked Philip Morris Ultra Lights and drank too much cheap wine. The wonderful meals Bibiane had prepared: rack of lamb, bœuf bourguignon, and pommes dauphinoise, finished with typically French desserts like floating island and crème caramel. She loved to talk about food. She was so proud of her cooking; it was a French badge of honor.

"Ah! In New York you will miss the French cuisine, *n'est-ce pas?*" Bibiane laughed, serving another heaping spoonful of gooey potatoes. As we talked into the night about Paris and New York and the future, I noticed Bibiane wasn't drinking much wine or smoking. This was strange. Perhaps she had discovered a new remedy for quitting?

"I'm pregnant!" Bibiane said suddenly, an ear-to-ear grin spreading across her face. She had privately pined for a third child, and it had not been easy to conceive again. We hugged and squealed. How could I miss the birth of this treasured child? *Tu dois revenir,* you must come back," Bibiane said, rubbing her stomach. "We want you to be the godmother!"

For a minute I thought she was kidding. Really? Me? *La Grosse Américaine?* Yes, it was true. I was finally, officially, part of the family.

A French family.

The night before I left, I threw a farewell party in my apartment on the rue Ernest Psichari. Most of the furniture had been packed up and shipped back to New York in the container. The living room was bare except for a bookcase, a few folding chairs, the boom box, and the IKEA foam couch. All of my close friends in Paris came: Domitille and Gilles, Virginie and her brother Christophe, Bibiane and Antoine, François,

Hervé, Christel and Jean-Marc, Tanya, and a few colleagues from the office. Nikki turned up late, with a bottle of champagne.

"I can't believe you're leaving, hey?" She smiled. "You always said you'd stay here forever! But New York? Wow. C'mon, it's going to be amazing! We all have to come visit. And you have to come to Sydney, hey?" Polo had promised to transfer Nikki back to Sydney. She was ready to go home; her boyfriend had dumped her and she wanted to get out of Paris, to start over.

I served Jeane Kirkpatrick's favorite salad with chèvre and miche from Poujauran. I wore the orange Chanel jacket I'd gotten at the sample sale and jeweled earrings the size of Ping-Pong balls. Everyone else dressed casually, in jeans and denim jackets, Converse sneakers. They were tan, ready for the summer ahead. We drank champagne. François turned up the volume on the boom box and we danced Le Rock. Michel Fugain sang. *"C'est une belle histoire."*

A few things I had been unable to fit into my container remained in the apartment, like the Formica kitchen table and the little plastic stools. Friends claimed pots and pans and odd knickknacks, like the salad spinner and the French extension cords. François took the bookcase and the IKEA sofa. Jerome took the boom box and some of my cassettes. I left the towels and sheets and the Art Deco bed for Hervé, with a note to say goodbye. He planned to pick them up the following week.

Cher Hervé,

I won't need this bed in the concrete jungle. I hope you can find a place for it. Thank you for making such a beautiful home for me in Paris. You will always be in my heart.

Ta Grosse Américaine

There was no sense of finality in leaving the rue Ernest Psichari or discarding those things. I had left that life a year before, when I left Hervé. The apartment had become a crash pad, nothing more. Leaving Paris would be different. I didn't know when I would be back. And even if I did return, would it ever be the same? I didn't feel nostalgic: At least

I didn't think so. In my heart I had already broken up with France. In my mind I was already seated at my desk at *Vogue.*

The next morning, Bibiane and Antoine picked me up before sunrise to drive me to the airport. I was taking the first flight out. As the heavy glass door clicked closed behind me for the last time, I paused for a minute to listen to the birds chirping in the cherry tree in the courtyard. The shuttered street was still, except for the occasional flutter of leaves and the rumble of Antoine's idling car. That streetlamp I'd stared at so many times from my bed flooded the sidewalk with light.

Antoine navigated his old gray Volvo down the place de l'École Militaire, around Les Invalides, and across the Pont Alexandre III. The gold winged horses glowed in the predawn darkness, beckoning us across the river. Through the morning mist I could make out revelers returning from nightclubs, crossing the Seine on their bicycles, not another car in sight. This was the same route I'd taken every morning to work, in a taxi or on foot. And it was the reverse of the route I took that late afternoon in January almost three years before, walking home from my first interview at Fairchild Publications, contemplating a life in fashion with Dennis as my consigliere.

"*Regarde Paris!* Take your last look at Paris," Bibiane exclaimed from the front seat. I buried my head in a magazine.

After I checked my bags, we stood at a counter in the airport café, sipping café crèmes, waiting for the gate to blink up on the big black board announcing departures and arrivals. Antoine smoked nervously and told jokes, making fun of me as he always did. *La Grosse Américaine.*

When the time finally came to say goodbye, I hugged Bibiane and Antoine, promised them I would be back—just another quick goodbye. I owed them everything. They had let me into their families and their lives when they had no reason to. They'd allowed me to live in a world I had no right to. Dennis and Mr. Fairchild had done the same: They'd introduced me to the world of fashion, helped me to develop professionally, to figure things out, to make mistakes, to run with ideas that could have amounted to nothing, and then they let me go, somewhat gracefully.

⚜

I read somewhere that when Benjamin Franklin returned from Paris in 1785, he brought back, among other things, a printing press and a sampling of mineral waters (I'm pretty sure it wasn't Chateldon). Thomas Jefferson had eighty-six packing crates shipped home from Paris. Among the many kitchen utensils, fabrics, and pieces of furniture, he also brought back champagne, French fries, and the recipe for crème brûlée. What did I bring back? A *plan de Paris,* a cantaloupe-colored Chanel jacket, several pieces of Quimper pottery I'd picked up in the flea market at Carnac, a Thonet chair that was a gift from Hervé on my twenty-fifth birthday, and a confidence I couldn't find at home. I had left behind so much more—a broken heart, a French family, and the Art Deco bed. I also left behind any remaining doubts about who I was and who I wanted to be.

Bibiane's Recipe for Chocolate Cake

INGREDIENTS:

8 ounces of dark chocolate
1 tablespoon of coffee
3/4 cup of butter
4 eggs, separated
3/4 cup of sugar
1 tablespoon of flour

PREPARATION:

Preheat the oven to 350 degrees.

In a double boiler, slowly melt the chocolate with the coffee and the butter. Mix together the egg yolks, sugar, and flour. Add the melted chocolate and mix.

Beat the egg whites and fold them into the rest.

Grease a large square metal pan and bake for 20 minutes.

CHAPTER TWENTY

Coming Home

On a late September morning I arrived at *Vogue* early, hoping to get some work done before the fashion and features meetings began. It had been over a year since I'd moved back from Paris. My closet-sized office was crammed with books, magazines, and color Xeroxes of double-page spreads from fashion shoots. The phone was ringing as I opened the door. Double threes flashed on the small screen: a call from Paris.

"Darling, it's Natasha." Her voice was small and sad. Usually when we spoke we were giddy with news, gossip, or jokes. One of our favorite phone pranks was to pretend we were someone else, mimicking Mr. Fairchild's shrill voice or Dennis's impatient twang. This time Natasha's voice was flat and serious.

"Dennis died last night," she said. "I thought you should know."

As she described his last few months in and out of the hospital, the image of Dennis that

Mrs. Kate Betts

Nº 71

first day on the job at rue d'Aguesseau came rushing back. I could so easily see him flirtatiously pushing the shock of blond hair off his forehead and smiling his wide Cheshire-cat grin. I could hear his voice, the way he said, *"You* know," or *"Kaaaaatherine,"* drawing out the flat "a" forever in his best Long Island accent. I had missed him more than I realized. The friends I had made at *Vogue,* market editors and other writers, were a lively bunch, especially over dinner at Café Tabac in the East Village, where they would kick off their Manolo Blahnik stilettos and swing their long, straight hair to the music, dancing on tables. But nobody at *Vogue* would ever burst into song in the office. *"Rivers belong where they can ramble."*

The best teachers impart knowledge through sleight of hand, like a magician. Dennis could pick up the phone without hesitation and call anyone. He could ask the questions nobody dared to ask. He used charm and a natural curiosity to pry information from his sources. He was a fearless and intrepid reporter in a business and a city where most journalists could be bought with favors or blocked by rigid social codes. He taught me how to overcome my trepidation about reporting in those moments when you feel thwarted, intimidated, or too paralyzed with anxiety to pick up the phone. Dennis taught me how to go for it. "You're a smart girl."

Years later, when I was the editor in chief of *Harper's Bazaar,* a young editor proposed an idea for a page in the back of the magazine. He worried that he couldn't do it because he wasn't a writer. "Of course you're a writer," I told him, hearing Dennis's voice in my own. "Everyone is a writer."

There were many days and nights at Fairchild when I questioned Dennis's logic and behavior, when he didn't seem aboveboard. But I never questioned his intelligence or his competence. Dennis always showed up, no matter what—that is, until he got too sick to show up. And even then, when he was dying, he tried to keep up appearances.

The last few months at Fairchild had been unbearably tense. The jealousies between Kevin and Dennis derailed the staff, discouraging teamwork. Every conversation and writing assignment was tainted with the exclusionary tone of the boys' club. If you couldn't join, what was the point? The buoyancy I'd felt early on at Fairchild—a sense that anything was possible with hard work and determination—collapsed when I recognized the limitations of my position. Constant finger-pointing took the joy out of reporting and writing. Even Dennis's obituary in *Women's Wear Daily* was tainted by the subtle insinuation that he had been responsible for the spat with Marie-Hélène de Rothschild over the Sleeping Beauty Ball. It was unfair. No, it was more than unfair. It was petty and absurd that some dumb socialite party or crisis would make its way into the obituary of a reporter. We had all pitched in on that story, Dennis perhaps more than anyone simply because he was so good at his job.

I hung on the phone with Natasha for an hour. She told me about Franco, Dennis's sweet Italian boyfriend who had tried to hold things together as Dennis grew weaker. A funeral service was planned in Paris. We recalled all the crazy things Dennis had made us do and say. He had been like a den mother, albeit one filled with mischief and a gargantuan appetite for Hermès and Brioni and Relais & Château hotel suites. We laughed, imagining him sashaying into the office as if he were walking onstage. He had a salesman's personality and a journalist's sense of irony. Dennis loved the good life and the trappings it brought, but he was not taken in by the wealth and fame that surrounded him.

After Natasha hung up, I closed my office door and cried. He was so incredibly young, only thirty-three. I wept out of sadness and shock but also out of guilt. Why hadn't I called Dennis more often from New York when I knew how sick he was? In his loyalty to Mr. Fairchild, Dennis had shut me out briefly when I left for *Vogue*. Rumors had trickled back about Fairchild colleagues spreading gossip about me, and Dennis was to blame, or so I thought. And so we never spoke again. Now it was too late.

The first few months back in New York City, I had immersed myself in my new life at *Vogue*. I didn't want to look back. I wanted to forge ahead and fit in. I wanted to fly like an arrow. And yet it came as such a shock to be back in the city. On one of my first days at *Vogue* I had lunch with the managing editor. On the way back to the office, we stood at the corner of Madison Avenue and 44th Street, waiting for the light to change. People rushed by. The air smelled faintly of garbage and exhaust from the buses roaring up Madison Avenue. I had forgotten about the crowds in Midtown at lunch hour. We made small talk about the awful humidity, and I wondered why on earth I was wearing black tights in May when all of the women in the office had long bronzed legs and bright-red toenails.

In my black leather Filofax, I still carried remnants of my Paris life: a business card from Bruno Dessange with my hairdresser's name and number on it, my French press card from Fairchild, and a canceled Carte Bleue credit card. Above my desk at *Vogue,* I had pinned up a few of the tear sheets that had been shoved under the glass on my desk in Paris: a Christian Lacroix sketch of a lace wedding dress, a postcard from Belle Île, and a Polaroid from the Chanel cover shoot for the first issue of *W Europe.* The memories associated with those events and images had started to fade, like the words to a song that you can't quite recall. I was in another world now, consumed with caption writing, submitting endless lists of story ideas to my editors, and finding a way to get more real estate in the magazine—more story assignments, more bylines.

The morning after Dennis died, I resolved to work my way back to Paris, to reconnect with my life there and that feeling of elation and ease I associated with Paris from the very first visit. I missed that part of myself. I was determined to find my voice at *Vogue,* but I understood that to do that I had to return to Paris.

A week or so later, one of Anna's assistants summoned me. "Anna

wants to see you," she said. Everyone at *Vogue* spent the better part of the day trying to anticipate what Anna wanted. A new headline? A better editor's letter? A cover reshoot? I thought she was going to ask me to "rethink" a set of captions I'd written for a fashion shoot of Christy Turlington cavorting in St. Barth's. I braced myself as I strode past the gatekeepers at her office door and sat down on one of the uncomfortable metal chairs in front of her desk.

"I'd like you to cover the shows in Paris," she said, looking up from a stack of color Xeroxes. "If you can figure out how to do it on a budget, I'll send you." My heart jumped. It was as if she had granted me a six-month vacation, or a lifetime of endless days meandering through the broad, leafy alleys of the Luxembourg Gardens. Forget the collections, I thought as my mind raced ahead, imagining the smells and sights of Saint-Germain and the Faubourg Saint-Honoré, far removed from Midtown Manhattan's dingy congested streets. I would have the chance to see my French friends again, to rediscover the city I loved! It was one of the few times in my life I wanted to hug Anna. "Yes, of course," I said, rising from the chair. "I'll stay with friends. No problem."

I rushed back to my office and called Bibiane, forgetting the time difference. It was already eleven o'clock at night in Paris. She answered the phone groggily. I could hear the baby—my goddaughter, Agathe!—cooing in the background.

"Je reviens! Je reviens!" I was so excited I couldn't contain myself. I hadn't yet met Agathe, and I hoped my trip would coincide with her christening. A group of assistants stopped in front of the door to my closet-sized office, dumbfounded at my outburst in French. Later that day, when I presented the business manager with my budget, she laughed.

"You can spend more than *this*!" But I didn't want to jeopardize my chance to go, I told her, explaining why I'd cut breakfast and lunch out of the budget. I could always live on Bibiane's Picard Surgelés supply.

"Next time, try getting a town car or something," the business manager advised. "You have to spend more money. That's the way it works around here. If you don't spend money, they don't respect you."

⚜

LANVIN
Kate
Betts

And so, on that first trip back to Paris, I slept on Bibiane and Antoine's couch, waking up in the middle of the night to the baby's cries and waiting my turn each morning for the bathroom. It was like I had never left, except that now, instead of Bibiane instructing me on fashion and style, I was telling Bibiane what to buy, which fashion shows were worth seeing, and where to find the latest beauty products in the pharmacy. I was Parisian still, wearing the usual mini-skirt and turtleneck and high heels. But my energy was now distinctly that of a New Yorker—high on adrenaline and low on patience.

"*T'es folle?!*" Bibiane would say, staring at me wide-eyed when I burst through the door at midnight, only to announce I would be departing for another party at Le Cabaret or a fashion dinner at Chez Georges. She would shake her head incredulously as I slipped out of a pair of tight Helmut Lang pants and into an even tighter Azzedine Alaïa dress. "This is fashion," I explained. "You need to dress the part."

"*Ah, bon.*" She would nod her head, rocking her baby in her arms as she surveyed the piles of discarded outfits strewn around my open suitcase—the hair dryer, a few Chanel tweed jackets tossed over a chair, discarded black Wolford stockings, bags of makeup, and envelopes stuffed with thick, shiny fashion-show invitations.

Natasha and I dissected every runway show. At night we would meet up with Christian Louboutin for raucous dinners at Natascha's, a trendy place in Montparnasse with red velvet curtains and terrible food. *Vogue* hosted dinner parties in restaurants and at nightclubs like Le Cabaret, a place just off the avenue Montaigne. Afterward, a whole group of editors would go dancing at Les Bains with Helmut and Christian.

On nights when I didn't have work obligations, I would kick off my heels and we would sit around the coffee table on the floor, just like old times, eating and drinking and talking about family and life. Bibiane would update me on her extended family and friends, itemizing each of her siblings' and in-laws' résumés as if she were checking off a grocery list. She talked about her parents and their summer vacations in Normandy, where their three children and ten grandchildren would gather in July and August. Stéphane didn't come around anymore; he lived with a ballet dancer now. Bibiane's friend Brigitte had moved her family back to Aix-en-Provence, but occasionally she brought her kids up to Paris to shop.

Hervé was living nearby, on the rue de l'Abbé Grégoire, behind Le Bon Marché. Bibiane said she had bumped into him a few times on the street recently. *Quelle coincidence!*

"*Alors*, Kate," Bibiane would say with a big smile. "When are you going to have kids?"

The idea of having kids seemed like a faraway deadline, something to check off the list in another decade. How could anyone think about kids before they'd established a career? The notion that it was possible to postpone the start of your so-called "real" life until age thirty-nine, to leave marriage and kids until the last possible moment, seemed strangely logical. Career first; family later—it was such an American idea, not at all the way my French friends imagined their lives. Bibiane didn't get it, and now, with three children, she was fulfilled in a way I didn't really understand. But she grasped the urgency of the moment, knowing what almost everyone in France knows, which is to say that life is not lived in the future. "Seize the moment," she said. "Pay attention to your life right now."

What I failed to see, sitting around the coffee table on those nights, was the possibility that I didn't have to keep looking for a family to belong to; I could create one of my own. I had conflated my deep need to belong to something bigger than myself with a more superficial need to fit in, to look and dress and act like others. But fitting in is not belonging. This seems so clear now, but at the time I didn't understand the difference. I was still floating between New York and Paris, at least in the sense that my identity was tied to both cities. I lived in New York and worked at a New Yorker's pace, but I couldn't let go of Paris—Paris, which had shaped me more deeply than college or even my Manhattan childhood. Returning to Paris felt as if I was reawakening some part of myself that had been asleep since I'd left.

My first Paris assignment for *Vogue* was to write a runway report and to manage the backstage photographer Roxanne Lowit. Roxanne was scrappy and quick. She had honed her skills shooting New York City nightlife in the days of CBGB and Studio 54. She knew everybody, and she reminded anyone who would listen about how much Gianni, Yves, and Karl liked her photos. She rattled off their names so matter-of-factly that even they believed her. With Roxanne's *culot*—chutzpah—anything was possible. We would scurry around backstage before the shows, shooting pictures of off-duty models as they lay around in their civilian clothes, waiting for hair and makeup. We raced from show to show in taxis, rental cars, borrowed limousines. We were the habitués of *les coulisses de la mode,* as the French called the backstage area. To anyone who denied us access— security guards, press attachés, even designers—we would wave our badges and bark, *"Vogue Américain."* When Pierre Bergé spotted us sneaking around backstage at Yves Saint Laurent shows, he would march over to shoo us out the door, and we would dive under tables piled high with accessories, hiding until the show began. We devised all sorts of

clever backstage strategies—climbing over fences, crawling under makeshift partitions, and bolting for the door when necessary.

We were reporters, bringing newspaper skills to the glossy magazine world. It was a niche at *Vogue* that Anna—the daughter of a journalist— seemed to appreciate. Fairchild's training came in handy, too, as I clocked larger cultural trends playing out in fashion. The world was changing quickly: The Soviet Union had collapsed, Margaret Thatcher had resigned, and the United States was mired in a deep recession. On the radio, Nirvana's hit "Smells Like Teen Spirit" had pushed Michael Jackson off the top of the charts, and on runways, supermodels like Cindy Crawford and Christy Turlington were appearing in Marc Jacobs's version of Seattle-style grunge. A young politician from Arkansas was making a play for the presidency. The Internet was giving everyone access to information and to one another. The cycles of fashion were accelerating. Manufacturers in Italy and France and the Far East were making clothing faster and cheaper.

Kal Ruttenstein cautioned me about keeping up with fashion's pace. "It's going so fast now," he said. "To survive in the nineties, you have to keep up. You can't just sit back and watch it happen." He was right. Fast fashion had already arrived; models on the cover of the hundredth-anniversary issue of *Vogue* wore the Gap. We knew what was coming and we were trying to express this enormous shift in sensibility, a shift that would only be clear in hindsight.

My professional life had taken off, but my personal life was a mess. I had resumed my relationship with Will. Returning to New York had awakened all of my old insecurities, and falling back in with him seemed natural and easy. He moved into my rent-stabilized apartment on East 88th Street. He was working around the clock, clerking for a federal judge, so we didn't spend much time together. On weekends he would go to Greenwich and play golf, while I stayed in the city, working, shopping, hanging out with friends. I was so determined to rack up bylines that I worked every single weekend, churning out story after story. My heart was in my job, not my relationship. So I pulled another fade. I traveled, I stayed at the office late, and I made new friends. When I complained to my mother about my job, she would say it wasn't my job that was making me unhappy.

Nora Ephron once said you cannot meet someone until you become what you're becoming. I always think of her when I remember those first few years at *Vogue,* jockeying to find my place, to find my voice. I was finally confident and driven. Professionally, this was where I wanted to be. This was who I wanted to be.

In late November 1994, Karen, a features editor at *Vogue* with whom I'd become friends, invited me to a book party at the Royalton Hotel on West 44th Street. The restaurant, with its pale-green velvet banquettes, had become the favorite lunch spot of high-powered Condé Nast editors. The wood-paneled bar area was dark and crowded. We bumped into Candace Bushnell, who was wearing a miniskirt and white go-go boots. She talked excitedly about her new column in *The New York Observer,* about the dating scene. Just that day her editor had given it a title: "Sex and the City." Bret Easton Ellis was there, too, as well as Tina Brown and a cast of Condé Nast editors. A group of writers and editors was headed downtown to dinner at Il Cantinori. I'd met one of the writers in Karen's office. He wore a long brown coat and purple glove liners—not something you saw every day at *Vogue*. He was funny and boisterous and sort of annoying, because he lingered outside my office while I spoke to friends in Paris on the phone. He tilted his head and smiled a kind of crooked smile as he studied me, as if he were studying some exotic creature in a zoo. His name was Chip Brown.

That night at Il Cantinori, Chip sat next to me at a big round table of ten people. Candace knew him and joked about including him in a sardonic column she was writing about "bicycle boys"—grown men who still pedaled around New York on bicycles even when they were on dates. Chip did that irritating thing of pushing his chair back on its rear legs. We talked about Paris and college and his early career as an investigative journalist at *The Washington Post*. He asked a lot of questions and he admired my shoes, a pair of black high-heeled Mary Janes I had bought at a Chanel sample sale for one hundred dollars. He had never seen as many high heels as he had at *Vogue:* Most of his girlfriends wore ugly shoes, he said, shoes that looked like slabs of meat.

It must have been toward the end of dinner, because I remember the red wine stains on the white linen tablecloth. I looked down at Chip's hand on the table as he rocked back in his chair. I remember thinking his hands were thick and hairy, very masculine. People around us were smoking cigarettes, loudly calling for more wine. Two editors were arguing about something, shouting at each other across the wide table. Then, all around me, the boisterous noise of the restaurant and the shouting seemed to fade away. As I studied Chip's hand gripping the edge of the table, a strange thought flashed through my mind like an electric current. *I'm going to spend the rest of my life with this person.* I pushed it away. How could that be possible? I hardly knew him, and he was dressed like a scarecrow!

Hemingway wrote that the seeds of what we will do are in all of us.

That night at Il Cantinori, I must have known something intuitively. A year later, on the Pont des Arts in Paris, when all the lights of the city had dimmed and we could hear the water shifting and swirling below, Chip asked me to marry him, offering his grandmother's diamond ring.

The following summer we said our vows in the Old Whalers' Church across the street from my father's house in Sag Harbor. Chip read a poem he had written. "Nothing is real that is not first imagined," he said, standing at the altar beneath the weathered azure ceiling of the church. Christian Louboutin danced so wildly at the reception on a bluff overlooking Gardiner's Bay that he had to wring out four sweaty shirts. Three years later I gave birth to our son, Oliver, and five years after that our daughter, India, arrived, punching the air with her tiny fists as the doctor held her up for me to see. Bibiane's words had often echoed in

my mind: *Attention! Pay attention to your life.* I couldn't have predicted that life. But that night at Il Cantinori, I must have known somewhere in my heart where I belonged—my tribe, my family, my future. They had been there all along.

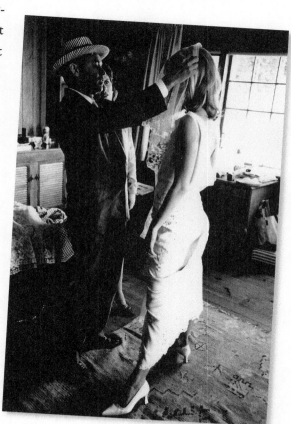

CHAPTER TWENTY-ONE

Up in the Attic

When my father died in the winter of 2011, I inherited the house in Sag Harbor where he'd lived for twenty-five years, a pristine reconstructed colonial on Madison Street. My husband, kids, and I planned to spend weekends and summers there. But first we had to make it our own. We repainted it, changing the interiors from bright Josef Albers–inspired primaries to soft Scandinavian grays—or were they Parisian?

I scoured the Internet for hours at a time, searching for the best shade of white for the living room and then the dining room and the hallways—Benjamin Moore Coastal Fog, Silver Cloud, Seashell, and, finally, French Canvas, my favorite. The repainting was clearly a physical manifestation of a deeper psychological metamorphosis. I was honoring and then letting go of an emotional presence and powerful figure in my life. My father was an architect. He loved order and color and the work of Josef Albers. I hung one of his Albers prints, *Homage to the Square*, above the fireplace near my grandfather's track-and-field medals from Princeton.

Upstairs, there was an attic that had been beautifully maintained by my father. He even left a vacuum in the corner in case one had the urge to purge dust. After we sorted through the things my father had left under the eaves—extra pillows, Moroccan rugs, a lonely white Eames rocking chair, and a needlepoint-covered Le Corbusier chair that had belonged to my grandmother—I moved the contents of my storage bin to his attic. There were boxes and boxes of journals and textbooks on French Impressionist painting, Baudelaire's *Les Fleurs du Mal,* handwritten notes from Karl Lagerfeld, Emanuel Ungaro, Gianfranco Ferré, and Christian Lacroix, and stacks of magazines—back issues of *W, Vogue, Harper's Bazaar,* and *Time:* It was a library-sized résumé.

But the real library, the one holding so many memories and so much meaning, was hanging in the sturdy garment bags: clothes I had once worn as a young reporter in Paris, as a *Vogue* editor, as the editor in chief of *Harper's Bazaar.* They were talismans, memories of who I had been. A gold-lamé Gucci leather coat I had pilfered from one of Tom Ford's first collections. The red velvet tuxedo I'd worn to a Tom Ford party in Los Angeles in 1996, where naked go-go dancers gyrated on Plexiglas pillars. A Vivienne Westwood plaid mini-kilt I bought at her store, Worlds End, on my first trip to London to cover the shows for *Women's Wear Daily* in 1989. The tomato-red bouclé Chanel jacket I bought in New York when I moved back to work for *Vogue,* the same one Pamela Harriman had admired at a *Vogue* party she hosted at the American ambassador's residence. Two Azzedine Alaïa suits—one in Donegal tweed, another in black barathea—that I'd worn religiously at *Vogue* the year I met my husband. Two Prada coats embellished with plastic petals. A white satin Dior gown, designed by John Galliano to lace up like a straitjacket.

My wedding dress, also a Galliano creation, was there, too, a slinky satin-backed crêpe dress with tiny eyelet flowers twisting down the torso. I could still remember the numerous fittings I had attended in Galliano's Bastille studio in Paris, accompanied by Natasha. The original design of the dress had been quite transparent, and Natasha had raised an eyebrow. She made Galliano recut the dress, lining it with something more opaque. Galliano had the dress delivered in a shoe box, and my mother had looked at the package with disbelief. "Your wedding dress is in here?" she said. Christian Louboutin had carried the veil—which Galliano had found in a Paris flea market—in an oversized envelope on a flight from Paris. Now the dress was carefully preserved in a properly sized box.

Why had I saved these pieces and not others? Helmut Lang funnel-neck coats, Calvin Klein cashmere suits, Narciso Rodriguez sequined slip dresses—they were all gone. I didn't save the A.P.C. coat I'd worn to my interview with Dennis or the air-hostess suit and the gargantuan dangly pearl earrings I'd scooped up at the Chanel sample sale in Pantin. The pieces I saved corresponded to seminal moments in my fashion life, like notches on a belt. More than books or notes or articles, they tell the story of my fashion education, how I grew up and matured and became a woman. They were pieces that defined my style when I had become the person I wanted to be.

I still hold out hope that someday my daughter will enjoy these clothes, even though in my heart I know it's unlikely. The shoulders are too broad, the buttons too big, the colors too bright. The red tweed jacket and the barathea suit were moments in time—my time. India will want something completely different, I hope. She will want to make her own statement, define her own style. Even I couldn't wear these clothes again. I'm not that person anymore.

I would return to Paris four or five times a year as an editor at *Vogue* and then *Harper's Bazaar* and later *Time* magazine. I revisited the same spots, like a record needle in a groove. Whenever I had an afternoon free, or an hour or two between runway shows, I would hustle over to Le Bon Marché to peruse the wooden toys in the basement or to wander aim-lessly through the racks of Dries Van Noten and Martin Margiela clothes on the third floor. Then I'd head down the rue du Bac, stopping in at the funny little hosiery shop before grabbing an open-faced roast beef sand-wich at the Bar de la Croix Rouge.

Bibiane and Antoine's youngest child, my goddaughter, Agathe, is twenty-three now. Her sister, Guillemette, was only six when I met her that first day I moved to Paris, and now she is the mother of a four-year-old boy named Adrien. Maxime studied to become an engineer. His days of snarling at strangers and screaming, *"Caca prout!"* are behind him.

I would meet Domitille and Gilles for dinner at the Coffee Parisien for a burger. Domitille still wore jeans with oversized V-neck sweaters. Her hair was longer, but she looked the same. She had started her own line of children's clothing called Soeur with her sister Angelique. They ran a shop on the rue Bonaparte. The walls were painted black, which sounds weird for a children's shop, but buyers and designers from the Gap and J.Crew came through the doors and marveled at the originality of Domitille's displays.

Christel had become a journalist at *Le Nouvel Observateur*. Nikki, back in Sydney, married a lovely Irish man and they had a son. Natasha had also married, a Frenchman, and had beautiful twin girls.

I lost track of some of my French friends. I never saw Hélène again, or Stéphane. After a few desultory dinners on the rue du Cherche-Midi in the early 1990s, I never saw Hervé again, either. We had run out of things to say, perhaps because we had both drifted so far from Paris. Hervé moved to Nantes, where he opened an antiques shop. Over the years I would hear snippets about his life from the Brittany gang. Domitille and Christel told me he lived with a woman who had four kids of her own. The sisters would see him every summer for dinner. When Christel flashed a photo of Hervé shucking oysters at the kitchen counter in Domitille's house on the Île d'Yeu, I thought for a moment it was Sean Penn. Hervé was unrecognizable, not just because of his long hair but also because years, distance, and children had erased his image from my memory. The only image I could conjure was that of a twenty-eight-year-old in his buttoned-up Lacoste polo and buzz-cut hair. I can no longer summon the smell of Eau d'Hermès.

Although he had sworn he would never speak to me again, eventually Mr. Fairchild came back to me. We had lunch a few times, he offered advice, and he continued to instruct me in his way. "Are you *really* ordering green salad at Le Bernardin?" he thundered one afternoon when we were seated at a power table in the famous Midtown restaurant. "What is wrong with you, Katherine?"

Many years later, when a job came up at French *Vogue* or Australian

Vogue—when I was eager to move on from American *Vogue*—he called me and repeated his favorite mantra.

"Never take one of those magazines," he instructed. "They don't make any money. You'll never be successful. Follow the money!"

Whenever I go back to Paris, or speak truck-driver French slang to business associates, or applaud a runway look, people ask me, "How do you know? How do you speak French like that? How did you learn about fashion?" I learned from the best.

Willa Cather believed that if you have a wish for something from a young age and you nourish it, if you continually make an effort to nurture this wish and stay connected to this dream, then you will live a fulfilled life. If you believe in something, it invests everything you do with meaning. Paris has always stayed with me, close to me, and I've continually felt nourished by it.

Each time I returned to Paris, Karl Lagerfeld would send me a big basket of roses from Lachaume, the exquisite florist on the rue Royale. He would always include a note on his personal stationery, tucked in the basket. Every note was signed: "Welcome back to Paris, your real French home."

12, Rue des Barres

On a dreary March afternoon I flew to Paris. I had an invitation for the Louis Vuitton show in the Cour Carrée. I dreaded the show. Several seasons had gone by since my last trip to Paris for *Time* magazine, and I felt out of it, behind the fashion curve.

I flashed my invitation at the security guard at the entrance to the Cour Carrée, remembering the guys in their white hazmat suits at Claude Montana's shows twenty years earlier, when the courtyard was mobbed with press and buyers, all waving their tickets, desperate to get in. Today there were no buyers in sight, just a few fashion bloggers with their cameras. I could tell by the empty courtyard that I was late; the show was about to start. I dashed across the cobblestones and scurried up the carpeted steps into the tent, which had been erected especially for the show. The lights had already gone down and it was hard to see. I spotted the American press area, the *brochette* of puffed-up editors poised in their seats.

"Katherine! Katherine!" It was Gilles Dufour, rushing by with Catherine Deneuve on his arm. They were late, too. He grabbed my arm and kissed me quickly on both cheeks, filling the air between us with the

smell of lemony eau de cologne. The Louis Vuitton press person was pulling me in the other direction, motioning to my seat behind a bunch of *Vogue* editors. "No, no, I'll just sit here," I said, pointing to an aisle seat in the fourth row.

All we could hear on the sound system was the clicking of heels as a cloud of smoke emerged at the head of the runway. We were sitting in the near darkness of what looked like a nineteenth-century train station, which had been constructed inside the tent; a wrought-iron roof soared above us. I could see the young editor next to me out of the corner of my eye. She had the look of a novice, full of anxiety and excitement and anticipation—and she was wringing her hands. She tapped me on the shoulder and whispered nervously, "That's actually my seat, and I need to sit there, because I have to see the shoes."

I ignored her for a minute. Oh, please. How could I explain to her that the shoes didn't matter? Then, in an instant, in the dark, I felt the familiar emotions come rushing back, the emotions of the first fashion show. I looked her in the eye and saw all of the excitement and terror of my younger self, those days of adrenaline-fueled second- and third-row striving. I could hear myself in her rapid-fire voice. It was here in *les coulisses de la mode,* in the Cour Carrée, where I had learned the ropes of the fashion business. I had been in her shoes once, a young editor, nervous, terrified that I wouldn't "get it." In the crucible of the Cour Carrée I had learned how to navigate the complex hierarchies of French fashion and to express my own opinion, to find my voice.

"Don't worry," I said, as we watched a shiny new locomotive pull into the station. "You will see the shoes."

The conductor in the window of the locomotive hopped out of his seat and opened the door to the car behind him, and a beautiful kohl-eyed model in a long devoré velvet coat and a big floppy fur hat stepped gingerly onto the platform. Suddenly I realized that I had lived this moment before. I'd seen this show before. John Galliano had created a similar effect fourteen years earlier on a broiling hot July afternoon at the Gare d'Austerlitz. A real steam-powered locomotive had pulled up to a platform where the editors and couture clients were seated. And one by one the models—Linda Evangelista, Nadja Auermann, Milla Jovovich, Naomi Campbell, and Kate Moss—had stepped off the train and onto the platform, which had been staged like a North African souk, with palm trees and golden sand underfoot. It was an astonishing show—not only the setting but also the breathtaking Dior couture outfits, inspired by a strange, incomprehensible combination of Navajo Indians, nineteenth-century courtesans, and Henry VIII.

Here we were, over a decade later, many seasons wiser, reliving something that had once seemed spectacular and unexpected and encompassing. Now it felt smaller somehow, less a uniquely poetic designer's fantasy come to life than a corporate marketing gambit of a global luxury brand. I wanted to grab the young editor and tell her: "Forget the shoes! Look at the whole picture; see the shape of fashion, what came before, what might come next, and what links them, what ties then to now and now to tomorrow." I could hear Mr. Fairchild telling me so many years ago: "Soak up the scene! Run through the lavender fields of Provence!" I remembered Yves Saint Laurent falling so movingly into the story he'd spun that day in his studio. I wanted to shake that young editor. "Get the story! Don't miss the forest for the shoes!"

When Marc Jacobs popped up from the conductor's seat to take his bow, I ducked out of my seat and sprinted for the exit, up the stairs and out into the sunlight. I didn't look back. I jogged across the now sparkling-clean paving stones of the Cour Carrée, passing the bloggers and the street photographers with their long lenses hunting for any stylish fashion person willing to stop and pose.

I did not know where I was going as I wound my way through the grid of waiting town cars and crossed the busy street. A light rain was falling. I ducked into Cador, a onetime tea salon with Napoléon III Corinthian columns and fresh pastries. The smoke-stained café was empty save for a couple seated by the window, nursing espressos. I ordered a crème at the bar and stirred the frothy milk for a minute, watching the rain slide down the plate glass. I recalled that in this very café I had once shot a *W* cover of a green 1960s-style Montana dress. I paid for the coffee and made my way out into the rain. It was coming down even harder now. I had no umbrella. A pair of young editors teetered by on lizard-covered platforms clutching their iPhones. My shoes suddenly seemed so last season. And then I thought, *Forget the shoes!*

I found myself walking like someone half asleep up the quai du Louvre, toward Châtelet and the big white Renaissance Revival Hôtel de Ville. I walked until my feet hurt and I was soaked to the skin: past the Pont Neuf and the smooth round turrets of the Conciergerie and past the Michelin-starred restaurant that had once been a cheap brasserie. The urine-soaked odor of the Métro wafted up through a sidewalk grate. The façades of the eighteenth-century limestone buildings lining the quai on the Île Saint-Louis looked luminous against the gray Parisian sky.

I turned off the quai de l'Hôtel de Ville onto the rue des Barres, a broad pedestrian passage, and suddenly I was standing before a flight of shallow steps made of wide paving stones. The steps glistened in the rain. At the end of the passage was a set of heavy wooden doors. Now it was a municipal office, but it had once been a youth hostel—the spartan shelter where I spent my first night in Paris nearly thirty years before with my boarding school roommates, a cone of Berthillon ice cream, and a head full of dreams and illusions. There was a young woman in a short skirt at the far end of the passage. She was skipping in the rain, chattering in French. She glanced back over her shoulder but did not see me standing there gazing at her. And then she turned the corner and was gone.

ACKNOWLEDGMENTS

In many ways my late mother, Glynne Betts, inspired this book. She pushed me to go to Paris and find my voice. She encouraged me to take notes and keep a journal. She published some of my journal entries as columns in a weekly newspaper she edited at the time. Many of the memories in this book are drawn from those columns, as well as from the boxes of journals, letters, notes, week-at-a-glance calendars, tear sheets, menus, Polaroids and photos, and invitations that I saved for nearly thirty years. They have helped jog my memory, to the extent that any memory can be flawlessly preserved. It's hard to believe my mother will never read *My Paris Dream;* so much of her spirit infuses its pages.

My agent, David Kuhn, saw something in my trove of keepsakes and urged me to write about Paris. Even when I doubted the viability of the idea, David pushed me forward, saying he felt this book in his gut. Luckily Julie Grau shared that feeling and framed and refined my story with her razor-sharp vision. I feel privileged to have benefited from their exceptional talent and to call them my friends.

The story—the dream—would never have lasted without the enduring friendship of Bibiane and Antoine Deschamps and their children, Guillemette, Maxime, and Agathe. This book is for them and for all of my French teachers: Hervé, Stéphane, Domitille, Gilles, Christel, Pierre-Yves, Bénédicte, Gérard, François, Edwige, Priscille, Jean, Vincent, Jacques, Joelle, Patrick, Jerome, Sabine, Denis, Brigitte, Marie, Bruno, Ervan, Virginie, Alex, Christophe, Olivia, and Hélène. I'm indebted to each of them for their patience with my language lapses and for their friendship.

I'm also grateful for the friends who shared my Paris dream quite literally: Natasha Fraser-Cavassoni, Nikki McCullough, Judy Goldman, Tanya Traykovski, Heidi Lender, Michelle Clark, Elaine Griffin, Warner Johnson, and Mary Beth Clemente. And for the editors who took a chance on me: John Fairchild, Anna Wintour, Steven Wagner, Dorothy Kalins, Bob McCabe, and Judy Fayard.

In Paris's *coulisses de la mode,* I was taught and humored by so many gifted designers, editors, writers, press attachés, and retailers: Carlyne Cerf de Dudzeele, James Scully, Marion Hume, Josh Patner, Jean-Jacques Picart, Christian Lacroix, Karl Lagerfeld, Christian Louboutin, Laura and Emanuel Ungaro, Azzedine Alaïa, Sophie Theallet, Diane Von Furstenberg, Helmut Lang, John Galliano, Tom Ford, Richard Buckley, Gilles DuFour, Brana Wolf, Bridget Foley, Etta Froio, Godfrey Deeney, Miuccia Prada, Victoire de Castellane, Donatella Versace, Rita Airaghi, Giorgio Guidotti, Laure de Pavillon, Laurent Suchel, Veronique Perez, Robert Farrell, Mesh Chibbr, Rose Marie Bravo, Barbara Weiser, Ellen Saltzman, Ines de la Fressange, Patrick McCarthy, Lorna Koski, Amanda Harlech, Rifat Ozbek, Manolo Blahnik, George Malkemus, Dominique Aurientis, Gerri Gallagher, Harriet Mays Powell, Lisa Schiek, Mary Lou Luther, Suzy Menkes, Franco Ferracci, and Robert Forrest. This list goes on; so many people in Paris inspired me.

I'm also extremely grateful for the friendship and support of friends from other chapters of my life: Andrea Topper, Lisa Podos, Blair Kloman, Alex Trower, Stephanie and John Golfinos, Johanna Herwitz, Alex Lebenthal, Burke Doar, Will Fleming, Lucy Hodder, Katrina Sorenson, Lize Burr, Margaret Laws, Sarah Pelmas, Lisa Pomerantz, Carol Brodie, Sharon Doram, Abigail Asher, Richard Sinnott, Karen Marta, Nancy Novogrod, Michael Boodro, Robert Pini, Billy Norwich, Lara Schriftman, Stephanie and Chris Clark, Jennifer Barr, Julia Van Nice, Melissa and Arthur Ceria, Madeline Weeks, and Naomi McNeely.

I so admire James Fallon's smart, calm, intrepid, and kind character, and I'm indebted to him for helping me piece together some of the *Women's Wear Daily* history, providing many laughs with the memories. Molly Monosky, Leigh Montville, and Jina Park were invaluable in guiding me through the *Women's Wear Daily* archives. Roxanne Lowit, François Dischinger, Pamela Hanson, Noa Griffel, Shoko Takayasu, Emmanuelle Hauguel, Don Ashby, Art Strieber, Philippe Costes, Dinh Thi Tien, and Thierry Bouët were also generous with their time and research for the photography in this book.

Without Laura Van der Veer's intelligence and patience, this book simply would not exist. Thanks to Cindy Spiegel at Spiegel & Grau and to Random House's Michelle Jasmine and Barbara Fallon for their enthusiasm and support. I'm so grateful to Beth Pearson, Kathleen Lord, and Allison Merrill for their thorough reading and copyediting of the manuscript, and to Caroline Cunningham and Greg Mollica for their beautiful interior and jacket designs.

I will never forget the friends and colleagues I've lost along the way, especially Dennis Thim, Kal Ruttenstein, Amy Spindler, Steven Robinson, Sandra Raymond, and Linda DeBoer.

A day doesn't go by when I don't miss my parents, Glynne Betts and Hobart Betts, but I'm lucky to have my wonderful sister and brother, Elizabeth and William Betts, who keep me on the straight and narrow.

Finally, to my family, my tribe, Chip, Oliver, and India Brown: *Je vous aime.*

LIST OF ILLUSTRATIONS

All photos are mine, unless otherwise noted.

Title-page spread (*clockwise from top left*): Me on the balcony of the Centre Georges Pompidou; an invitation to an Yves Saint Laurent show; an outtake from a shoot on the beach in Brittany (photo by Emmanuelle Hauguel); a map of the Île de Brehat off the coast of Brittany; Karl Lagerfeld and me at Café de Flore (photo and captions by Art Streiber); a seating card; an outtake from a *W* cover shoot in the Bois de Boulogne; a card from Miravile Restaurant.

4 The card from Le Flore en L'Île, a brasserie on the Île Saint-Louis where they sold Berthillon ice cream.

5 A snapshot of me taken in front of the chapel at Princeton that ultimately appeared in the university yearbook.

18 A narrow city street not unlike the ones behind the rue de Grenelle, where I lived at number 17. (Photo by Petrina Tinslay)

ABOUT THE AUTHOR

KATE BETTS has been covering the world of style for twenty-five years, first as a reporter in the Paris bureau of *Women's Wear Daily* and later as an editor at *Vogue, Harper's Bazaar,* and *Time* magazine. The youngest person ever to serve as editor in chief of *Harper's Bazaar,* she is also the author of the critically acclaimed book *Everyday Icon: Michelle Obama and the Power of Style.* Betts lives in New York City with her husband, the writer Chip Brown, and their two children.

www.katebetts.com
@katebetts

This book was set in Bembo, a typeface based on an old-style Roman face that was used for Cardinal Pietro Bembo's tract *De Aetna* in 1495. Bembo was cut by Francesco Griffo (1450–1518) in the early sixteenth century for Italian Renaissance printer and publisher Aldus Manutius (1449–1515). The Lanston Monotype Company of Philadelphia brought the well-proportioned letterforms of Bembo to the United States in the 1930s.